T0288025

Someone Will Make Money on Your Funds— Why Not You?

Someone Will Make Money on Your Funds— Why Not You?

A Better Way to Pick Mutual and Exchange-Traded Funds

GARY L. GASTINEAU

WILEY

John Wiley & Sons, Inc.

Published by John Wiley & Sons, Inc., Hoboken, New Jersey.
Published simultaneously in Canada.

For general information on our other products and services or for technical support, please contact our Customer Care Department within the United States at (800) 762-2974, outside the United States at (317) 572-3993 or fax (317) 572-4002.

Wiley also publishes its books in a variety of electronic formats. Some content that appears in print may not be available in electronic books. For more information about Wiley products, visit our web site at www.wiley.com.

Library of Congress Cataloging-in-Publication Data:

Gastineau, Gary L.
    Someone will make money on your funds—why not you? : a better way to pick mutual and exchange-traded funds / Gary L. Gastineau.
        p. cm.
    Includes bibliographical references.
    ISBN-13 978-0-471-74482-5 (cloth)
    ISBN-10 0-471-74482-4 (cloth)
    1. Mutual funds.   2. Exchange traded funds.   3. Stock index futures.   4. Portfolio management.   I. Title.
        HG4530.G37   2005
        332.63'27—dc22

                                                          2005012270

Printed in the United States of America.

10 9 8 7 6 5 4 3 2 1

CONTENTS

ACKNOWLEDGMENTS

A s I worked on the manuscript for this book, I was privileged to have help and suggestions from a number of people whose collective knowledge of investments is extraordinary.

Special thanks go to Dan Dolan (who suggested the title), Frank Fabozzi, Edward Hynes, Craig Lazzara, Burton Malkiel, Seth Varnhagen, and Wayne Wagner, who read the manuscript and gave me extensive comments. I also benefited from conversations with Jay Baker, John Bogle, Todd Broms, Don Cassidy, Paul Charbonnet, Michael Dickerson, Scott Ebner, Roger Edelen, Gary Eisenreich, Dennis Emanuel, Deborah Fuhr, John Gambla, Martin Gruber, Dodd Kittsley, Mark Kritzman, Todd Mason, Paul Mazzilli, Dan McCabe, Ian McDonald, Kevin McNally, Richard Michaud, Michael Porter, James Ross, Geert Rouwenhorst, Lawrence Strauss, Robert Tull, Cliff Weber, and Jim Wiandt.

Tina Lazarian took on much of the statistical research, the preparation of exhibits, and the revisions of successive versions of the manuscript. She deserves special recognition.

Special thanks also go to Ruth Weine. Ruth edited my first book a number of years ago and she came out of retirement to help make this one more useful to readers. She is still at the top of her game.

Of course, I accept full responsibility for the book's shortcomings.

One of the most frustrating tasks facing any writer over the past 30 years has been finding a way to deal sensitively with the sex distinctions embedded in English pronouns without calling unwanted attention to the issue with "he/she" or the artificial "one." In this book, I have tried a different approach. I use what I intend as a genderless "he" in most places, but I have given all the portfolio management jobs to "she's." Ideally, the reader will not notice this. If he/she does, this is my explanation.

INTRODUCTION

To make the objective of this book as clear as possible, consider two very different investors, both in their late twenties. The first investor, Joe, subscribes to several financial publications. He spends an hour or two a month working on and thinking about his financial plan and his portfolio. He examines his account statements carefully. He reads the periodic reports from each fund he owns. Joe has also read this book.

After he finished reading, Joe sold several high-cost **equity funds** he had been carrying in his **401(k) plan** account and replaced them with a large position in a low-cost fixed-income fund and a smaller position in a U.S. total market index fund. He used most of the money market balance in his personal brokerage account to buy some tax-efficient equity **exchange-traded funds (ETFs)**. Joe used the free retirement planning software that comes with his 401(k) plan to get a clearer picture of what his financial situation might look like after retirement. He has made an appointment with a financial planner to ask some specific questions. Joe is more comfortable with his financial position and his understanding of his investment risks and opportunities than he has ever been before. He is also convinced that he has improved the annual return on his portfolio by at least 2 percent.

The second investor, Pete, has a few stocks in his personal brokerage account. He bought them on enthusiastic recommendations from friends, but they have performed badly. Most of the assets in his brokerage account are in a low-yielding **money market fund**. When he joined his employer's 401(k) plan, he signed up to put 50 percent of his payroll deductions into an intermediate-term bond fund and 50 percent into a large-cap equity fund. Pete puts his unopened 401(k) statements in a drawer, hoping the fund will grow to take care of him in retirement. He has not taken an inventory of his financial assets and liabilities since he filled out a mortgage application five years ago. He does not know the **expense ratios** or the performance of the funds he owns in his 401(k) account. Pete has not read this book.

Joe and Pete, if they are like most investors, do not realize how great the difference in their respective retirement outlooks has become. Joe is correct in concluding that the changes he has made in his portfolio will increase his return by at least 2 percent per year. Pete, of course, does not have a clue.

What do Joe's changes mean in terms of the value of the two men's accounts and the amount they can spend each year after retirement? If Joe earns a 7 percent return and Pete stumbles into a 5 percent return, the difference is striking. As Exhibits I.1 and I.2 show, with a single modest investment of $10,000, at a 7 percent return Joe will have $149,745 at the end of 40 years and Pete will have $70,400 if he earns 5 percent—less than half of Joe's total.[1] If, instead of a one-time deposit, each man makes an annual contribution of $2,000 a year beginning in year 0, Joe will have $431,178 after 40 years at 7 percent and Pete will have $256,350 after 40 years at 5 percent.

EXHIBIT I.1   Impact of a 2 Percent Difference in Return

	Joe's 7 Percent Return	Pete's 5 Percent Return
One-Time Investment	$ 10,000	$ 10,000
Value after 40 Years	$149,745	$ 70,400
Annual Contribution	$ 2,000	$ 2,000
Value after 40 Years	$431,178	$256,350
Annual Withdrawal from Year 41	$ 30,000	$ 15,000
Value of the Account after 40 Years of Withdrawals	$467,610	Account Exhausted

EXHIBIT I.2 $10,000 One-Time Investment

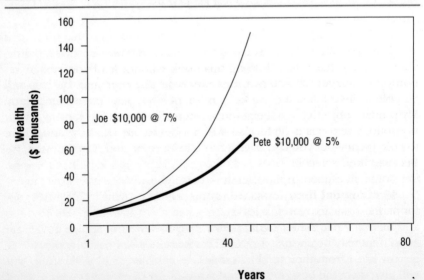

In some respects, the most dramatic difference is in what happens to Joe and Pete after retirement (see Exhibit I.3). Based on the $2,000 annual deposit at a 7 percent return and a continuing 7 percent return during 40 years of retirement, Joe will be able to withdraw $30,000 a year from his investment portfolio and the value of the account will still increase slightly over the next 40 years. If Pete withdraws $15,000 a year, the value of his account will be exhausted in the 40th year of his retirement.[2] A few simple changes in his approach to his fund holdings have put Joe on track to significantly greater wealth and higher income for what will probably be more than one-third of his life.

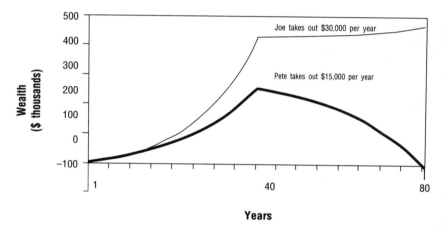

Years

EXHIBIT I.3 $2,000 Investment Each Year for 40 Years

This book should help you improve your portfolio's expected performance, as Joe has done. Reading this book will not lead you to the one portfolio manager who outperforms everyone else next year. But you will be able to invest smarter and keep more of what your investments earn. My primary objective is to help you select the best possible funds for your portfolio. The focus is on funds—which ones to use and how and where to hold them—but you also need a basic investment and planning strategy. Because fund selection does not take place in a vacuum, I discuss some important investment and planning issues in the early chapters.

Most **mutual fund** books describe how funds work and discuss performance, basic expenses, sales charges, and the relationship between risk and return. If you are a trusting person and do not want to look under the hood, that may be enough for you. This book is for investors who want to get the most from their fund investment portfolios. They want funds that will give them the best possible performance and they want to understand why *their* funds *should* do better than other funds. You can achieve that understanding by reading parts of most chapters and learning some simple rules and techniques. The idea that you can improve your investment results by cutting costs is not new, but I apply this principle to specific costs and specific funds in more detail than other fund book authors have done.

This book is about what to look for and how to use what you find to evaluate and compare funds. Each chapter discusses a number of important investment and fund evaluation issues. At the beginning of each chapter, you will find a brief summary of what the chapter covers and, sometimes, how that chapter fits into the investment process. For readers who are not **financial planners** or financial **advisers**, these chapter summaries may give you all the information you need on a particular topic. The summaries describe what is covered in the balance of the chapter and you will be able to decide quickly how much more you need to read in that chapter. If you want to come back and read the balance of the chapter later, the detailed material will be there for you. At the end of most chapters is a brief summary and, in some cases, a list of books or articles for additional reading if you want more information on the topics discussed in the chapter.

Some of the calculations I consider essential for effective fund evaluation are not routinely extracted from fund reports and published by fund data and advisory services. Furthermore, some of the fund services are not as committed to accuracy as they should be. Unless your tax situation is pretty complicated, you will not have to do much detailed work on your own to evaluate a specific fund. That fund's annual report will have the data you need. Unfortunately, comparing more than a few funds can be time-consuming.

Appendix A provides supplementary information, including the web addresses of some useful sites. Some important words are in bold type at least the first time they appear in the text. Those words and a few other fund terms are defined in the Glossary. If you come across a word or phrase in the text or in other reading that does not appear in the Glossary or in an ordinary dictionary, use the online version of the *Dictionary of Financial Risk Management* at www.amex.com/dictionary/frinit.html to look up the word or phrase.

I have tried to make this book as easy to read and understand as I possibly can. To that end, I avoid unnecessarily complex discussions in the beginning of each chapter. Depending on your personal needs, you will find useful details in the body of the chapters and in the notes. Discussions of some special topics are separated from the narrative into topical text boxes. The text boxes are referenced in the text and in the Index. I promise that you will find useful information on topics that are not discussed in any other fund book you have read. I challenge some conventional wisdom, so you will find viewpoints that you have not encountered before. If you want to learn more about controversial issues, I have provided sources in Appendix A, in the notes, and in the reference list.

Funds Under Fire

People's capitalism—small investors buying shares of funds that offer investment **diversification** at low cost—has been one of the stated objectives of the U.S. mutual fund management industry since it was founded in the 1920s.[3] To date, the creators and managers of funds have not consistently succeeded in meeting this goal. Congressional hearings during the 1930s uncovered abuses from the early years of investment company sales and management. One result of those hearings was the Investment Company Act of 1940, which, with only minor amendments, still serves as the primary basis for fund regulation in the United States.

A more recent series of mutual fund scandals that began to surface in 2003 stimulated new reform efforts. To date, these recent attempts at reform have increased the costs borne by fund shareholders without any meaningful improvement in shareholder protection. Cost-effective regulation by market forces has been rejected in favor of bureaucratic changes expected to improve fund governance. Shareholders also have to pay for a new, but unproven, compliance function.[4] Useful disclosure and improved fund operating rules have been rejected in favor of disclosures that are of little use to investors or fund analysts. The safest and most realistic assumption that fund investors can make is that they have to look out for their own interests, rather than counting on the fund regulatory framework.

Apart from differences in the size of the average transaction, much fund marketing differs little from the sale of soap or breakfast cereal. One of the major marketing innovations of recent years is even called the mutual fund "supermarket" (discussed in Chapter 4). Many fund marketers promote hot managers and hot market segments. Both are easy to sell, even if they are not necessarily the right choice for the investors who buy them. Of course, some fund companies have delivered good performance at reasonable prices and without hype. But the inverse correlation of funds' expense ratios with fund performance—the funds with the highest expenses tend to have the worst performance—suggests that many investors do not have access to information that will help them make higher-quality, lower-cost choices. Some index funds have provided good investment performance, partly as a result of lower expenses and reduced portfolio **turnover**. But the concentration of indexed assets in funds using a small number of popular indexes has hurt index fund performance in recent years. Concentration of indexed assets in funds linked to a few overused indexes continues to increase.

In the aftermath of the 2003–2004 scandals, the fund industry is at a crossroads. Most **fund managers** who pursue business as usual will survive, and some of them may continue to prosper. A better strategy for most fund managers will be to develop funds that deliver better value to investors. This book is about finding and selecting better funds. If enough of us are looking for better funds, the incentive for the fund companies to offer them will grow.

Exchange-Traded Funds

Most investors have a reasonably clear understanding of how mutual funds work, but investors can also choose from another important group of funds. A new type of exchange-traded fund (ETF) was introduced in the United States in 1993. The first of these ETF shares were the Standard & Poor's Depositary Receipts (SPDRs, pronounced "spiders"), shares in an S&P 500 index fund. In most respects, ETFs fit into the regulatory and tax pigeonholes long occupied by conventional mutual funds, but the ETFs have some distinguishing features.

The most obvious difference between an exchange-traded fund and a conventional mutual fund is that most investors buy ETFs at a price determined by the interaction of buyers and sellers in the open market. The price at which an ETF share is purchased or sold will usually be close to the per-share value of the underlying fund portfolio at the time of the transaction. However, in contrast to a conventional mutual fund, most investors do not buy ETF shares precisely at **net asset value (NAV)**. The ETF investor will trade at a market-determined price and will usually pay a commission charge and a **bid-asked spread**. Consequently, it costs more to *trade* ETFs than to trade conventional funds.

However, it usually costs more to *hold* conventional funds than to hold ETFs. Expense ratios on indexed ETFs are generally lower than the expense ratios on conventional index mutual funds because of cost savings inherent in the ETF structure. Furthermore, the mutual fund scandals have made it clear that *long-term* mutual fund shareholders often pay dearly for the "zero cost" trading offered by mutual funds. Active traders of mutual fund shares trade without readily measurable cost, but they trade at the expense of the ongoing shareholders in the fund. In an ETF, the traders pay the cost of their entry to and exit from the fund. The ongoing shareholders in the ETF are protected from the trading costs of in-and-out shareholders.

Next to shareholder protection from other investors' fund share trading costs, the most significant advantage of ETFs is their inherent tax efficiency. A well-managed ETF should be able to avoid **capital gains distributions** and defer all capital gains taxation until investors sell their

ETF shares. This feature means that ETFs can offer a significant advantage to all investors who use funds in taxable accounts. While ETFs are often good substitutes for mutual funds in tax-deferred accounts, they are the funds of choice in taxable accounts. It took U.S. ETFs less than 12 years to attract more than $226 billion in assets. Conventional mutual funds needed more than 66 years to accumulate as much.[5] This growth record suggests that many investors have concluded that ETFs are worth a close examination. In Chapter 3, I explain the in-kind creation and **redemption** process for ETFs that is behind both the shareholder protection and the tax efficiency inherent in ETFs. As in other chapters, you can decide how much detail on this topic is important to you.

All currently available ETFs are index funds. Actively managed ETFs are somewhere over the horizon and I have tried to anticipate them where appropriate throughout the book. The introduction of actively managed ETFs is important because conventional actively managed mutual funds cannot compete effectively with index ETFs in taxable accounts.

Fund Information and Analysis

The dominant purpose of this book is to help you pick the best mutual funds and exchange-traded funds from among the thousands of funds that the fund companies offer. If you decide to do your own research, the effort you will have to make to find the best funds is greater than it should be because some of the information that investors need to help them make informed fund selections is hard to find. The information routinely provided to investors in periodic fund reports or on fund and **Securities and Exchange Commission (SEC)** web sites is not as comprehensive or as user-friendly as it should be. Some fund advisory services assemble and organize fund information, but many of these sources do not help investors distinguish between useful and trivial information. Data errors in available fund adviser databases are far too common.

Availability and usefulness are two information problems that regulators and advisory services have not solved. Key information is often missing or distorted. Here are two examples:

1. The most important indicator of the cost of the liquidity that mutual funds offer to traders in their shares, fund share **flow**, is not calculated or reported by any mutual fund or mutual fund service I have examined. See the "Cost of Providing Free Liquidity to Mutual Fund Share Traders" and "Flow" sections in Chapter 5 (pp. 101–110).
2. When regulators require information, or when fund companies, advisory services, and fund sales representatives provide it, a misleading calculation is often chosen over a useful one. Examples include

inappropriate measures of the average expense ratio for a group of
funds (see Chapter 5, pp. 92–93), the use of turnover as an indication of a fund's trading activity (see the "Portfolio Composition
Changes—Turnover" subsection in Chapter 5, p. 99), and fund rating systems that have little value in helping investors select the best
fund for their purposes (see "Fund Ratings" in Chapter 7, p. 155).

Apart from the fact that the data that fund services use are not always accurate or compiled appropriately, the analysis behind recommendations
from fund advisory services is often shallow—or even nonexistent. By the
time you finish reading this book, you will know what to look for and
where to look. I lament the fact that this will be harder than it should be
because you may have to dig for useful fund information. If enough investors demand it, fund advisory services may undertake to publish more
useful data. The fund industry and its principal regulator, the SEC, need to
do a great deal more to assure useful disclosure designed to permit intelligent analysis of each fund and meaningful comparative evaluation of competitive funds.

Market forces are by far the best regulators, but they cannot do their
job if accurate information is not easy for market participants to get. One
would expect accurate, meaningful fund comparisons to be the staple
product of advisory services. In fact, there is no useful, accurate, comprehensive, and affordable fund database available to investment advisers or
small investors either directly or through public libraries. Advisory services seem to go out of their way to avoid comparisons among competitive funds that go much deeper than historic returns and expense ratios.
Some risk-adjusted return information is available, but marketers are free
to emphasize comparisons that favor the product that pays them best.
Any data underlying recommendations are often not available, not relevant, or not reliable.

Mutual funds and exchange-traded funds are increasingly the individual investor's preferred vehicles for investing financial assets. But the
choices offered an investor are often limited by a 401(k) provider to include
just one fund in each category, or by a salesperson from whom one fund or
one family of funds is offered to fit all needs. These limited choices are justified only if the choices are based on an intelligent analysis of the best interest of the investor. Some employers try to provide a desirable fund
selection in 401(k) and similar plans, but you cannot count on that.

Getting the Most from Your Fund Investments

I am often puzzled by the contrast between how much effort individuals
make to earn or keep more income from their primary occupation and

how little attention they give to improving investment decisions in small ways that could double or triple their net worth over a period far shorter than their expected remaining lifetimes.

Useful techniques for improving mutual fund or exchange-traded fund selections rely on an analysis of probabilities. By this, I mean that the search is not for *certainty* of performance improvement, but for *probable* better performance. The expected degree of performance improvement along any single path will be small and uncertain, but the cumulative return improvement from improvement in the fund selection process along several dimensions can be substantial and virtually certain. Correspondingly, over a short time period, the expected value of a small performance improvement will not be great. However, as the comparison of the prospects for Joe's and Pete's portfolios illustrates, the expected value of a number of small performance improvements combined and compounded over many years can have a dramatic effect on terminal wealth or on the annual income an investor will have available after retirement. A small performance improvement can have a large enough impact on an investor's standard of living to justify far more effort than following my suggestions requires.

If you doubt that there are substantial opportunities to add value through fund selection, I offer a glaring example based on S&P 500 index funds. Many investors are aware that there are substantial differences across fund groups in the quality of their index fund management. An astute index fund manager who transacts at a time other than the moment of the official index composition change can often add substantial value for the fund's investors. For the S&P 500, the annual value added by the best managers has been about 25 **basis points (bps)** or 0.25 percent. More dramatic evidence of the magnitude of differences in index fund performance has come from Elton, Gruber, and Busse (2004). They compared the expenses and performance of *all* the Standard & Poor's 500 index mutual funds offered in the United States from the beginning of 1996 through the end of 2001. There were 52 open-end S&P 500 index funds available over the entire six-year period. The best of these 52 funds outperformed the worst fund by an average of 209 basis points (2.09 percent) per year over the six-year period. This study demonstrates that index funds are clearly not as commoditized as many investors have believed. It also suggests that there is even more scope for adding value through fund selection when the entire fund universe is available to you. Most importantly, it raises the question, "If the difference between the best and worst S&P 500 index fund was this great, why didn't SEC-mandated disclosures and fund advisory services get that information to us clearly and promptly?" I will take the argument one step further in Chapter 6 by arguing that you should avoid S&P 500 index funds entirely. The S&P 500 index is inefficient as a fund template.

Any serious attempt to help investors improve their fund selections must include an examination of relevant academic literature on fund performance, like the Elton, Gruber and Busse paper. I have tried to discuss appropriate academic studies in as reader-friendly a way as possible, extracting relevant findings and using them to offer realistic suggestions for achieving better investment results. These papers are cited in the text with full publication details in the References. Most readers will not want to read the original studies, but improved library services and the Internet make these papers widely available.

There are a number of reasons why the amount and type of mutual fund information available to investors is far less extensive and less usefully organized than we would like. Mandatory disclosure by funds is neither as extensive nor as standardized as it should be. The formal reporting process discourages funds from offering additional information that might help investors. The commitment to data integrity and timeliness varies greatly among fund advisory services and database managers. It is not clear that willingness to pay for an extensive fund database with a high level of integrity is great enough among individual investors and independent fund advisers to support even one high-quality investor service, let alone several effective competitors. I try to point out how the conscientious investor can find and extract useful information from the sea of data, but this problem needs formal SEC or fund industry attention.

The next few years will see some significant changes in fund reporting. Barring a significant change in focus by the SEC, however, these changes will increase the usefulness of available disclosure only marginally. For the astute investor there is a bright side to this sad state of affairs. The more difficult it is to analyze and evaluate funds, the greater the payoff will be for the small number of investors who make the effort to improve their fund selection process. You can be one of that number.

CHAPTER 1

A Framework for Saving and Investing

This book is not primarily about the "why" of investing, but about the "how." Our principal topic is the process of putting your savings and investment flow to work to earn the best return possible at an acceptable level of risk. In that context, this chapter and Chapter 2 are big picture chapters. In these two chapters, I am concerned not just with the risks of losing money on a specific investment, but with the risks of failing to meet a specific **investment objective**—the risk of being unable to cover a specific future need or obligation. More generally, I am concerned with investment choice—the task of selecting effectively and efficiently from a large menu of investment offerings to implement an investment plan. To understand the significance and interaction of risks and investment choices adequately, it is useful to look broadly at risks and investment returns—and at the reasons for saving and investing. Joe, the astute investor mentioned in the Introduction, found these chapters helpful in developing a perspective on his investment program and the motivation to create a plan.

The founders of political economy—the eighteenth- and nineteenth-century name for economics—felt they needed to explain the motivations behind saving and investment. Some of their explanations were relatively complex and, even by today's standards, sophisticated. An important element in nearly all of their explanations for saving was the idea of putting something aside today to finance future consumption.

We save and invest to cover our future needs and obligations. Most savers and investors have relatively clear objectives. These are often formal and specific: to accumulate enough money to buy a new car without borrowing, to pay for children's education, or to provide for a variety of lifestyle choices when the saver/investors reduce their participation in the workforce.

In this chapter, I offer an eclectic personal perspective on some of the financial planning and investment implementation issues that every investor must deal with. My perspective reflects my perception that many investors embark upon investment choices without understanding what is possible and what is not, and without understanding the magnitude and nature of some kinds of risk. Of course, the essence of risk is that it makes outcomes uncertain.

Most investors who buy a book about selecting mutual funds and exchange-traded funds have very specific expectations. I intend to meet those expectations fully. However, to put the fund selection objective in focus, I will devote a few pages to discussing some aspects of wealth management—investment planning, risk evaluation, and risk management—that are often overlooked. One purpose of what may seem a digression to some readers is to amplify the Introduction's demonstration of the importance of improving an investor's fund selection by even a small margin. If your plan is clear and you appreciate the importance of small performance improvements, do not hesitate to scan the section headings and exhibits in the balance of this chapter and in Chapter 2. If nothing in between grabs your attention, go on to Chapter 3.

A Life-Cycle Approach to Investment Planning

Many of the people and organizations that offer investment advice to individual investors emphasize the importance of taking a long-term—even a life-cycle—approach to financial planning and investing. These recommendations are certainly appropriate, but the way they are often stated fails to consider some important realities that affect an investor's ability to implement the advice.

A young family unit typically has relatively few liquid assets to invest. The principals are paying off student loans, incurring mortgage debt, and spending most of their income (which does not yet reflect their peak earning capabilities) on goods and services. Any inheritances from their parents' generation usually lie in the future, and retirement and college tuition bills for their children seem years off, relative to the resources the young family can commit immediately to a saving and investment program. The adults in such families should certainly begin to learn about financial planning and investments. But it is not realistic to expect a young family to cut back sharply on current consumption to increase their savings rate or to adopt a sophisticated portfolio management process to handle a small portfolio. Subject to some minor qualifications, young adults should invest as much as they can in various tax-sheltered retirement funds, such as

401(k)s, 403(b)s, and individual retirement accounts (IRAs). Their initial portfolios should probably be relatively aggressive. Their human capital will be largely converted to financial assets in their remaining years in the workforce. Most investors do not have enough financial assets before age 45 to worry excessively about **asset allocation** or aggregate portfolio risk. Nonetheless, the example of Joe and Pete in the Introduction demonstrates the importance of starting early and earning a good return to take advantage of the power of compounding returns.

By the time the earning members of the household reach their high earning and asset accumulation years—typically mid-forties through mid-sixties—financial planning should become a high priority. Commitments and requirements for family education expenses, lifestyle choices, and retirement objectives should become clearer during that period.

One of the secondary objectives of this book is to help readers reach appropriate "make-or-buy" decisions at various stages in the financial planning and implementation process. In this case, "make-or-buy" means—at the extremes—do-it-yourself or pay one or more advisers to do the work for you. Most individuals who like the idea of understanding and controlling every aspect of their financial lives can certainly learn enough to do an adequate job of basic personal financial planning and they can implement the plan in an intelligent way. However, a full understanding of all possibilities and pitfalls is beyond the scope of most do-it-yourself efforts. The greatest mistake most investors make is failing to obtain necessary information and advice from professional advisers. The second greatest mistake is to accept bad advice. You cannot count on avoiding either of these mistakes if you do not have some personal understanding of investment and financial planning principles.

A financially sophisticated individual can certainly take on most aspects of a financial plan and its implementation. In general, the quality of the result the individual achieves will be, at least in part, a function of the time and effort committed to the process. Not every intelligent and financially sophisticated person will be prepared to make the commitment necessary for a total do-it-yourself approach. In fact, the more sophisticated do-it-yourselfers are, the more likely they will recognize what they do not know. A discussion with a tax planner or investment manager who has a complementary skill set to your own will help ensure that major issues have not been overlooked.

At several points in later chapters, the need to monitor your investment portfolio will become apparent. Hiring a planner or other adviser is not a substitute for watching your own nest egg. For most family breadwinners who have reached the age of 60, their investment portfolio and vested benefits will affect their living standard for the remainder of their lives far more than current or future employment income. The time they devote to their portfolio rarely reflects this fact.

The Trade-Off between Risk and Reward Works Only within Limits

One of the axioms of a beginning course in finance is quickly understood by virtually every student: Within the range of investment choices where most investors operate, an investor can usually expect a higher return for a given period in exchange for willingness to accept a somewhat greater risk. This relationship and the range of probable return variations are illustrated in Exhibit 1.1.

Historic data on performance of various categories of investments can give an indication of the nature of the risk/return trade-off, but it is the essence of risk that future returns cannot be known in advance. For a specific period or for a sequence of periods, the effect of accepting greater risk will be greater dispersion in returns. The cumulative return for a risky investment policy over a long period may be higher or lower than the return from a lower-risk investment.

The fact that a specific outcome is not favorable does not invalidate the general association of higher risks with higher returns. An unfavorable outcome does highlight several important effects of risk on long-term results. First, the result of a sequence of risk/return choices may give results that are substantially better or worse than the investor anticipated at the time each of the choices was made. Second, a principal characteristic of risk is that it increases the range of possible returns on both the upside and the downside. The range of return variations over a 5th to 95th percentile range illustrated in Exhibit 1.1 is wide even for a single period as risk increases. A single high-risk investment, particularly if taken on a

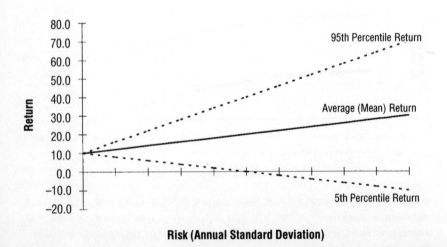

Risk (Annual Standard Deviation)

EXHIBIT 1.1   Expected Return Increases with the Acceptance of Greater Risk

leveraged basis, can wipe out an investor's financial assets. It may be impossible to play again in a subsequent period. The dramatic effect of high-risk investment on cumulative returns is best illustrated by the effect of risk (volatility of return) on the compound return expected from a portfolio in Exhibit 1.2.

The graph of results expected from compounding 12 percent and 20 percent arithmetic or simple returns at various standard deviation (risk or volatility) levels illustrates the possible effect of return volatility on long-term investment results.

Annual volatility in the range of 30 to 50 percent has been common in recent years for some undiversified equity investments. When volatility gets this high, the risk increases that substantial losses cannot be recouped even in the long run. As the right-hand side of the graph shows, the compound expected return at high levels of volatility drops sharply. The 20 percent average return provides a compound expected return of about 12 percent at a 50 percent volatility level and the 12 percent average return gives a compound expected return of less than 3 percent at a 50 percent volatility level. Volatilities of individual stocks and portfolios of stocks with similar risk characteristics often measure over 50 percent. The technology-stock-heavy Nasdaq-100 index and the QQQQ exchange-traded fund (ETF) based on it traded at 50 percent volatility levels for long stretches around the turn of the millennium. At a given average return, this high risk

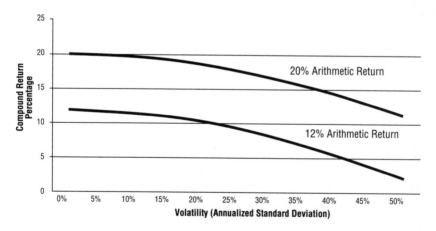

EXHIBIT 1.2 Effect of Volatility (Greater Risk) on the Compound Return of a Portfolio
Assumption: Arithmetic or simple return is compounded annually for 40 years. Results are not very sensitive to use of a shorter period or a higher compounding frequency.
Source: Richard Michaud.

level reduces longer-term expected returns. The risk is greatest with single stocks or baskets of highly correlated stocks like the portfolio of the QQQQs. A catastrophic loss can nearly eliminate the chance to recover in the long run.

The point of this graph is that at a reasonable *average* return, leverage and volatility can *reduce* the compound return to the vanishing point. This graph is based on the return pattern of an equity portfolio. Single stocks, like some of the dot-coms, had recorded volatilities off the right side of the graph in the run-up to the peak of the technology bubble in 2000—and in the subsequent run-down. The prices of some of these stocks dropped so far that recovery was/is hard to imagine. Simple tools to measure diversification—and, hence, the concentration of risk—can improve long-term return expectations and reduce risk.[1]

Most of the risks reflected in the risk/return trade-offs illustrated in Exhibits 1.1 and 1.2 and the most common types of risks examined and evaluated by investors are market risks. There are, however, a number of risks that are best examined and evaluated outside the relatively simple framework of securities market risks.

Thinking About the Big Risks

In the early years of the twenty-first century, most American investors take comfort in the relative stability that the U.S. economic system has enjoyed since the Great Depression of the 1930s. The United States has been an example of a stable social environment for an even longer period, dating back at least to the end of the Civil War in the 1860s. The absence of foreign armies in the settled portions of the United States since Revolutionary War times supports the belief that direct involvement in armed conflict is improbable for most U.S. citizens. Events since September 11, 2001, have shaken public confidence, but most Americans view risk in a very different way from investors who live in many other countries.

Citizens of Western Europe have seen their immediate environment in turmoil as recently as World War II. Citizens of the Middle East, Eastern Europe, Asia, and many parts of Africa have witnessed great social, political, and economic changes and military activity even more recently. On a global basis, the American experience of long-term political and economic stability is almost unique. Only in Britain and the United States have securities markets operated relatively continuously since the end of the eighteenth century, and even the London and New York markets closed for several months during World War I (Brown, Goetzmann, and Ross 1995).

Addressing the global fragility of social stability and financial continuity is not to suggest that buying a mountain cabin and stocking it with several years' supply of freeze-dried food and some heavy weaponry is an appropriate part of any American's retirement strategy. However, anyone making a financial plan should consider the possibility of major structural change in the social and economic environment that will affect the value of investments and the range of lifestyle choices available. On a historical, global basis, these changes have been more frequent and more profound than the North American experience implies.

Most financial plans do not look beyond normal market risk—a level of return volatility substantially less than that experienced in the United States in the 1930s or around the turn of the millennium. Little or no attention is paid to hard-to-anticipate systemic risks—risks that the economic system could have a very different appearance and function in the time period that is relevant to an adult with a remaining life of 50 years or more.

During the cold war, military planners had a phrase for such hard-to-anticipate risks. They called them "unk unk" risks, short for unknown unknown risks. It is impossible to know what you do not know that should worry you, especially over a long time horizon. There are, of course, some major known risks that can be appraised. Looking at known risks will sometimes provide a degree of perspective on systemic risks and unk unk risks. Among the known risks are the risks of inflation and of extreme longevity and the peculiar risk of relying on what is sometimes called "time diversification" to help a risky investment policy meet retirement savings objectives. So-called fat-tailed risks even challenge the analytical framework typically used to evaluate risk.

Inflation

Exhibit 1.3 shows the average annual rate of inflation by decade in the United States from World War I through the more recent period of relatively modest inflation.

Overall, the United States has a good record of controlling inflation. By way of contrast, Exhibit 1.4 and Exhibit 1.5 show two examples of hyperinflation from the twentieth century.

During the Weimar Republic hyperinflation in Germany (1920–1923), the value of the reichsmark declined by a factor of 100 billion to 1 relative to the British pound. By the end of this episode, the money needed to buy a sausage weighed more than a dozen hogs. More recently, Brazil experienced inflation rates averaging more than 25 percent per month from 1988 through 1994.

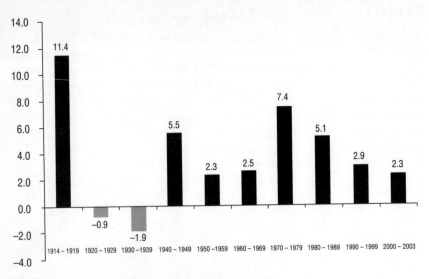

EXHIBIT 1.3   Average Annual U.S. Inflation by Decade
Source: U.S. Department of Labor, Bureau of Labor Statistics.

Any investor dependent on a long-term fixed flow of income—whether from a long-term bond or from a fixed annuity—is subject to significant inflation risk. Social Security payments are theoretically indexed for inflation, but this protection is not an absolute. There is a high probability of change in the inflation protection now built into Social Security. The age at which an individual can begin to receive Social Security payments has changed and will surely change again. More subtly, the way Social Security distributions to retirees might be taxed, particularly if the retiree has other sources of income, may erode the value of the inflation protection in Social Security payments.

In the long run, the only thing that seems relatively certain, assuming reasonable political and economic stability, is that low-income retirees will continue to receive Social Security payments and that there will be a degree of inflation protection embedded in those payments. Anyone who expects to enjoy retirement living above a subsistence level will have to obtain some protection from inflation independent of Social Security cost-of-living adjustments. With the exception of the popular Treasury inflation-protected securities (TIPS) issued by the U.S. Treasury, most inflation protection available to investors lacks an irrevocable guarantee. Even the TIPS version of inflation protection may become subject to punitive taxation.

EXHIBIT 1.4 The Rising Circulation of Reichsbank Notes Issued and Their Equivalent Sterling Values

Date	Paper Marks (Billions)	Rate of Exchange (Marks for Pounds)	Sterling Value of Notes in Circulation (Millions of Pounds)
Dec. 31, 1919	35.7	184.8	193.2
Dec. 31, 1920	68.8	258.0	255.5
Dec. 31, 1921	113.6	771.0	147.3
Dec. 31, 1922	1,280.1	34,000.0	34.4
Jan. 31, 1922	1,984.5	227,500.0	8.7
Feb. 28, 1923	3,512.8	106,750.0	33.0
Mar. 29, 1923	5,517.9	98,500.0	56.0
May 29, 1923	8,563.7	320,000.0	26.8
June 30, 1923	17,291.1	710,000.0	24.3
July 7, 1923	20,341.8	800,000.0	25.4
July 14, 1923	25,491.7	900,000.0	28.3
July 23, 1923	31,824.8	1,600,000.0	20.0
July 31, 1923	43,594.7	5,000,000.0	8.7
Aug. 7, 1923	62,326.7	15,000,000.0	4.1
Aug. 15, 1923	116,402.5	12,400,000.0	8.9
Aug. 23, 1923	273,905.4	23,000,000.0	11.9
Sept. 15, 1923	3,183,681.2	410,000,000.0	7.8
Oct. 15, 1923	123,349,786.7	18,500,000,000.0	6.8
Nov. 15, 1923	82,844,720,743.0	11,000,000,000,000.0	8.4
Nov. 20, 1923	180,000,000,000.0	18,000,000,000,000.0	10.0

Source: www.gold-eagle.com/editorials_02/phillips121302pv.html.

EXHIBIT 1.5 Brazil—Inflation Measures 1987–1995 (Percentage Change over a 12-Month Period)

Year	Consumer Price Index[a]	Wholesale Price Index[b]
1987	367.1%	400.7%
1988	891.7	1,055.4
1989	1,635.9	1,732.4
1990	1,639.1	1,425.3
1991	458.6	471.9
1992	1,129.5	1,160.9
1993	2,491.0	2,635.7
1994	941.3	1,031.4
1995	23.2	6.6

Source: Boletim do Banco Central do Brasil (BCB) 32, no. 3 (March 1996).

[a]IPC-Fipe.

[b]Total wholesale price index.

Longevity

Exhibit 1.6 shows the increase in female life expectancy. Starting about 160 years ago, female life expectancy began to increase by one-quarter of a year for each year that passed. Men have not done quite as well. The researchers who assembled these life expectancy data characterize them as the "most remarkable regularity of mass endeavor ever observed," and "an extraordinary constancy of human achievement" (Oeppen and Vaupel 2002). Even if the increase in life expectancy slows or stops, most of today's retirees are financially unprepared for 30 years or more in retirement. This increase in life expectancy has changed the work and retirement dynamic throughout the world.

Improvements in nutrition and medical treatment have extended the period the average individual can expect to enjoy good health and the ability to cope physically with a diverse environment. Neither extrapolating the trend reflected in Exhibit 1.6 to greater longevity nor predicting an abrupt end to the trend is necessarily the appropriate way to plan for longevity. The growth in the number of retirees already has been so great that the active workforce will not be large enough to provide goods and services to maintain current lifestyles.

A generation or two ago, in an environment where life expectancy for an adult was not many years beyond the normal retirement age and the number of healthy centenarians was small, the extreme longevity of a few

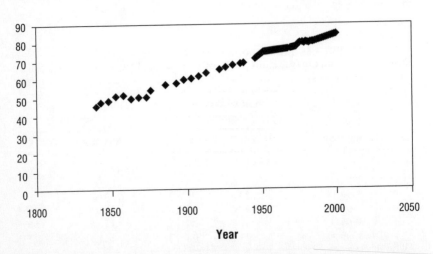

EXHIBIT 1.6   Female Life Expectancy Has Been Increasing by One Quarter of a Year per Year for 160 Years

Data source: Jim Oeppen and James W. Vaupel, "Broken Limits to Life Expectancy," *Science* 296, issue 5570 (May 10): 1029–1031.

retirees placed little or no strain on the retirement savings and investment system. Trustees of defined benefit pension funds now find the growth in plan liabilities overwhelming the growth in assets. The architects of these plans did not anticipate the dramatic increase in the lifespan of retirees receiving payments from the funds. Planning for a possible retirement period of as long as 50 years for a significant number of retirement plan beneficiaries is a great deal more complex and much more risky than planning for a retirement period that was unlikely to extend beyond 15 years for more than a small number of plan beneficiaries. It is no accident that only 17 percent of the private sector workforce is covered by defined benefit plans today, down from 44 percent just 30 years ago (Clowes 2004).

The Pension Benefit Guaranty Corporation (PBGC) pays only a fraction of the benefits the employer promised to the higher-income beneficiaries of failed pension plans turned over to the PBGC. In spite of its ability to reduce the benefit obligation, the PBGC is sinking under its burden. A few government officials are beginning to address the growing public employee pension liability that affects taxpayers from the federal level down to some small school districts with inadequate tax bases.[2] The problem for society is compounded when the lengthening expected retirement period coincides with growth in the population approaching retirement.

Exhibit 1.7 shows **median** and **mean** pretax income and net worth by age range for heads of households in the United States. Although the Forbes 400 have been systematically removed from the data set, the mean net worth after age 65, let alone the median net worth, is not great enough to finance a long retirement in the style most of us would choose.

EXHIBIT 1.7   Pretax Income and Net Worth Median and Mean by Age Groups (2001) ($ Thousands)

Age of Family Head	Annual Pretax Income		Net Worth	
	Median	Mean	Median	Mean
Less than 35	$33.4	$44.2	$ 11.6	$ 90.7
35 to 44	51.4	77.1	77.6	259.5
45 to 54	54.5	93.2	132.0	485.6
55 to 64	45.2	86.9	181.5	727.0
65 to 74	27.8	58.1	176.3	673.8
75 or more	22.4	36.7	151.4	465.9
All families	$39.9	$68.0	$ 86.1	$395.5

Note: Excludes the present values of defined benefit pension and Social Security entitlements and unpaid capital gains taxes.

Source: Federal Reserve Bulletin, January 2003.

Time Diversification Is a Fallacy—The Risk of Speed Bumps

In an environment where longevity has significantly increased and shows no sign of abating, the possibility of outliving one's assets cannot be ignored. As a practical matter, no institution—not even a sovereign government—can provide absolute protection for retirement assets and guarantee adequate returns on those assets for the expected lifetime of many individuals alive today. The popular notion that risk declines over time because good years and bad years tend to cancel out and the long-term return will become increasingly stable over time is misleading. In fact, the *accumulated return* on any investment becomes *more* uncertain over time. The effect of high risk on expected return was illustrated in Exhibit 1.2. A retiree must also consider that, in contrast to the accumulation phase of the investment process, retirement will require drawing down assets over time to meet living expenses.

If the risk of investing for the long run did decline because of some combination of time diversification and return compounding, then we should be able to buy insurance against a shortfall in a savings/investment program. If risk declines over time, that insurance should cost *less* the longer we live. In fact, that insurance, a put option on the forward value of a portfolio, actually costs *more* as the term of the insurance increases.

A clear picture of the uncertainty in the long-term value of one's retirement portfolio can be gleaned with retirement planning software provided by Financial Engines and by Advisor Software, Inc., among others.[3] This software helps investors gauge the amount of annual retirement income they can count on over their remaining life expectancy with, say, 95 percent confidence that they can withdraw a target amount each year. The analysis from the software is based on actuarial tables for life expectancy. Of course, the date of everyone's expected death recedes by a significant fraction of a year for each year of life that passes, just as one's remaining assets will decline if drawdowns to meet living expenses exceed annual dollar returns. The 95 percent confidence level for covering a specified minimum distribution will also change after a period of adverse market performance.

Software tools for planning a living standard in retirement are very useful and are a marked improvement over anything available to individual investors even a few years ago—but investors who want to understand the risk of outliving their assets must understand the limitations of such software. No savings or investment program and no planning software can offer 100 percent assurance that you will not outlive your assets.

Then there is the problem of fat tails.

Fat-Tailed Risks

The normal distribution in Exhibit 1.8 is one of the wonders of statistical analysis. The normal distribution illustrates the behavior of a wide range of natural phenomena. Whether someone is flipping coins, counting the average number of kernels on ears of corn, or measuring the distribution of investment returns, the normal distribution illustrates a pattern found in a broad range of natural and human-influenced phenomena: namely, that a large percentage of observations are concentrated near the mean of the distribution and the number of observations declines more or less in the manner illustrated in Exhibit 1.8 as one moves to either higher or lower levels.

The normal distribution curve never really touches the baseline. There is always some probability of an observation beyond, say, five or six standard deviations above or below the mean, but such extreme observations are rare in a truly normal distribution. For example, only 0.13 percent or 13 events out of 10,000 occur beyond three standard deviations away from the mean in each direction. Yet a wide range of phenomena display a larger number of observations in the tails of the distribution than the mathematics of the normal distribution predict. Many actual distributions have what are called "fat tails." This phenomenon is particularly well documented in the behavior of securities markets and, of course, for a potential retiree it is particularly dangerous when the market return's fat tail occurs

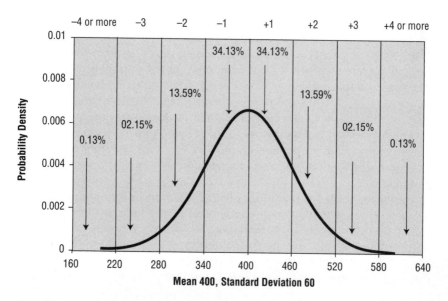

EXHIBIT 1.8 Generalized Normal Distribution

on the left-hand side of a portfolio return distribution. Exhibit 1.9 overlays a **fat-tailed distribution** on the normal distribution to illustrate the increased frequency of extreme outcomes under some circumstances.

The 1987 market crash is often described as a seven-standard-deviation event. By the scale of the normal distribution in Exhibit 1.8, this means that we should expect to see such an event less than once in the entire span of human history. In fact, however, extreme events are much more common than the normal distribution predicts. The problem of fat tails is not with statistics. The problem is simply that many real-world distributions—market returns being one of them—are influenced by a wide range of forces. Among the factors affecting a securities market return distribution are events that could wipe out the value of the entire market, such as a war, an extreme natural calamity, or a political change leading to confiscation of privately held assets and/or the abrogation of government promises. The best retirement planning software in the world cannot anticipate the impact of a specific fat-tailed event on the value of your retirement portfolio, and, of course, insurance against many types of fat-tailed events is simply not available. If it were available, there is no chance that the guarantee of the entity offering the insurance would survive *every* possible fat-tailed event.

This discussion is not meant to be disconcerting; it simply reflects the limits on the range of certainty in any financial planning.

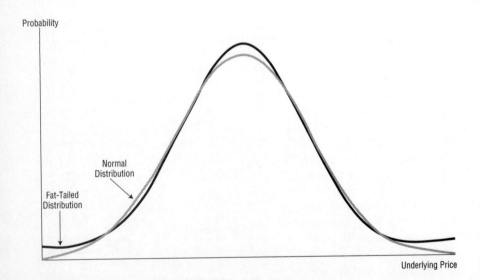

EXHIBIT 1.9 Comparison of Normal and Fat-Tailed Distributions
Source: Gary L. Gastineau and Mark P. Kritzman, *Dictionary of Financial Risk Management*, John Wiley & Sons, 1999.

What Is an Appropriate Expectation from an Investment Program and from Financial Planning?

Software programs can provide an estimate of the probability that investors will achieve their retirement income objectives under certain scenarios. Such an estimate is just that: an estimate of the probability that they will meet their objectives *if the investment environment in the future is broadly similar to the investment environment in the period on which the assumptions of the software are based.*

This software can be extraordinarily useful and extremely revealing to the investor who takes all of its lessons and implications to heart—and understands the risk of fat tails. First, the software reveals that the further out in time one looks at the results of a realistic long-term saving and investment program, the more diverse the possible outcomes are. As the extreme high gets higher at a more distant horizon, the extreme low gets lower at that same horizon. More importantly, the risk of a catastrophic outcome resulting from a market crash or some combination of adverse economic developments *never completely disappears.* The point of this discussion of the characteristics of long-term investment results is not just that there is no totally safe harbor, but that continuing diligence is essential.

A financial planner can help an investor understand and deal with the uncertainty that is an inevitable part of the future. From a plan implementation perspective, the principal effect of growing longevity is that a family must maintain and extend the usefulness of its human capital. Older members of the household should expect to continue to work to earn a significant part of the family's income after they reach what was considered a normal retirement age for their parents.

The expected term of a family's income needs in retirement planning is far longer than it was a few years ago. Yet investments that can provide adequate protection from inflation, from changing asset values, and from greater longevity are less available and less reliable today. The U.S. government may reopen the issuance of 30-year Treasury bonds, but the longest new issue Treasury security is now the 10-year bond. Insurance companies offer fixed-rate annuities for the balance of your lifetime, but they have to invest the amount you are paying for the annuity somewhere, and their investment opportunity set is only modestly broader than what is available to you as an individual. If their reinvestment risk is higher because they cannot buy 30-year or longer investment-grade bonds, your risk that they may not be able to meet their commitment to you is also higher.

Employers are increasingly declining to offer **defined benefit pension plans** to new employees, and new companies are not offering these plans at all. General Motors has been described as a pension plan with an automobile company attached. When and if a corporation turns its pension liabilities over to the PBGC, the maximum amount pensioners dependent on the PBGC can receive is often a fraction of the amount originally promised to them by their employer. In general, companies with defined benefit pension plans are old economy companies with older workforces and lower rates of sales and earnings growth. More of their pension plans will be turned over to the PBGC as time goes by.

Do Not Despair

The message of this chapter is not a cause for despair. There are a number of things that an investor can do to increase the probability of good investment results and increase the likelihood of attaining the investment objectives necessary for a comfortable lifestyle into the indefinite future. While I will offer a number of suggestions, the topic I stress is picking the best funds. By the best funds, I mean those with the highest probability of delivering good results without adding to the other risks that are an inevitable part of the world we live in. The basic idea is to find funds with lower costs and/or higher gross (pre-expense) returns. These funds should permit investors to maximize their returns relative to risk. A 2 percent a year return improvement from careful fund selection is a realistic expectation for most investors. An improvement of this magnitude can lead to a very satisfying improvement in long-term performance, as the comparison of financial outlooks for Joe and Pete in the Introduction illustrated.

The relatively simple comparison illustrated in Exhibits I.1, I.2, and I.3 shows the value of a slightly better return. Most investors can achieve the same return improvement as Joe simply by reducing expenses such as:

- Operating expenses.
- Sales expenses or fees.
- Transaction costs embedded in a fund's management process.
- Taxes.

In contrast to many of the exhibits in this chapter, Joe's example shows substantial reason for optimism and illustrates the importance of improving returns by small amounts.

The next several chapters cover some of the basic issues of financial planning in the context of the material discussed in this introductory chapter:

- The relative attractiveness of separate investments versus pooled or collective investments like funds.
- Basic information about funds.

- Structuring an investment program to minimize tax expense.
- The range of choices available.
- What choices seem likely to provide the best results.

Later chapters offer a fairly extensive critique of the products currently offered by all segments of the fund industry and even some suggestions on how funds might be improved to provide better results for investors. I show how investors should go about finding funds likely to deliver the best possible results at whatever level of market risk they choose.

I examine the relative merits of active and passive investments as reflected in actively managed mutual funds and index funds. Passive investment in a well-designed and well-executed index fund can be an extremely attractive investment strategy. In contrast to most commentaries on fund choices, my viewpoint is that most of today's index funds are poorly designed. The best index funds available are far superior to the average index fund. Furthermore, I believe there can be a role for active management of some portfolio segments, but active managers likely to deliver superior results are hard to find.

Summary

The purpose of this chapter and Chapter 2 is to set the stage for a nontraditional approach to the selection of mutual funds and ETFs. No fund selection decision takes place in a vacuum. It is part of a complex investment process that begins with basic financial planning. Many of the choices that investors make—especially the amount of risk that they accept—will be determined by a very personal decision-making process. This chapter and Chapter 2 describe the earlier stages of that process—before specific fund decisions are part of the picture. The macroeconomic and demographic issues discussed in this chapter should be part of any individual's thinking about the future.

Supplementary Information

The popular press and many specialized publications have done a good job of highlighting some of the long-term issues that stem from increased longevity. Shoring up Social Security and corporate and government employee pension plans is a topic that should be of concern to everyone—as retirement plan beneficiaries and as taxpayers. Longevity also has serious implications for inflation and for the value of investment portfolios. While the issues are long-range issues, the focus of policy changes and the debate should be monitored by every investor. Two particularly thoughtful books are:

Kotlikoff, Laurence J., and Scott Burns, *The Coming Generational Storm: What You Need to Know about America's Economic Future*, Cambridge, MA: MIT Press, 2004.

Peterson, Peter G., *Running on Empty: How the Democratic and Republican Parties Are Bankrupting Our Future and What Americans Can Do about It*, New York: Farrar, Straus & Giroux, 2004.

CHAPTER 2

Assets, Liabilities, and Financial Planning

The purpose of this chapter is to help you resolve some essential investment and risk management questions. My focus is asset/liability matching and the investment aspects of financial planning. At the risk of gross oversimplification, the planning and investment process involves at least three significantly different skill sets.

The first skill requirement is the kind of planning and budgeting skill that is usually memorialized in a computerized spreadsheet and is approached best with a series of questions. Financial planners are usually adept at developing or using questionnaires and transforming your answers into a framework for analysis and action. Some of the books listed at the end of this chapter can provide a good start on the planning process if you want to do it yourself or if you want to be in a better position to work efficiently with a financial planner.

The second skill or knowledge requirement is familiarity with the federal tax code and the tax code of your family's state of residence. The degree of familiarity with taxes that is necessary is usually a function of a family's assets and income. The larger your assets and income, the more sophisticated the tax evaluation, analysis, and planning needs to be. Chapter 3 addresses some of the most important tax issues associated with funds and should help you decide how much tax help you will need.

The third skill requirement, and the primary one I address in this chapter, is the ability to plan and implement an investment program. Your allocation of assets should be linked to the evaluation and projection of your liabilities and financial objectives—and your attitude toward risk.

With respect to at least these three distinct processes and skill requirements, a family needs to consider "make or buy" decisions. The family needs to either develop and polish the skills necessary to do these things themselves or hire someone to do one or more of them. The systematic evaluation of your needs and resources is outside the scope of this book. While I will offer tax tidbits from time to time, particularly in Chapter 3, I am not a tax specialist. Any tax comments I make are in the context of investment discussions and they are certainly *not* meant to serve you as tax advice.

In the balance of this chapter, I stress the investment side of the planning process. Some essential fund tax considerations and asset location issues are covered at length in Chapter 3. The balance of the book is devoted to fund-specific investment selection and implementation issues.

Asset/Liability Matching

An extremely important part of any financial plan is an estimate of needs—the amount needed, the timing of the onset of the requirement, and the duration of the expenditure that needs to be covered. Until recently, it was possible for a financial planner to do for an individual investor what actuaries for life insurance companies and pension plans have long done to manage institutional risks. Risk management for insurers and pension plans has been done by matching the maturity and risk of their investment portfolios to the expected requirements for payouts to policyholders and beneficiaries. These institutions assembled a portfolio of investment-grade fixed-income securities with varying cash flows and maturities. Specialized life expectancy tables guided their selection of fixed-income securities with coupons and maturities that provided cash flows designed to meet their estimated liability stream.

With the interruption of new issues of 30-year Treasury bonds, the increased tendency of investment grade corporate borrowers to issue shorter-maturity debt (virtually all under 10 years), and the continued increase in the population's longevity, there is a dearth of assets with a long-enough maturity to cover the growth in long-term liabilities.

One of the most interesting—and disconcerting—aspects of the asset/liability mismatch is that unless you can create a fixed-income portfolio with the maturities you need, the changes in the value of your assets and the changes in the value of your needs or liabilities are frequently different. In today's markets, matching the returns and market risks of assets with the discounted value of liabilities is not practical more than 10 years into the future.

Exhibit 2.1 assumes we use a set of Treasury STRIPS[1] selected to match the timing of the annual cash flows out of a defined benefit pension plan as a measure of needs or liabilities. Recognizing that there are not enough Treasury STRIPS available, particularly at distant maturities, to meet risk

EXHIBIT 2.1   A Comparison of Defined Benefit Pension Fund Assets and Pension
Liability Returns

	1996	1997	1998	1999	2000	2001	2002	2003	2004
Assets	15.21	22.98	21.37	13.69	−2.50	−5.40	−11.41	20.04	8.92
Liabilities	−3.70	19.63	16.23	−12.70	25.96	3.08	19.47	1.96	9.35
Assets − Liabilities	18.91	3.35	5.14	26.39	−28.46	−8.48	−30.88	18.08	−0.43

Assets: 5% Cash, 30% Lehman Brothers Aggregate Bond Index, 60% S&P 500
   Index, 5% MSCI EAFE International Index.
Liabilities: Equal-weighted Treasury STRIPS (at one-year maturity intervals).

Source: Ryan ALM, Inc.

management needs more than 10 years into the future, the return on the typical pension plan asset portfolio and the changing value of the liabilities as the applicable discount rates change over time give very different patterns of returns for assets and liabilities. Without long-term (30 years or longer) debt instruments, investors can achieve asset diversification but they cannot match asset and liability returns with any confidence.

In contrast to the matching process practiced by insurers in the past, the ability to meet liabilities with a specific pool of assets is now much more tentative. The financial planning tools that estimate an investor's probability of achieving the cash flows needed to meet retirement goals can never deliver more than a probabilistic estimate based on uncertain returns. A combination of fluctuations in the value of assets and fluctuations in the value of liabilities makes the endeavor multidimensional.[2] The growing liabilities of the defined benefit pension plans offered primarily by public sector employers and the more mature companies in Western economies have had a distinct effect on differences in the relative performance of new economy companies that do not have defined benefit pension obligations and old economy companies that have pension obligations that, in some cases, are greater than the company's net worth.

Asset Allocation

Partly because the basics of asset allocation are simple and most of the asset allocation that is performed is done in a rudimentary way, asset allocation gets a lot of attention. Because it gets so much attention, asset allocation is probably the most overrated aspect of investment management. Two studies, the first of which was made in the mid-1980s, have distorted perceptions of the role of asset allocation. In their studies, Brinson, Hood, and Beebower (1986) and Brinson, Singer, and Beebower (1991) were asking a specific question and evaluating a specific process. They came to a conclusion that was applicable to their question and process, but not to all asset allocation decisions. Misinterpretations of these studies and different definitions of what asset allocation includes have led many observers to the misleading conclusion that these studies demonstrated that asset allocation accounts for more than 90 percent of the value of the investment process.

Asset allocation has traditionally been defined as dividing investment funds among markets or **asset classes** to achieve diversification and/or a combination of expected return and risk consistent with the investor's investment objective. Depending on how finely someone wants to break down markets or asset classes, there might be anywhere between 2 and 20 markets or asset classes to spread investments over. Unless someone defines asset allocation to include selection of specific securities, asset allocation is a framework for risk management, not a list of specific investment positions. If someone offers you the "asset allocation is more than 90 percent" argument, ask for a definition of asset allocation and encourage a reading of Ibbotson and Kaplan (2000), Jahnke (2004), and, especially, Kritzman and Page (2002 and 2003) for more contemporary discussions of **asset allocation** and **risk budgeting**.[3]

I am not suggesting that asset allocation is unimportant, but the notion that it is more than 90 percent of the solution to a very complex problem is patently absurd. Your appreciation for the limitations of asset allocation relative to such issues as fund selection and even specific security selection will change significantly as you read the last two-thirds of this book— and as you make the kind of investment choices that Joe made for your own portfolio.

In practice, asset allocation is a relatively easy decision for most investors to make because the asset allocation issues are usually presented to them in a very simple way. A typical asset allocation for a wide range of portfolios is reflected in the allocation used on the asset side of the Ryan ALM asset/liability return table in Exhibit 2.1. This asset allocation is 5 percent cash, 30 percent Lehman Brothers Aggregate Bond index, 60 percent S&P 500 index, 5 percent Morgan Stanley Capital International Europe, Australasia, Far East (MSCI EAFE) international index. The asset allocation is frequently broken down more finely than this simple allocation with separate allocations to large- and small-capitalization stocks and corporate and Treasury debt, but the amounts distributed among domestic and international equities and various fixed income instruments rarely differ greatly from the totals reflected in Exhibit 2.1. Small allocations to real estate and commodities add flavor around the edges, but the basic allocation for most institutional portfolios varies remarkably little from this pattern. Some portfolios have more equity and less debt and others have more debt and less equity. Portfolios for individual investors often avoid the international equity diversification entirely. Variations in the amounts assigned to equities and debt are the major asset allocation change recommended to individual investors over their expected life spans.

Although I downplay the complexity of asset allocation, it does fill an important role. It provides an appropriate degree of comfort that fluctuations in the value of one's assets under most circumstances can be modified by differences in asset allocation. Virtually all mutual fund companies and investment planners provide questionnaires that ask the investor about the ages of family members, financial resources and responsibilities, and, most importantly, attitude toward risk of loss in the value of invested assets. The investor answers these questions; the provider of the questionnaire feeds the answers into a very simple computer program and the computer returns a suggested asset allocation. Some investors indicate in response to the questionnaires that they are uncomfortable with wide fluctuations in the value of their assets and are willing to accept a lower, more stable return to reduce the fluctuations. These investors are told that they should have fewer assets that show highly volatile returns and more that are generally relatively stable (that is, less equity and more fixed income). The suggested asset allocation also usually reflects the postulate that investment aggressiveness should decline (i.e., some portion of equity should be replaced by fixed-income securities, which typically have lower return volatilities) near the time of retirement.[4] It is hard to argue with this simple approach, as long as the investor understands the implications of accepting a lower expected return on investment in exchange for stability. The investor who chooses a more conservative allocation *must* be reconciled to the probability of a lower expected return.

Every investor should take a few of these quizzes, consider carefully the answers that seem appropriate, and recognize the role that specific answers play in the asset allocation recommendation proceeding from the questionnaire. To understand better how these quizzes work, it might be useful to take the same test a number of times, changing answers as to age and attitude toward risk to see how the proposed asset allocation changes.

The principal purpose of these questionnaires is to find a portfolio with a level of return volatility the investor can live with, so the purpose of the questionnaire should be taken seriously. Investors who cannot tolerate large fluctuations in asset values *should* have a relatively conservative portfolio because they will abandon an aggressive portfolio in a weak equity market—and will probably abandon it near the bottom of the market. In Chapter 1, I mentioned programs used to develop forecasts of the likelihood that an investor will meet certain investment objectives, usually with respect to retirement. A more aggressive (risky) portfolio will generally show a greater probability of achieving specific retirement objectives than a less aggressive asset allocation. This is primarily because these programs assume a higher average or expected return, as well as greater dispersion of returns, from a more risky portfolio.

The return expectations assigned to the more volatile investment components of the portfolio reflect past experience that might overstate the equity return premium likely in the years ahead. Consequently, an investor should not take too much comfort from the fact that a questionnaire—actually the success forecasting program—shows a higher expectation of meeting his investment objectives if he accepts more risk. Few, if any, investors should have all of their assets in government securities, and few, if any, should have all of their investments in leveraged equity positions. Between these extremes, I would expect the relative riskiness of most portfolios to vary over a narrower range than they have in the past. If your equity allocation is below 40 percent or over 90 percent, you are probably taking a lot more risk than most of the rest of us that your investment return will be too low or your risk too high to achieve a comfortable retirement.

Going forward in time, the asset allocation between equities and debt in particular is likely to have relatively less impact on overall performance than it had in the second half of the twentieth century. Asset and liability returns are often only weakly correlated, as suggested by the magnitude of the annual asset/liability return mismatch in Exhibit 2.1. Asset returns, in general, are positively correlated across asset classes. In other words, when equities show good returns, there is a general tendency for corporate debt, which is covered by a stream of income from the same pool of earning assets as common stocks, to show positive returns. And when the outlook for profits is poor, the stocks and bonds of the companies will tend to go down in value together.

There has been an increasing tendency in recent years for correlations among asset classes to increase during periods of economic and market stress. The notion that cross-border equity diversification provides valuable diversification because other economies will do well when the U.S. economy is doing poorly has not worked well in most recent years. International equities have tended to become much more highly correlated with domestic equities, particularly in weak markets, when you need diversification the most. The increased linkage of domestic and foreign equities is probably a result of globalization of economic activity and a reduction in differences in cross-border rates of economic growth. When the U.S. equity market has declined sharply in recent years, other equity markets have declined along with U.S. stocks, reducing the benefits that cross-border equity diversification brought to portfolios in earlier market cycles. Much of the remaining difference in cross-border equity rates of return is attributable to currency fluctuations, which are often hedged away by fund managers. If you own non-U.S. equities either directly or through a fund, most of the diversification you obtain today comes from currency fluctuations.[5]

The greatest asset allocation return diversification benefit is the decoupling effect of U.S. government bond markets from equity markets during periods of stress (Gulko 2002; Harper 2003). When equity markets domestically and internationally are performing poorly, there is a long-standing tendency for investors to flee to quality—to purchase U.S. government securities as a haven from the storm. This does not work with corporate debt, and even Treasury returns and equity returns tend to be correlated under most circumstances. The greatest value of diversification into Treasury securities is concentrated in brief periods of severe economic stress.

Diversification

While correlations of investment returns across the traditional asset classes are higher today than they have been at most times in the past, diversification is still a valuable tool to reduce the risk of specific securities in a portfolio. Exhibit 2.2 illustrates the effect of adding additional positions to a portfolio of domestic stocks in terms of the standard deviation of the return on the portfolio. Keep in mind as you look at this figure that standard deviation is not the only risk measurement used to evaluate diversification. Portfolio **tracking error** relative to a broad market index will not drop below 1 percent until you have a diversified portfolio with several hundred stock positions.

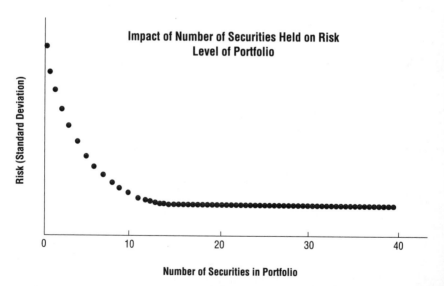

EXHIBIT 2.2 Diversification—Increasing the Number of Positions in a Portfolio Decreases Risk

Source: Gary L. Gastineau and Mark P. Kritzman, *Dictionary of Financial Risk Management,* John Wiley & Sons, 1999.

If the stocks in a portfolio have a wide range of size (e.g., large and small cap), style (growth and value), and industry characteristics, the diversification effect will be greater. If the stocks are all large cap or all in related industries, the diversification effect will be less. An investor who has a highly concentrated portfolio of low-cost-basis stock in one or a small number of companies in the same industry is subject to concentrated risk because a large percentage of the assets are subject to common risks. This portfolio can be stabilized by diversifying within the equity universe and from equities into fixed-income securities, real estate, commodities, and so on. The beauty of diversification is that adding a risky diversifying asset to a portfolio often reduces the total risk of the portfolio because the risks are partly offsetting, not entirely additive.

While most asset returns are positively correlated, with the limited exceptions of Treasuries in the event of severe market stress and some commodities, an investor should try to achieve a lot of diversification as long as there is no specific obstacle such as tax payments on realized capital gains which make obtaining that diversification costly. Diversification is, after all, the first line of risk management. In addition to its exposure to the overall economy, an individual company has its own set of risks. Many investors who invested heavily in some of the recent scandal-ridden companies, like Enron and WorldCom, and investors in the dot-com companies would have benefited substantially from greater diversification in their portfolios.

Beyond Asset Allocation—Risk Budgeting

Once an investor has reached the appropriate basic asset allocation breakdown, there is still more work to be done. Exhibit 2.3 illustrates a useful approach to one type of decision an investor must make: where should he take specific active management risks if he feels he can take them effectively? As Exhibit 2.3 illustrates, the opportunity for significantly better (or worse) returns in a particular asset class or subclass varies widely over the investment universe. Selection of specific securities, particularly in small **capitalization** stocks, or sector allocation strategies, can add value with appropriate management. There is less return variability and, consequently, less opportunity to improve returns by making typical changes in asset class or country allocations.

Of greater significance, there are many ways to take positions in a particular group of assets where the drag of investment costs on portfolio performance can be substantially reduced. From the what-goes-where analysis of Chapter 3, which is designed primarily to reduce taxation, through the analysis of how to find the most efficient funds for your tax-deferred and taxable accounts, to some thoughts on selecting active man-

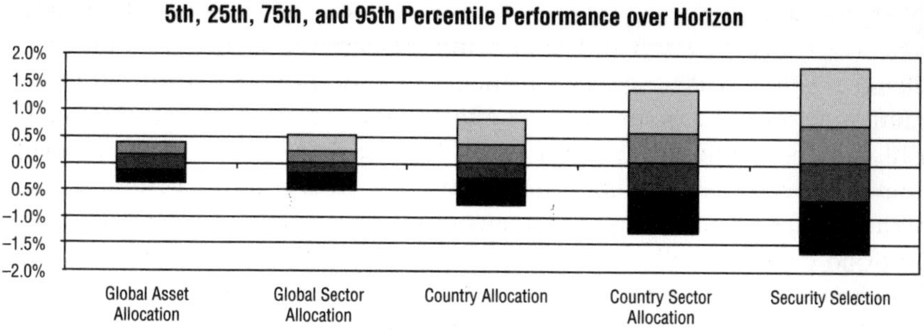

5th, 25th, 75th, and 95th Percentile Performance over Horizon

EXHIBIT 2.3   Return Dispersion for Selected Active Management Choices
Source: Mark P. Kritzman and Sebastien Page, "The Hierarchy of Investment Choice,"
Journal of Portfolio Management (Summer 2003): 11-23.

agers, the remaining chapters focus on the most efficient ways to implement your asset allocation plan.

Practical Significance of This Chapter

Consider how large a part you want to play in developing and implementing a financial plan—and what help you will need.

Asset allocation's significance for most investors will be limited. When the questions about risk are answered carefully and thoughtfully, the asset allocation decision is surprisingly easy to make.

Diversification is important. If you are starting from cash, buy a small number of widely diversified funds that suit your attitude toward risk.

Implementing the asset allocation with specific financial instruments is a manageable task that offers numerous opportunities for improved results within the framework of the risk/return trade-off embedded in the asset allocation discussion.

Summary

This chapter provides a basic discussion of the assets and liabilities that dominate the family financial planning process, and the role of asset allocation and diversification in the development and management of a portfolio. The primary purpose of the chapter is to provide a framework for a family's make or buy decisions on components of the financial planning process.

Supplementary Information

Many financial firms offer retirement planning information ranging from simple brochures to financial planning software. A short but well-done booklet from Fidelity Investments, "Planning for Retirement Income," touches on some of the issues discussed in Chapters 1 and 2.
Other useful planning references include:

Brenner, Lynn, "The Right Advice," *Bloomberg Personal Finance*, September 2001, pp. 64–71.
Brenner, Lynn, *Smart Questions to Ask Your Financial Advisers*, Princeton, NJ: Bloomberg, 1997.
Jaffe, Charles A., *The Right Way to Hire Financial Help*, Cambridge, MA: MIT Press, 1998.
Longo, Tracey, "How to Pick a Planner," *Mutual Funds*, October 2001, pp. 44–47.
Trone, Donald B., William R. Allbright, and Philip R. Taylor, *The Management of Investment Decisions*, New York: McGraw-Hill, 1996.

Four useful articles that have implications for financial planning, for investment selections, and for the allocation of assets to an actively managed fund are:

Ibbotson, Roger G., and Paul D. Kaplan, "Does Asset Allocation Policy Explain 40, 90, or 100 Percent of Performance?" *Financial Analysts Journal*, January/February 2000, pp. 26–33.
Jahnke, William W., "Death to the Policy Portfolio," pp. 17–37, in Harold Evensky and Deena Katz, eds., *The Investment Think Tank*, Princeton, NJ: Bloomberg Press, 2004.
Kritzman, Mark P., and Sebastien Page, "Asset Allocation versus Security Selection: Evidence from Global Markets," *Journal of Asset Management*, December 2002, pp. 202–212.
Kritzman, Mark P., and Sebastien Page, "The Hierarchy of Investment Choice: A Normative Interpretation," *Journal of Portfolio Management*, Summer 2003, pp. 11–24.

CHAPTER 3

Tax-Efficient Financial Planning and Investing

The body of this chapter contains more information than most readers will want about fund taxation. Fortunately, you do not have to read all of it to make intelligent fund choices and to put the right kind of fund in a taxable account to get good performance while minimizing your tax bill.

Tax provisions affect different investors in different ways, and tax rules are subject to change from time to time. I am not a tax professional and I am not qualified to offer specific tax advice appropriate to your situation. These introductory comments and the more detailed tax discussion in the body of the chapter describe my understanding of the economic effects of some tax issues and principles involving funds. No part of this material is a substitute for the advice of your own tax adviser.

The key tax-related conclusions I have reached are relatively straight-forward and small in number.

■ A well-managed exchange-traded fund (ETF) should not have to make any taxable capital gains distributions to its shareholders. The significance of this point is that if you hold an ETF in a taxable account, un-realized capital gains should increase the value of your fund share position if the fund performs well. If the portfolio manager does her job well, you should not have to pay any capital gains taxes until you decide to sell your ETF shares.

■ Conventional mutual funds, particularly actively managed mutual funds, are rarely as tax efficient as most ETFs. Distributions of taxable capital gains by mutual funds are largely a function of the underlying portfolio management process, fund performance, and the tax aware-ness of the portfolio manager. Depending on the index, index funds may be more tax efficient than actively managed funds, but certain indexes like the Russell 2000 and most growth and value style indexes are unlikely to be templates for tax-efficient funds unless the funds use the ETF format.

- **Capital gains overhang**—a fund's net unrealized gains less any accumulated realized losses as a percentage of a fund's assets—is the best indicator of a conventional mutual fund's likely future tax efficiency. The higher the capital gains overhang, the more likely a capital gains distribution becomes.
- After you have determined your asset allocation between **fixed-income securities** and equities, taxable fixed-income securities or funds holding them should be placed first in tax-deferred accounts such as 401(k)s and individual retirement accounts (IRAs). If your fixed-income allocation more than fills these accounts, additional fixed-income positions in your taxable accounts should usually be in the form of federal tax-exempt municipal securities or funds holding these tax-exempt debt instruments.
- If you have room in your tax-exempt accounts for equities after buying all the bonds or bond funds your asset allocation calls for, the least tax-efficient equity portfolios, such as actively managed equity mutual funds or a stock trading account that generates short-term gains, should go in the tax-deferred accounts. Taxable accounts should hold tax-efficient exchange-traded funds as their preferred equity holdings.
- Any rebalancing transactions between debt and equity positions to get back to your target asset allocation are usually done most tax efficiently in your tax-deferred accounts. If the boundary between fixed-income and equity assets falls in your taxable account, try to realize as few net gains as possible and consider making rebalancing changes less frequently.
- In contrast to common advice to adopt a more conservative asset allocation after retirement, only an abrupt change in your wealth or attitude toward risk justifies a significant change in asset allocation at the time of a planned retirement.
- If you are subject to the **Alternative Minimum Tax (AMT)**, you might try to pay for services you obtain with fees deducted from income in your taxable accounts.

There are at least four important questions to ask your tax adviser. They are:

1. Given the nature and size of my income and deductions, how concerned should I be about the AMT?
2. How is my tax bracket likely to change after retirement?

3. Should I do anything specific to reduce probable estate taxes?
4. Is a traditional IRA to Roth IRA conversion permissible in my income bracket? If so, is it advantageous to convert?

Given the tax changes embedded in the current law through 2011 and the possibility of additional changes in the tax code, it makes sense to ask these questions every year or two.

If this is enough detail on tax issues to meet your needs, you may want to skim through the remainder of this chapter, read the chapter summary (pages 64–65) and go on to Chapter 4.

Plan of the Chapter

Thanks largely to the in-kind redemption feature of exchange-traded funds, the phrase "tax efficiency" has come to be associated with the ability of ETFs to avoid realizing capital gains inside the fund and, consequently, to avoid the taxable capital gains distributions that have been the bane of many conventional mutual fund investors. Taxable capital gains distributions by conventional funds are particularly annoying to taxpayers who find their careful tax planning upset by the sudden arrival of a capital gains distribution at—or even after—year-end. ETFs offer simple and increasingly reliable capital gains tax deferral.

This kind of tax efficiency is an important feature of exchange-traded funds, and ETFs enjoy significant advantages over conventional funds in this respect. However, the scope of this chapter is considerably broader than reliable capital gains tax deferral. The chapter covers what goes where in the various types of accounts an investor might own. The emphasis is on choosing what to put in tax-deferred retirement accounts such as 401(k)s and IRAs and what to put in an investor's taxable accounts. This is an important issue affecting fund selection, because tax efficiency is very important in taxable accounts and irrelevant in tax-deferred accounts. The chapter concludes with a discussion of the AMT and an opportunity to obtain a modest degree of relief from that provision of the tax code.

Fund tax efficiency comes first because it has implications for asset location and, marginally, for asset allocation.

What Tax Efficiency Means

One of the most significant features of an investment fund from the viewpoint of the taxpaying *long-term* investor is the fund's tax efficiency. The ideal tax-efficient investment will earn a high return, but very little of the return will come from ordinary (dividend or interest) income each year. Of more importance, the fund will distribute little or nothing in the form of taxable capital gains. Most of the fund's total return will be in the form of *unrealized* capital gains. These gains will continue to accrue; but investors will not pay any tax on them unless and until they sell some of the fund shares.

Mutual funds and other pooled portfolios vary greatly in their tax efficiency. In general, funds managed by an active manager will realize more taxable capital gains than equally successful index funds where portfolio composition turnover occurs only as a result of changes in the index. Even conventional index funds vary considerably in tax efficiency, based in part on the stability of the index composition and in part on changes in the size of the fund.[1] An open-end exchange-traded fund may offer its shareholders the probability of capital gains tax deferral that is substantially more reliable than that offered by any other type of fund. This feature of ETFs is important enough that most fund investors should try to understand how it works.

Why ETFs Are Tax-Efficient

From a tax efficiency perspective, the most significant difference between conventional funds and ETFs is in the process by which fund shares are redeemed. Unlike a traditional mutual fund that will ordinarily sell stocks inside the fund and pay cash to a fund shareholder who is redeeming shares, the redemption mechanism for an ETF is usually "in kind." This means that the fund delivers some of its portfolio stocks (the in-kind distribution) to a redeeming dealer that has turned in shares of the fund for this exchange. By United States statute, this in-kind exchange is not a taxable transaction from the point of view of the fund so *there is no realization of taxable gain or loss inside the fund.*[2] Occasionally, a conventional mutual fund will deliver stock in kind to a large redeeming shareholder, but opportunities to redeem fund shares by delivering portfolio stock in kind are limited in most conventional funds. Usually, a traditional mutual fund will experience a tax event from selling portfolio securities when holders of a significant number of the fund's shares redeem their positions for cash.[3]

Other things being equal, changing a fund portfolio to implement a manager's decisions or changes in the composition of an underlying index will have the same pretax effect in the open-end ETF as in the traditional mutual fund. Essentially, the fund will buy new stock, sell the old stock, and, perhaps, adjust weightings in the rest of the portfolio. This basic procedure will be followed in some form whether the portfolio is an index portfolio or an actively managed portfolio. However, other things are not equal and this pretax similarity may increase the probability that the ETF will be able to avoid making a capital gains distribution.

The in-kind redemption process for exchange-traded funds enhances the ETF's tax efficiency in an additional way by *reducing the tax cost of portfolio composition changes that lead to stock sales inside the fund.* The lowest-cost shares of each stock in the ETF portfolio can be delivered against redemption requests, leaving the fund with relatively high-cost positions. A conventional fund will tend to sell its highest-cost stocks first, leaving it with low-cost positions in the portfolio and making the fund vulnerable to substantial capital gains realizations when the portfolio composition is changed or when the fund suffers net redemptions. In addition to portfolio composition changes, tax events occur inside a fund when a portfolio company is acquired for cash or when stock must be sold to cover a cash redemption. The lowest-cost shares of any stock held by the ETF are tendered first to redeeming shareholders. The shares remaining in the portfolio after in-kind redemptions have a relatively high cost basis, which means that these stocks generate smaller taxable gains—or even tax losses—if they leave the fund in a cash sale.

If the portfolio manager prefers, ETF redemptions do not have to be in kind. The ETF manager can remove positions that the fund is carrying at a loss from the in-kind redemption basket and sell them for cash to realize losses inside the fund. Realized losses build up additional protection from taxation on future gains. These realized losses can be carried forward by the fund for up to eight years before they expire. The fact that an ETF retains its highest-cost positions makes realization of losses inside the fund easier for an ETF than for a conventional fund. If all else fails, the ETF portfolio manager faced with the need or desire to eliminate low-cost-basis stock from the portfolio can deliver it as part of a customized redemption basket if someone wants to redeem during the period when the manager needs to sell the stock.

One feature of in-kind redemption occasionally causes confusion: the tax position of the redeeming shareholder. The redeeming shareholder *does not acquire the fund's cost basis* in the stocks delivered in a redemption. The fund's basis is the fund's basis, and the shareholder's basis is the shareholder's basis. There is no necessary or usual link between the two. A redeeming fund shareholder pays taxes on gains over his cost basis in the fund shares, not on gains over the fund's basis in the portfolio basket that the fund tenders the shareholder upon redemption. The redemption is a taxable transaction for the redeeming shareholder. The proceeds to the redeeming shareholder are the net asset value of the fund shares redeemed. The shareholder's cost basis in the securities received is their value at the market close on the day of the redemption, the same value used in the net asset value calculation of the fund shares. Redeeming shareholders are invariably dealers who are not affected by the **wash sale**

rule. The wash sale rule does not delay realization of the loss if a dealer has a loss on the fund shares. (See "Wash Sale Rule" subsection on p. 220 in Chapter 11.)

There is no unequivocal statement we can make about the net tax impact on a traditional mutual fund from the purchase and sale of fund shares by investors over a period of time. The stock market has generally risen over time, and many traditional funds have accumulated substantial unrealized capital gains. Consequently, it is a safe generalization that the most likely impact of the ordinary cycle of portfolio changes and fund share cash purchases and cash redemptions will be to generate taxable capital gains distributions for a traditional mutual fund. These gains generally will be in excess of the taxable capital gains that are generated by changes in the portfolio of a similar actively managed or indexed ETF that redeems in kind. Thus, the redemption of ETFs in kind will make them more tax-efficient investments under nearly all circumstances because capital gains taxes usually will be deferred until an investor sells the fund shares. In fact, more shareholder turnover will typically cause more in-kind redemptions and greater tax efficiency for long-term ETF holders.[4]

Not all ETFs are pure ETFs. A pure ETF is characterized by having all entry and exit of assets through the ETF creation and redemption process. In this process, purchase and redemption of fund shares are generally in kind with a basket of the fund's portfolio securities exchanged for fund shares at net asset value. Secondary trading of the shares does not change the composition of the fund. Vanguard has introduced an extensive line of ETF share classes of most of its index funds, calling these shares Vanguard Index Participation Equity Receipts (VIPERs). Most of the shares of these funds are conventional mutual fund shares. There are no VIPERs shares on the Vanguard 500 index fund, Vanguard's largest fund. To the extent that the VIPERs might become the dominant share class of one of Vanguard's index funds, that fund might have tax efficiency comparable to pure ETFs. If the VIPERs do not largely supplant the conventional shares of the Vanguard index funds, their impact on tax efficiency will be limited. It is too early to judge the importance and effectiveness of Vanguard's approach to ETFs, but a discussion of the price competition among various funds ("Fidelity, Vanguard, and the Great Index Fund Price War" in Chapter 6, pp. 142–145) provides more information and data for analysis of this share class.

Capital Gains Overhang

Few investors fully appreciate the significance of the tax efficiency that the ETF structure provides. Exhibit 3.1 offers an arresting comparison of the capital gains tax status of the Vanguard 500 mutual fund and the Standard

EXHIBIT 3.1   Capital Gains Overhang or Underhang, Vanguard 500 versus SPDR

Date of Fund Annual Report	9/30/2004	Adjusted to 12/31/2004[a]	12/31/2004
Fund	SPDR	SPDR	Vanguard
Net Assets	100.00%	100.00%	100.00%
Unrealized Gains (Losses)	(20.73%)	(11.04%)	27.32%
Accumulated Net Realized Losses[b]	(7.29%)	(6.70%)	(4.17%)
Capital Gains Overhang (Underhang)	(28.02%)	(17.74%)	23.16%
S&P 500 Index Level	1,115	1,212	1,212
Actual Fund Assets ($ billions)	$45.7	$55.9	$106.6

[a]Adjusted for appreciation in the S&P 500 from 9/30/2004 through 12/31/2004. This adjustment reduces realized and unrealized losses as a percent of adjusted net assets for the SPDR. The adjusted net assets for the SPDR as of 12/31/2004 would have been $49.7 billion.

[b]Realized losses in a fund may be carried forward for up to eight years.

Source: Vanguard and SPDR annual reports and Standard & Poor's.

& Poor's Depositary Receipt (SPDR) ETF, two funds tracking the S&P 500 index that have been in existence for a number of years—more than 12 years for the SPDR and over 25 years for the Vanguard 500. Both funds have had high rates of asset growth in a generally rising equity market. To make the comparisons as clear as possible, the relationships in the table are stated as percentages, with each fund's net assets set at 100 percent.

The dates of the latest available annual reports for the two funds are different—September 30, 2004, for the SPDR and December 31, 2004, for the Vanguard 500 fund. To make the tax positions comparable, I adjusted the relevant realized and unrealized loss figures for the SPDR forward to December 31, 2004. In making this adjustment, I assumed that the SPDR had no losses or gains during that quarter other than an increase in net assets and *unrealized* appreciation from the rising market in the final quarter of 2004. The appropriate columns for the capital gains overhang comparison, then, are the adjusted SPDR column for 12/31/04 and the Vanguard 500 column for the same date.[5] The striking difference between the funds is that the SPDR investor is protected from a capital gains distribution by unrealized losses while the Vanguard 500 shareholder eventually faces capital gains distributions if accumulated gains have to be realized.

Vanguard's response to the vaunted tax efficiency of ETFs has been that conventional funds have the ability to realize losses in the fund to offset gains that might be realized on stocks sold at a profit. In fact, the accumulated net realized losses as a percent of the fund's projected 2004 year-end net asset value were greater in the SPDR (6.70 percent) than in the Vanguard 500 (4.17 percent). Vanguard also notes that mutual funds can redeem fund shares in kind, just as ETFs do. Vanguard did succeed in redeeming shares in kind to shelter an impressive $372 million in capital gains during 2004. However, this amount pales in comparison to the $2.6 *billion* in unrealized gains that the much smaller SPDR redeemed out in its 2004 fiscal year.

The most important difference between the two funds is in the level of unrealized gains or losses. The Vanguard 500 had unrealized gains of 27.32 percent of net asset value at 12/31/04 whereas the SPDR had 11.04 percent of net assets in unrealized *losses* after adjusting the 9/30/04 portfolio forward to 12/31/04. The SPDR's accumulated book losses provide a cushion against any possible capital gains distribution. To use standard terminology, the Vanguard 500 had a capital gains overhang of 23.16 percent at the end of 2004 and the SPDR had a capital *loss* overhang or a capital gains "underhang" estimated at 17.74 percent of net assets as of that date.[6]

Vanguard has done an excellent job of managing its Vanguard 500 index fund to defer the realization and distribution of capital gains. The task has been simplified by a steady stream of new assets that has kept the average cost basis of the fund's holdings from falling too far behind a generally rising market. However, asset growth is not likely to be as dependable in the future for the Vanguard 500. Dollar inflows equal to the inflows the Vanguard 500 has experienced in the past will have a smaller impact as the fund grows. The historic growth rate of the fund seems unsustainable at its current size and in an increasingly competitive fund environment. Fidelity's challenge to Vanguard with its 10 basis point expense ratios on S&P 500, Total (U.S.) Market, and Extended Market mutual funds will draw tax-deferred accounts away from the Vanguard 500, as some 401(k) providers replace Vanguard index mutual funds with lower-fee Fidelity funds. The clear long-term tax advantages of the two available S&P 500 ETFs (the SPDR and the iShares S&P 500 fund) seem likely to reduce the Vanguard 500's growth rate by attracting taxable investors to ETFs. In its fiscal 2004, for example, the SPDR added a net $5.3 billion in assets from shares purchased compared to the Vanguard 500's net purchases of $4.7 billion for calendar 2004. The increase in SPDR net assets in the fourth calendar quarter of 2004 suggests that the SPDR took in an additional $5 billion to $6 billion in that quarter alone. The Vanguard 500 is a much larger fund, making the recent growth rate in the SPDR even more significant. Vanguard responded to the Fidelity and ETF challenges by sharply reducing the expense ratios on its broad-market VIPERs ETF share classes. Those fee cuts will also tend to cannibalize the Vanguard 500. (See "Fidelity, Vanguard, and the Great Index Fund Price War" in Chapter 6, pp. 142–145.)

The Vanguard.500's use of the S&P 500 benchmark index may increase the fund's vulnerability. A few investors may respond to my argument that the S&P 500 is an inefficient, overused index[7] and choose funds based on more efficient index templates. When merger and acquisition activity in the United States brings turnover in the S&P 500 index back to historic levels in a rising market, capital gains distributions in the 500 fund will be even harder for Vanguard to avoid.[8]

SPDR shareholders need not worry that *their* fund will accumulate meaningful unrealized gains. In-kind redemption opportunities are plentiful for the SPDR. Even with the fund's strong growth in net assets, SPDR redemptions in fiscal 2004 were equal to about half of end-of-year net assets.

It is not appropriate to extrapolate the relative security of SPDR shareholders from capital gains distributions to all ETFs. The SPDR has been very actively traded, and the rate of SPDR redemptions relative to fund size has been higher than the rate experienced by most other ETFs. Nonetheless, it is clear that there is substantially greater likelihood of a capital gains distribution in most conventional funds than in comparable ETFs. Dependable **long-term capital gain (LTCG)** tax deferral in taxable accounts is much more likely if you own equity ETFs than if you own conventional equity funds.

As the SPDR/Vanguard 500 table in Exhibit 3.1 suggests, a mature ETF can grow in tax efficiency over time. This point is important enough to merit at least a brief discussion. When fund assets are growing in a generally rising market and changes in the portfolio composition are modest, avoiding capital gains distributions is easy in most funds. If growth stops, or if the fund faces net redemptions as most funds do at some times in their life cycle, avoiding capital gains distributions is easy for an ETF. The ETF's lowest-cost tax lots in each of the securities it holds are the first positions delivered to redeeming shareholders. Securities that can be sold at a loss are sold inside the fund with losses to be offset against possible gains. The fund's average tax basis on remaining portfolio securities rises as fund assets decline. In the case of the SPDR, net redemptions would increase realized and unrealized losses as a percent of assets under most scenarios. The opposite is usually true of mutual funds. The portfolio and tax management processes in a conventional mutual fund are likely to become more and more constrained over time as low-cost-basis positions reduce the portfolio manager's flexibility. Rising stock prices, significant portfolio changes, and periods of net fund share redemptions are likely to lead to substantial capital gains distributions in a conventional mutual fund.

Neither the SPDR nor the Vanguard 500 is likely to distribute capital gains for 2005 or 2006. However, any investor looking for tax efficiency beyond, say, 2010 will find the SPDR to be the obvious choice of the pair. The Vanguard 500's first capital gains distribution after a number of tax-efficient years will highlight that fund's tax vulnerability as taxable investors look at what will eventually be a formidable capital gains overhang.[9]

Any investor who is concerned about tax efficiency should look carefully at a fund's capital gains overhang. Capital gains overhang is far more useful than the Securities and Exchange Commission (SEC) after-tax return calculation in predicting a fund's long-term tax efficiency. A conventional mutual fund with accumulated capital losses may have some significant portfolio management shortcomings, but book losses in an ETF usually reflect appropriate tax management. Capital gains overhang (or underhang) is easy enough to calculate from a fund's financial statements, but it is not emphasized by fund advisory services.[10]

Capital Gains Tax Deferral

In some circumstances, deferral of capital gains in an ETF can mean that the capital gains tax never has to be paid. These circumstances include the step-up of basis at the death of a taxpayer and the gift of an appreciated asset to a qualified charity.[11] Under current United States tax law, capital gains that are unrealized by the date of death of a natural person are never subject to a federal capital gains tax. Generally, the market value of the investment on the date of death is included in the decedent's gross estate for estate tax purposes.[12] The decedent's heirs use the asset valuation from the estate tax calculation as their tax basis in the ETF shares. This provision steps up the tax basis of the shares and offers a substantial incentive for many taxpayers to defer capital gains for as long as they live.

Taxpayers who give a share of stock or a share of a fund to a qualified charity may be able to deduct nearly all of the market value of the gift from their personal income tax return in the year of the gift without paying the capital gains tax on the unrealized gain. Conventional mutual fund shares are rarely the basis of such gifts because those funds are required to distribute net realized capital gains each year. There will usually be less unrealized gain in shareholders' long-term holdings of conventional funds than in ETF share positions held for the same period.

Unless the tax-efficient fund is held for life or the appreciated shares are given to a charity, tax efficiency means only deferral, not avoidance of the capital gains tax. In fact, if the shares are sold during the holder's lifetime, the government may even collect more tax from gains in a tax-efficient fund than it collects from gains in an ordinary fund because the assets stay invested longer and, other things being equal, build greater capital gains. From the shareholders' perspective, of course, a capital gains tax-deferred fund will have more assets working to increase their wealth.

There is another side to this picture. Today's low tax rate on capital gains may be replaced with a higher rate in the future. Also, the tax law provisions that promise to eliminate the estate tax (and the basis step-up) in 2010 (and bring them back in 2011) could be revised and/or the basis step-up provision could be eliminated permanently. Generally, however, the typical investor will be better off with tax deferral—even with the threat of adverse tax legislation changes.

The principles that (1) capital gains should be taxed at a lower rate than most other income and (2) capital gains should be taxed only when realized are well established in the United States.

The capital gains tax efficiency available in ETFs is a semiautomatic feature of the ETF creation and redemption process. ETF managers do not have to go out of their way to assure a high degree of tax efficiency, and, consequently, this should not entail extra costs in an ETF. Tax-efficient portfolio management in an ETF is fully consistent with all sound portfolio management principles.

Discussions of tax reform often stimulate proposals to defer taxation of some or all fund capital gains distributions until investors sell their fund shares. Damato (2004) describes some of the persistent mutual fund capital gains tax-deferral proposals that have not yet made the tax cut list. Deferral of mutual fund capital gains taxes until you sell the fund shares is certainly possible, but counting on a favorable change in the tax treatment of mutual fund capital gains distributions would be, as Samuel Johnson said in another context, a "triumph of hope over experience." Using tax-efficient ETFs in taxable accounts is a much more promising strategy.

What Goes Where—Tax-Deferred versus Taxable Accounts in Tax-Efficient Financial Planning

A number of investors hold significant assets in both tax-deferred and taxable personal investment accounts. For investors with both types of accounts, it is usually important to decide what goes where (i.e., what types of assets should be held in taxable accounts and what should be held in tax-deferred accounts).[13]

Financial planners regularly emphasize to their clients the importance of the differences between tax-deferred and taxable accounts. Long-term capital gains, particularly unrealized LTCGs that can be deferred indefinitely, are clearly the most valuable form of investment return in most investors' taxable accounts. In taxable accounts, taxes are usually due in the year when income is credited or capital gains are realized. In tax-deferred retirement accounts, such as 401(k)s and IRAs, all returns are tax deferred until the investor makes a withdrawal from the account.[14] When money is withdrawn from the retirement account, the entire withdrawal is usually taxed at the ordinary income rates in effect at the time of the withdrawal. A mandatory withdrawal period begins for most tax-deferred retirement plans soon after the investor's 70th birthday.

Financial advisers have been consistent in urging their clients to maximize the tax-deferred savings opportunities available to them. Furthermore, professional advice has been relatively consistent that taxable fixed-income positions should be held first in tax-deferred savings plans and that equity positions should be concentrated in taxable accounts, with the possible exception of some high-yielding securities or tax *inefficient* funds. In general, a high-bracket taxpayer holding fixed-income securities in a taxable account will find it most attractive to hold tax-exempt municipal bonds rather than taxable bonds. A prize-winning paper,[15] Dammon, Spatt, and Zhang (2004) (hereafter DSZ), analyzes the question of what goes where in greater detail and with greater precision than past studies. The discussion in the following paragraphs is based largely on their work.[16]

First, with some notable qualifications, DSZ found that the traditional recommendation to maximize tax-deferred savings is, indeed, the best policy. For younger investors, this recommendation has always been grounded on the implied assumptions that borrowing is possible in the investor's personal account and that the investor is not likely to face a liquidity shock or a "consumption gulp" large enough to require premature withdrawals from tax-deferred accounts. Premature withdrawal[17] usually requires payment of income taxes due on the amount withdrawn, plus a 10 percent penalty. With the exception of an individual who faces a high probability of needing to make a premature cash withdrawal, maximizing tax-deferred savings throughout an investor's active earning years is the best policy.

DSZ also concluded—and these conclusions appear robust to any reasonable variation in assumptions—that taxable fixed-income positions should be held in tax-deferred accounts up to the maximum allocation the investor makes to fixed-income securities. In a two-asset class model, once the maximum allocation to fixed-income is reached, any balance in tax-deferred accounts should be committed to equities. Higher-yielding stock positions might be placed in the tax-deferred accounts in preference to the taxable accounts, but only after the taxable fixed-income allocation is fully satisfied in the tax-deferred accounts. If this policy is followed with the two broad asset classes, either the tax-deferred account or the taxable account will be all one asset class—either all taxable debt in the case of the tax-deferred account or all taxable equity in the case of the taxable account.

The difference in the tax treatment of the two accounts may have a modest effect on an investor's asset allocation, but the tax effect is predominantly one of location rather than asset allocation. On the margin, asset allocation may be sensitive to the fact that tax deferral of interest income improves the return on taxable fixed-income instruments relative to equities in the tax-deferred account. Correspondingly, LTCG tax-deferral opportunities, favorable dividend tax rates, and the step-up of cost basis at death all increase the relative attractiveness of equities in the taxable account.

An investor following the DSZ recommendations will occasionally sell securities in his taxable personal account to meet liabilities, emergencies, or other cash requirements rather than maintain a substantial emergency fund in fixed-income instruments in the taxable account. Even if the investor might have to liquidate some equity positions in emergencies, occasional sales of part of the taxable equity portfolio are generally preferable to holding substantial taxable fixed-income positions in the taxable account and tax-efficient equities in the tax-deferred account.

DSZ made a number of assumptions that are listed in Exhibit 3.2. Their assumption of high prospective returns, particularly on equities (9 percent from capital gains plus 2 percent from dividends or 11 percent annually versus 6 percent on taxable interest), affects the allocation between fixed-income and equity positions. The high return on equity assumption combines with other features to keep an investor's allocation to equity high throughout retirement years. DSZ's emphasis on a (realistic)

EXHIBIT 3.2 Dammon, Spatt, and Zhang Study Assumptions

Asset Returns:	
Riskless one-period taxable interest rate	6%
Dividend yield on equity	2%
Expected capital gain return on equity	9%
Standard deviation of capital gain return	20%
Inflation rate	3.5%
Tax Rates:	
Ordinary income tax rate (no special rate for qualified dividends)	36%
Long-term capital gains tax rate	20%
Utility and Bequest Functions:	
Utility discount factor	0.96
Relative risk aversion	3.0
Years of consumption investor wants to provide beneficiary	20
Labor Income and Retirement Savings:	
Annual labor income as percent of total wealth	15%
Retirement contribution rate as percent of annual labor income	20%
Retirement (mandatory) withdrawal rate	1/Life expectancy
Mandatory retirement age	65

Source: Robert M. Dammon, Chester S. Spatt, and Harold H. Zhang, "Optimal Asset Location and Allocation with Taxable and Tax-Deferred Investing," *Journal of Finance,* June 2004, pp. 999–1037.

longer life expectancy than posited in many earlier studies—and on the bequest motive with the step-up in basis when assets are passed to the investor's heirs—leads DSZ to this asset allocation conclusion.

Where the Dammon, Spatt, and Zhang Conclusions May Be Vulnerable

The major conclusions of the DSZ analysis are robust to realistic changes in investment returns and most changes in the tax rate schedule that seem at all likely.

Asset Location

Only fundamental changes in the United States approach to taxation such as (1) taxing capital gains as they are accrued instead of when they are realized or (2) elimination of the step-up in basis at death when securities are passed on to one's heirs would lead to an appreciable change in DSZ's conclusions on asset location. In fact, some recent tax changes reinforce their conclusions. The current low capital gains tax rate, the low qualified dividend tax rate, and the temporary reductions in the federal estate tax all reinforce the appropriateness of their principal conclusions. Two other major papers, Shoven and Sialm (1998) and Poterba, Shoven, and Sialm (2004), concluded that holding equity mutual funds in tax-deferred accounts and municipal funds in taxable accounts was a more appropriate initial location approach from 1962 to 1998. The authors of these papers agree that the current lower tax rates for dividends and capital gains and, more importantly, the availability of tax-efficient ETFs make the DSZ conclusions more appropriate going forward.

The DSZ assumption on equity returns, both absolute and relative to taxable fixed-income returns, is aggressive in the view of many market observers, but the return and estate tax assumptions affect asset *allocation* far more than they affect asset *location*. The implicit rejection of a major systemic investment disruption (DSZ posit a 20 percent standard deviation and a normal distribution of annualized equity returns) is probably their most vulnerable investment assumption, given the frequency of fat tails in equity market returns.

Changing Asset Allocation at Retirement

As to the DSZ risk and utility functions, generations of financial advisers have recommended a directional shift from equities to fixed income as the conversion of their clients' human capital to financial assets was essentially completed at retirement. Most financial planning processes, including most of the simple asset allocation computer programs described in Chapter 2, operate on the widely held assumption that portfolios should be invested more conservatively after the principal holders of the assets retire from the workforce. **Life strategy funds** that make automatic allocation shifts to less equity in tax-deferred accounts over time have become increasingly popular.[18] The tax-efficient life strategy fund described in the text box later in this chapter (pp. 62–63) is also based on a change in asset allocation. DSZ (2004) postulates no deliberate policy change in asset allocation around retirement and, for many investors, the DSZ asset allocation process would slightly increase the equity allocation after retirement, particularly for a family that was highly likely to meet its retirement income coverage goals.

While the tradition of reducing equity exposure at or near retirement is widely accepted, a number of astute observers do not subscribe to this approach. Ellis (2002), for example, has thought deeply about this issue and reached the conclusion: "Don't change investments just because you have reached a different age or have retired" (p. 146).

Most economists also take a very different perspective from the planners' traditional recommendation. Samuelson (1969) and Merton (1969) offered proofs that simply aging or implementing a planned voluntary retirement was not an appropriate reason to change your portfolio's risk characteristics. More recent analysis by Gollier and Zeckhauser (1998) and Gollier (2001) suggests that the picture may be more complicated than either the planners or the economists have believed. My interpretation of the economists' consensus today is, stated as simply as possible: Barring an *unexpected* change in circumstances such as a decline in wealth, an increase in expenses, or an increase in expected longevity, there is no reason to adopt a different asset allocation just before, at, or just after retirement. As the DSZ analysis suggests, very wealthy investors might find holding more equities to pass on to the next generation to be highly appropriate if their wealth unexpectedly increases. The dominant influence on any change in asset allocation is likely to be a wealth effect on risk tolerance that comes from unanticipated changes in the market value of your assets.

Rebalancing

The most common criticism of how 401(k) and similar tax-deferred savings plans are used is that investors ignore what goes on in their accounts. Most plan participants select a specific asset allocation for their contributions at the time they become eligible participants and keep that allocation until they leave the company or retire. They do not rebalance the allocation in the account to reflect differences in the performance of equity and debt portfolio components. A study of a large number of defined benefit pension plans and 401(k) plans found that the pension plans performed much better than the 401(k) accounts for the bear market years of 2000–2002 after three years (1997–1999) when the 401(k) plans outperformed.[19] The investment discipline imposed by the pension plans' investment policy caused those plans to enter 2000 with equities at 58 percent of assets while the bull market of the late 1990s had increased average 401(k) equity holdings to 72 percent of assets.

If a 60/40 equity-debt asset allocation is appropriate for a specific individual, then the appropriate way to maintain that asset allocation is to sell some equity fund holdings after the stock market has done particularly well and to liquidate fixed-income positions to buy more stock after a period when the stock market has performed badly. Most 401(k) providers and IRA custodians offer suggestions on rebalancing, and some will rebalance your account automatically. In practice, relatively few investors rebalance their 401(k) or IRA accounts.

Rebalancing is widely discussed, if not widely practiced, in connection with fund positions held in tax-deferred accounts. There are no tax consequences from a rebalancing transaction in these accounts. Also, most rebalancing transactions will be effected at a mutual fund's net asset value, so there is no apparent transaction cost associated with the rebalancing.

If your asset allocation transition point between fixed-income positions and equity positions falls in your taxable account and if you are not using conventional mutual funds for all positions, there will be transaction costs associated with a rebalancing transaction. Furthermore, to the extent that you realize any taxable gains (or losses), there may be a tax cost (or benefit) associated with a rebalancing transaction in the taxable account. Rebalancing might be more appropriately done at less frequent intervals in taxable accounts because of these costs, but do not ignore the effect of asset allocation drift on the risk and return characteristics of your portfolio.

Importance of Tax Efficiency in Taxable Accounts

The tax efficiency of ETFs is of no particular importance in a tax-deferred account, though other features of ETFs such as lower expense ratios and shareholder protection, which will come up in later chapters, may make ETFs desirable in tax-deferred accounts as well. The basic idea behind the DSZ analysis and any other financial planning effort that takes a very long-term view of the taxable investment portfolio is that the tax efficiency of the components of that portfolio is extremely important when looked at for a period that could last for 50 years or more. The drain on portfolio return from taxes on capital gains distributions can be substantial over that much time.

The difference between a 5 percent return and a 7 percent return illustrated in the Introduction suggests the toll that taxes on capital gains distributions might exact in a realistic case. The value of ETF tax efficiency is a powerful argument for using ETFs exclusively in taxable accounts. Even the less-than-stellar performance of many index ETF managers, which is often only partly offset by the lower average expense ratios of index ETFs, is not a good reason to use conventional index funds or conventional actively managed funds in taxable accounts if a satisfactory ETF choice is available. A tax-aware portfolio manager of a conventional mutual fund can attempt to put off capital gains distributions. Eventually, the tax-motivated contortions that the portfolio manager will have to use will take a toll on pretax performance. When you look at the looming differences between the SPDRs and the Vanguard 500 in Exhibit 3.1, the appropriate fund choice for any taxable account seems clear. Consider that you might be making a commitment that you will want to keep in a tax-efficient instrument for 50 years—or even longer depending on your life expectancy. I recognize that not every investor will be totally persuaded that any of the current crop of ETFs are the correct choices, particularly when better ETFs, including actively managed funds and funds using more efficient indexes, may be available within a few years. In that context, what might an investor look at when evaluating conventional funds for a taxable portfolio?

The Securities and Exchange Commission (SEC) has adopted rules for publishing pretax and after-tax returns for mutual funds. As is often the case with regulatory requirements, the rules oversimplify the tax issue, and going from the reporting rule to fund selection is a doubtful exercise. Most investors who have examined the pretax and after-tax return comparisons understand that the reported numbers indicate the difference between the pretax results and after-tax results under specified assumptions. Unfortunately, the assumptions used in the SEC rules do not provide a useful framework for analysis by a long-term-oriented taxable investor. Very long-term investors are not so much interested in the tax impact of closing out all the positions in the fund as they are in the ability of the fund to defer most or all capital gains distributions indefinitely. ETFs are the answer to the need for long-term tax efficiency.

A low capital gains overhang is the best indicator of a conventional fund's tax efficiency over the next few years. Estimating the long-term value of ETF tax efficiency relative to a typical conventional indexed or actively managed fund is difficult. Top-bracket individual investors may pay a tax rate as low as 15 percent on realized long-term capital gains if they do not pay a state income tax or the Alternative Minimum Tax. If they pay both those taxes, the effective tax rate on a long-term gain might approach 40 percent. In addition to great variability in the effective tax rate, capital gains distributions tend to be substantial or nonexistent, depending largely on stock market returns. Allowing for some accumulation of capital gains in the conventional fund, the value of ETF tax efficiency could be anywhere between 0.5 percent and 2.5 percent per year for a long-term shareholder. With a tax *penalty* as high as 2.5 percent per year, it is very hard to justify holding a conventional equity mutual fund in a taxable account when tax-efficient ETFs are available.

Roth IRA Accounts

DSZ (2004) did not discuss the features of Roth IRA accounts or incorporate them into their analysis. Roth IRA accounts are funded with after-tax income. Not only do they permit investments to grow without interim taxation, they permit withdrawal of assets from retirement savings without payment of any federal income tax at the time of withdrawal. Roth accounts are extremely attractive for most investors who are eligible to create them. To the extent that an individual can make a deposit to a Roth IRA or, under certain conditions, convert a traditional IRA or 401(k) account into a Roth IRA by making a tax payment, these accounts are even more desirable than the traditional tax-deferred retirement account. Relative to 401(k) and other traditional tax-deferred accounts, Roth IRAs hold fewer total assets and place more income level and contribution restrictions on investors. However, proposals to expand Roth IRA eligibility and opportunities available to many investors over 70½ years of age to convert regular IRAs to Roth IRAs justify a brief discussion of where they fall in the asset placement hierarchy.

Using the DSZ approach, Roth accounts should hold taxable fixed-income positions if the fixed-income allocation is not exhausted by positions in traditional tax-deferred accounts. They should hold equity positions if the fixed-income allocation is covered by the other retirement accounts. Since there is no mandatory withdrawal requirement on Roth accounts, they will be the last account on your liquidation list as long as capital gains get preferential treatment in taxable accounts. Roth accounts can be shifted from equity to fixed-income positions without a tax penalty as your other tax-deferred fixed-income accounts are liquidated.

Applying Cost Analysis to 401(k)s and Other Tax-Deferred Retirement Accounts

The wave of corporate governance and mutual fund scandals that served as the impetus for the Sarbanes-Oxley legislation and for mutual fund reform efforts by the SEC has led a number of observers to focus more attention on the expenses of 401(k) plans.[20] It pays to analyze your tax-deferred account choices carefully, especially when you change employers.

Third-party administrators (TPAs) and other 401(k) providers, not affiliated with the 401(k) sponsor (the employer) but sometimes affiliated with a mutual fund group, are the traditional providers of a broad range of services to 401(k) plans and to employee-investors using the plans. The costs of investing through a 401(k) plan are not always easy for a plan participant to determine without help from the employer's human resources department or the 401(k) web site. Human resources administrators should be able to provide the cost information routinely; but there is strong evidence that the human resources staff at your firm may not be able to get good cost information on these plans. A survey by *Plan Sponsor*, the leading publication for retirement plan sponsors, found that at least 12 percent of the employers who responded to the survey were not confident they could determine the cost of these plans to the firm and to the participants. See *Plan Sponsor* (2004 and 2005).

Funds offered to 401(k) plan participants may carry either much higher or much lower expense ratios than comparable funds available to investors who buy funds directly from fund sponsors in taxable accounts or tax-deferred (IRA) accounts. Employers have a wide range of policies toward the level of investor costs embedded in their 401(k) plans. Funds offered in some 401(k) plans carry service or marketing fees to offset some or all of the employer's costs of providing 401(k) plan administration and account-holder reporting. Other employers pick up all administrative costs and insist that the service provider offer ultralow fee institutional fund share classes. The net effect can be an aggregate (fund plus account) expense ratio difference of 100 basis points (1.0 percent) or more between two 401(k) plans or between an IRA and a 401(k). You will need to phrase your questions to the human resources department carefully because all funds available to a 401(k) participant may not have the same cost characteristics. Your interest in managing costs may not persuade your employer to make a change in the agreement with the 401(k) administrator. If fees paid by plan participants do not cover the cost of offering the 401(k) plan, the employer will have to cover any shortfall. Your interests and the interests of your present or former employer may not be perfectly aligned.[21]

If your 401(k) assets exceed $100,000, the most important measurable cost to you is likely to be the funds' expense ratios. If you can keep retirement assets in the extremely low-cost 401(k) plan of a current or former employer, by all means consider doing so. If you do not have that choice, you can use an IRA to minimize the assets you keep in a high-cost 401(k) account. It is common practice for an investor moving from one firm to another to roll over the old firm's 401(k) plan into the new firm's plan for administrative simplicity. Before making a rollover, an investor should compare the annual costs of the old employer's plan, the new employer's plan, and the cost of rollover into an IRA. Though some employers go to extremes to offer low-cost 401(k)s, my experience has been that a separate IRA often makes more economic sense than transferring assets to a new employer's 401(k) plan. Purveyors of IRA services operate in a competitive market. An employer has a captive audience for a 401(k) plan. You will not be surprised to find a wider range of investment options available to IRA investors. You also have more ways to extend the life of an IRA than to extend a 401(k).

Until mid-2005, there was one caveat on converting from a 401(k) to an IRA: Most assets in employer-sponsored retirement accounts are protected from creditors by federal law. A 2005 Supreme Court decision and new legislation extended similar protection to most assets in IRAs.

The tax and transfer rules for 401(k)s, IRAs, and similar retirement accounts can be as complex as any government program you may encounter. Slott (2003 and 2005) are the best sources of information on these accounts that I have found. Unless you are confirmed in the do-it-yourself approach, you will want to consult an IRA specialist if your assets in these accounts total more than $100,000.

A Simplified Look at the Economics of Tax Deferral

As the table in Exhibit 3.3 illustrates, the after-tax economics of a tax-deferred account such as an IRA, 401(k), or other qualified defined contribution retirement plan are very different from the economics of a taxable account. The tax rates assumed in Exhibit 3.3 are the top brackets in effect before 2003 for an individual investor. These rates—including the estate tax rate—are scheduled to change dramatically (and in both directions) through 2011. Many investors will be subject to lower rates, to state and city income taxes, and/or to the AMT. Some investors will have special risk concerns (e.g., an outsized position in the stock of their present or a former employer) that affect the risk and tax characteristics of their entire portfolio and constrain their asset allocation decisions. The variations among investors in risk exposures and tax concerns are too diverse to cover all the possibilities adequately in a simple table, but this exhibit does illustrate a number of interesting features of tax-deferred and taxable accounts.

As the numbers in line (a) indicate, an investor in the top income tax bracket would have to earn $16,556 to pay federal taxes and have $10,000 left over to go into a taxable investment account. As line (d) indicates, the tax on distributions from tax-deferred accounts will usually be higher than taxes paid on distributions from the taxable account when assets are liquidated after retirement. Some of the gains in the taxable account are taxed

EXHIBIT 3.3 Simplified Tax Effects of Savings and Distributions—Tax-Deferred and Taxable Accounts

| | Tax-Deferred Accounts[a] | | | | Taxable Accounts | | | | |
| | Corporate Bonds | | Equities | | Municipal Bonds | | Equities | | |
Description of Step	Amount	Tax Rate	Amount	Tax Rate	Amount	Tax Rate	Commentary	Amount	Tax Rate
Accumulation									
(a) Initial pretax income to make $10,000 contribution to account	$10,000	0.0%	$10,000	0.0%	$16,556	39.6%		$16,556	39.6%
(b) Available to invest	$10,000		$10,000		$10,000			$10,000	
(c) Average annual tax rate before distribution		0.0%		0.0%		0.0%	Dividends and short-term capital gains		39.6%
							LTCG		20.0%
							Unrealized capital gains		0.0%
Distributions									
(d) Initial pretax income needed to provide $10,000 after tax	$16,556	39.6%	$16,556	39.6%	$16,556	0.0%	Principal	Various	0.0%
							Dividends		39.6%
							LTCG		20.0%
Residual needed to distribute $10,000 to next generation									
(e) Pre-income and estate tax	$36,791		$36,791		$22,222			$22,222	
(f) Available to beneficiary	$10,000		$10,000		$10,000			$10,000	
Federal tax rates									
Income tax			39.6%						
Long-term capital gains tax			20.0%						
Estate tax			55.0%						

[a]401(k), 403(b), IRA, SIMPLE, and SEP accounts. For Roth IRAs *Accumulation* and *Residual needed to distribute $10,000 to next generation* are like a taxable account. Distributions from the Roth account are exempt from federal income tax.

as long-term capital gains and the original cost basis of the investment and accumulated dividends in the taxable account have already been taxed. The advantage of the tax-deferred accounts is in compounding the investor's pretax contribution for many years before *any* taxes are paid.[22] As the DSZ study concluded and as financial planners usually stress, an investor should elect to defer the tax on as much income as possible for as long as possible to let returns compound tax free. It usually makes sense to take full advantage of compounding in tax-deferred retirement plans by delaying distributions from them for as long as the law and your other assets permit.

High income tax bracket/wealthy investors usually have relatively fewer of their assets in tax-deferred accounts like 401(k)s and IRAs than middle-income taxpayers, because of the contribution limits imposed by the tax code. Even if a taxpayer does not plan to live exclusively on Social Security checks and mandatory distributions from tax-deferred accounts, these accounts offer a safety net that even an extremely wealthy investor should use: They can shelter some income from taxation for many years and they can increase the value of a charitable contribution after the deaths of the taxpayer and spouse.[23] Unless an additional tax shelter mechanism is added, the combination of the estate tax and the income tax on distributions makes it difficult for a wealthy investor to pass much of the value of non-Roth accounts to the next generation. To appreciate this, look at lines (e) and (f) of Exhibit 3.3 to see the taxation cost of passing tax-deferred account assets to the next generation.

There is very different tax treatment of taxable equity positions (lines (c) and (d) of Exhibit 3.3) depending on holding period and ability to defer realization of long-term capital gains. In general, an active equity trading program that is even modestly successful at generating short-term capital gains should be in a tax-deferred account if these accounts are not filled by the investor's fixed-income allocation. Even a trading account that realizes only long-term gains should be on the tax-deferred side relative to a portfolio that accumulates *unrealized* long-term gains. Unrealized long-term gains are most valuable in a taxable account. If equity returns are high, the ability of well-managed ETFs to defer capital gains taxes indefinitely is extremely valuable to high-bracket investors because of the tax reduction during their lifetimes and the value to their heirs of the step-up in basis of the fund shares.[24]

Many investors have an intuitive grasp of the value of putting long-term equity investments in a taxable account where the tax advantage of deferred long-term capital gains can be significant. They also appreciate the value of putting taxable fixed-income positions in retirement accounts to defer taxes on the interest income. However, it is clear from conversations with investors and a variety of studies of 401(k) accounts that, as a group, investors do not pay enough attention to where they carry specific assets. Many investors need to obtain and use advice on the nuances of taxation and the tax-efficient location of investment positions.

Employee stock options and employer stock holdings in many investors' accounts create unique tax and risk issues. Many investors who do not have large positions in their employer's shares have similar problems caused by successful investments in one or a few stocks that dominate their portfolios. Even after the stock market decline from early 2000 levels, low-cost-basis stock positions dominate some investors' net worth calculations, frustrate attempts at diversification, and inhibit tax planning. ETFs are part of one logical answer to the question of what to do with whatever cash an investor can extract from these dominant positions, but many investors need specialized advice on how to manage the diversification and tax issues these positions present.

In general, the older and the more successful an investor is, the more difficult it is to achieve and maintain a diversified equity portfolio without paying some capital gains taxes. Some advisers specialize in the needs of such investors. Appropriate solutions vary greatly, but an investor in this circumstance should spare no more than a few moments for self-congratulations on the skill or good fortune that led to this "problem" before addressing possible paths to increased diversification and risk reduction that can be followed without a substantial tax penalty.[25]

Many investors with substantial embedded capital gains should consider realizing some of these capital gains at the 15 percent tax rate. Of course, they will need help from a tax adviser to test what their *actual* tax rate will be. The 15 percent LTCG tax rate promise is clouded for many investors by the prospect of the Alternative Minimum Tax, which can make the *effective* tax rate on a long-term gain much higher at some income levels.

One specific conclusion seems clear: the higher the effective LTCG tax rate, the more attractive ETFs will be relative to conventional funds. This relative attractiveness will be retroactive to the purchase date of the ETF.

Alternative Minimum Tax and Embedded versus Separately Billed Costs

The AMT can cause long-term capital gains to be taxed at a much higher effective rate than the 15 percent nominal maximum rate. Raising the rate on long-term gains is not the only problem the AMT creates. *The AMT can cause expenses for things like state income taxes, property taxes, and investment advisory fees to lose their tax deductibility.* Taxpayers who live in high-tax states or who make extensive use of itemized deductions are

A Tax-Efficient "Life Strategy" Fund: The Product Niche

Life strategy funds, or similar products with names suggesting a similar investment policy, provide either (1) a static asset allocation or (2) an asset allocation that changes in response to market opportunities or to the passage of time. Generically, the more flexible of these funds might be called variable asset allocation funds. Because these funds hold taxable fixed-income positions and may also realize significant capital gains, they are designed and sold almost exclusively for use in tax-sheltered accounts such as 401(k)s and IRAs.

I believe there is a substantial market for funds with similar investment policies but designed to operate efficiently in a taxable environment. The tax-efficient variable asset allocation fund would be designed to hold and defer taxation on equity positions in the early years of heavy stock ownership and would morph (without tax impact) to lower equity risk exposure and greater fixed-income participation (in tax-exempt municipal bonds) in the later years of the fund shareholder's life. This approach contrasts to some of today's life strategy funds, which are often either static or opportunistic in their asset allocation and very tax-inefficient.

The table in Exhibit 3.4 shows a possible asset allocation pattern for a fund that an investor might purchase at age 20, and that would be designed to convert to a much more conservative asset allocation

EXHIBIT 3.4 Percentage Composition of a Tax-Efficient Life Strategy Fund—Inception to Maturity

Investments—All Domestic	Years from Start of Fund					
	0	10	20	30	40	45
Large-Cap Indexed Equities	45%	45%	45%	45%	45%	8%
Large-Cap Sector Allocation	15	15	15	15	15	
Small-Cap Equities	10	10	10	10	10	2
Debt/Equity Asset Allocation	20	20	20	20	20	
Taxable Fixed Income	10	10	10	10	10	
Tax-Exempt Fixed Income	0	0	0	0	0	90
Total	100%	100%	100%	100%	100%	100%

when the investor reached age 65 (if that is what an investor decides to do). A series of such funds converting to a more conservative asset mix at five-year intervals could provide a range of choices of target asset allocations at retirement for a specific individual, and for a more gradual pattern of conversion for an investor who might invest in several such funds to customize the conversion to a more stable return portfolio over a longer interval. An ETF fund or **fund of funds** structure would permit asset allocation changes without taxable capital gains realizations or distributions. All entry to and exit from the funds would be through an ETF share class.

Any international equity diversification should be obtained with a 10 to 25 percent position in one or more *separate*, predominantly non-U.S. stock funds. Holding a small foreign stock position in a predominantly domestic fund is not tax-efficient.

The basic product structure would be an actively managed ETF of ETFs and other funds (a fund of funds). The SEC has been routinely granting exemptions from the rules of Section 12(d)(1) that limit the holdings of an umbrella fund in the shares of funds held in its portfolio. The only remaining exemptions necessary would permit limited active management of the ETF fund of funds. Because the fund's objective limits the range of choices open to the manager, obtaining the exemption should require much less effort and legal cost than a full active management exemption.

The obvious reason for choosing this variant on the ETF structure is the opportunity it provides to accomplish redemptions of the fund's positions in kind. When the fund is making a transition, either in investment policy or to a more conservative asset allocation, redemptions in kind could defer *all* taxes from appreciation of securities in the portfolio. Gains would not be realized by the ultimate investor unless and until that investor liquidated holdings to cover living costs in retirement. The use of the ETF format will provide opportunities for tax deferral at all stages in the life cycle of these funds and step-up of the investor's basis on remaining shares for heirs in the next generation.

The fund board would have broad powers to modify the fund's policies to pursue the tax and investment objectives shareholders will need in a changing investment or tax environment. These powers will also permit the fund to take advantage of broader ETF exemptive relief available in the future.

finding that their tax planning is turned on its head by the presence of the AMT structure.

The AMT is a parallel tax structure that exists side by side with the traditional tax rate schedule familiar to most investors. The AMT was originally designed to extract tax payments from a small number of high-income individuals who were paying little or no federal income tax. In practice, it has trapped a number of moderate-income taxpayers in a situation where the effective tax rate they pay is above the statutory rate for their tax bracket after some traditional expense deductions have been disallowed. With the AMT, which is truly an alternative to the traditional tax structure, a variety of expenses including state and local taxes and many other itemized deductions are excluded in calculating an investor's tax liability.

The reason for bringing the AMT up in the context of funds is that the effective expense ratio of a fund can be lower than the stated rate if you can use part of the pretax income in the fund to buy something else. For example, many financial planners and financial advisers are eligible to receive payments from funds pursuant to 12(b)(1) plans or **contingent deferred sales charges (CDSCs)**. The investor may be able to determine who gets the fees—and the fees might be used to pay for services other than fund marketing. Because these fees are paid through the fund, they reduce the investor's taxable income from short-term gains, dividends, and interest by reducing the investor's top-line income. In this way the fees become deductible when you calculate your AMT liability.

To the extent that fund fees can be used to pay for expenses that would not be deductible under the AMT structure if they were billed separately, they can reduce taxes for an investor who slips into the AMT net. Employing a fee-only adviser avoids some potential conflicts, but it may not be tax-efficient.

Summary

This chapter began the serious process of finding the right investment for each spot in your portfolio. The chapter started with a discussion of tax efficiency, both in general terms and as it applies to mutual funds and ETFs. The primary purpose of this discussion was to clarify and emphasize the value to a long-term investor of a tax-efficient fund carried in a taxable account. A tax-efficient fund will defer the taxation of capital gains indefinitely, allowing gains to compound on a pretax basis. Because of their tax efficiency, ETFs have an unmatchable advantage over conventional funds in this application. The long-term after-tax value of ETF tax efficiency is probably between 0.5 percent and 2.5 percent per year.

The second major topic covered in the chapter was the distribution of assets over different types of accounts held by the same individual or members of the same family. Recent research emphasizes the importance of placing taxable fixed-income assets first in tax-deferred accounts and tax-efficient equity assets first in taxable accounts. While the expected return and risk characteristics of the two instruments can have implications for the family group's overall asset allocation, the dominant implication is where various assets should be carried for tax efficiency.

Exhibit 3.3 shows a simple schematic of the economics of tax-deferred and taxable accounts both for the current generation and for assets to be passed on to future generations.

The chapter also touched on a point that every investor should give some personal thought to: Is it appropriate to change the character of a family portfolio when the senior members of the family pass from their working years into retirement? Should retirement be accompanied by a change in portfolio composition to increase fixed-income exposure and reduce equities?

Supplementary Information

Dammon, Spratt, and Zhang (2004) and Ellis (2002) are worth your attention as you wrestle with the issues raised in this chapter:

> Dammon, Robert M., Chester S. Spatt, and Harold H. Zhang, "Optimal Asset Location and Allocation with Taxable and Tax-Deferred Investing," *Journal of Finance*, June 2004, pp. 999–1037.
> Ellis, Charles D., *Winning the Loser's Game*, McGraw-Hill, 2002.

This could be an excellent opportunity to review your thinking on retirement planning. Consider the absolute and relative risks associated with what might happen in the world over your remaining life expectancy and how well or how poorly your financial plan would be likely to cope with these risks.

> Slott, Ed, *The Retirement Savings Time Bomb*, Penguin Books, 2003, and Slott, Ed, *Parlay Your IRA into a Family Fortune*, Viking Penguin, 2005, are excellent sources of information on handling the complexities of IRAs and other retirement accounts.

Updegrave, Walter, *We're Not in Kansas Anymore*, Crown Business, 2004, provides a clear discussion of the different types of tax-deferred accounts.

Wrestling with fund reports, especially tax reports, is often the worst part of owning funds. *Mutual Funds for Dummies* by Eric Tyson (John Wiley & Sons, 2004) provides detailed instructions for reading all fund reports and a great deal of other useful fund information. Be sure to get the fourth edition.

CHAPTER 4

Controlling Investment Costs: Money Market and Brokerage Account Economics, Separate Investments versus Funds

This chapter is largely about paying what you have to pay as efficiently as possible and getting full value for what you pay. If you get useful investment advice or help from a planner, a registered investment adviser, or a securities broker, you should expect to pay for that service. This chapter discusses the mechanisms that various financial organizations have in place to collect their fees, and how you can determine what you are paying in cases where there is no obvious price tag. The body of the chapter offers a number of suggestions on how to calculate some of the hidden fees. The key points are:

- Most of the money a brokerage firm makes on your securities account comes from two sources (and trading commissions are not one of them):
  1. Service fees embedded in the expense ratio of a money market fund used to hold cash balances or from the below-market interest rate paid on a money market deposit linked to your brokerage account.
  2. Service or 12(b)(1) fees paid to the broker by funds bought for no transaction fee (NTF) through the broker's fund supermarket.
- The traditional sources of brokerage income from commissions and order flow preferencing payments continue to decline in size and economic significance.
- Investors who use investment managers directly (as opposed to using them only through funds) might reduce their costs by using a manager who builds most of a client's portfolio from low-cost funds rather than from individual stocks and bonds in an unnecessarily customized separately managed account (SMA).

The most important single feature of this chapter is a discussion of the economics of short-term cash management and the closely related economics of your brokerage account. Like fund trading costs, important brokerage account cost elements are not always easy to identify or quantify.

Funds—both conventional mutual funds and ETFs—have relatively few distinct investment characteristics that are unique to the fund structure. For the most part, funds acquire their risk/return features from the risk/return features of the components of their portfolios. A financial planner, an investment manager, or an individual managing his own investments can either take a position in separate securities or hold equivalent positions in funds. Funds are vehicles of convenience and vehicles with cost advantages or disadvantages. Also, there are efficient and inefficient ways to buy funds.

For some funds and some purposes, you may be well served by a broker's fund supermarket, but you will want to avoid many funds that are sold through supermarkets. The supermarket structure can still be used by market timers to trade some funds. Most funds using the supermarket distribution channel will be vulnerable to abuse by market timers until late 2006—and even longer in some cases.

Most of the issues in choosing a fund versus separate positions in individual securities are expense ratio and transaction cost issues, but occasionally fund tax treatment will be different from separate-position tax treatment in significant ways.

Many readers will find the section entitled "Your Cash Balances Pay Your Broker" revealing. If you have a fund purchased through a fund supermarket or are considering the purchase of any fund that uses this distribution channel, you will find the "Mutual Fund Supermarkets" subsection of interest. Other sections can be omitted or scanned quickly unless the topic is of particular interest to you.

Thrift and Bank Savings Products versus Money Market Funds and Other Short-Term Fixed-Income Deposit Choices

Money market funds, banking institutions and brokerage firms all compete aggressively at times for your short-term transactional and emergency balances. The range of services, fees, and yields on the various products and accounts available is wide, and the regular appearance of new products shows that the opportunities for innovation have not been exhausted. Extremely low short-term interest rates in 2003 and 2004 blunted the competition between and among banking and brokerage entities and money market funds because none of the competitors could pay a very high rate in absolute terms. In high-rate and fluctuating-rate environments, investors who hold significant transaction balances or other short-term funds often switch among providers of money market investments to obtain some combination of a better net yield, an appropriate level of risk, and desired ancillary services including checking and cash transfer privileges. As in the case of 401(k) accounts, where most investors do not change their choices or their allocations after they sign up for the plan, most investors do less shopping among various types of short-term money market accounts than the economics of the range of choices might justify.

Money market mutual funds enjoyed their initial success because they were exempt from restrictions on bank interest rate payments on demand deposits. Money market fund yields still tend to vary over a wider range than the rates banks pay on deposits, and the competition among bank, brokerage, and fund products changes in intensity over time. The federal deposit insurance that banks offer can be worthwhile compensation for a slightly lower yield. The safety record of money market funds has been good, but there have been anxious moments when money funds have held the debt of defaulting borrowers.

An investor interested in maximizing interest yield from month to month will find that moving funds can pay off because many providers of short-term investment fund (STIF) services rely on the fact that fund flows are sticky: Most investors do not move their balances in response to small rate differentials. A common practice of money market funds has been to waive some expenses to attract assets with a higher yield and then end the fee waiver quietly. If you have enough assets in short-term deposits to consider moving your assets around to capture a higher return, you will want to check competitors' yields (including the yields on tax-exempt money market instruments and funds) every few months.

An important trend has been for some brokerage firms, particularly those affiliated with banks, to bypass money market funds and simply pay a low interest rate on cash deposits to accounts with small balances. This approach may not mean that deposits are held in an insured account with a banking affiliate, but it internalizes the cash management product, simplifies processing, and usually increases the broker's profit margins. In this case, as in many other relationships between financial intermediaries and their customers, a charge against income before the investor receives the income is less obviously painful than an explicitly stated fee charged after the income hits your account. As the discussion of the Alternative Minimum Tax in Chapter 3 indicated, for many investors, deducting fees before income is calculated can be more tax-efficient than paying an explicit fee. In either case, it is important to know that earnings on customer cash balances are the dominant source of brokerage firm profits on most of their customer accounts. As a cost-conscious investor, you want to understand how and how much you are paying your broker. That is the subject of the next section.

Your Cash Balances Pay Your Broker

My emphasis is on understanding and controlling expenses. Nonetheless, this seems like a good place to suggest a constructive—as well as an aggressive—attitude toward expenses. Anyone who needs the services of a financial intermediary (a bank, brokerage firm, fund, investment adviser, financial planner, etc.) should be aware of what is perhaps the most fundamental rule of economics after the law of supply and demand. It frequently goes by the acronym TANSTAAFL. The letters stand for "There Ain't No Such Thing As A Free Lunch." The grammatical challenge associated with the use of *ain't* may be a holdover from frontier days when many saloons advertised a "Free Lunch" in the window beside the swinging doors. The lunch was free only if you bought drinks at the bar. The rule long antedates the promotion of free lunches by saloons, however.

A satisfactory relationship between a customer and a financial intermediary requires that both parties find something useful in the arrangement. Before banks were permitted to pay interest on demand deposits, they offered customers "free" checking as compensation for leaving their deposits with the bank. Of course, so-called free checking was available only to investors who kept specified minimum balances in their demand deposit accounts. If your balance fell below the minimum or if you wrote more than the maximum number of checks each month, there was a charge for checking. The bank set its terms for free checking to provide adequate profits and hoped that some investors would let their cash balances grow to levels that would provide the bank with an additional windfall profit. Today, most brokerage firms use the TANSTAAFL model and treat customer cash balances and investor services in exactly the same way that banks treat free checking.

Watching the broker's toll charges on your cash balances is usually much more important than comparing commission rates. Since brokerage firm commissions became negotiable in 1975, a number of different profit models have been embraced by brokerage firms.[1] At times, extremely low commission rates with a wide range of free services were subsidized by payments many brokerage firms received for directing their customers' orders to certain markets. If your broker charges more than, say, $50 to execute a trade, the broker is probably earning something from the commission payment. Unless you are an extremely active trader, however, this source of revenue for the broker will be very modest. The broker's profit comes from holding the cash or fund assets of its customers. Not all brokerage accounts work this way, but it is by far the most common contemporary business model for brokerage firms. Brokerage firms advertise their low commission rates to divert attention from the interest you earn—or do not earn—on your cash balance. As long as the income from your cash balance is large enough to cover its costs and provide a modest profit, the brokerage firm does not care if you never trade a share. The broker knows what it costs to provide you with the range of services that you typically use. Correspondingly, you can make a good estimate of the revenue the broker is realizing on your account.

Unless you are paying an unusually high commission charge per trade, your broker has set the transaction fee schedule at a level designed to cover the costs of your trading—and to encourage you to leave securities and cash with the firm. Full-service brokers charge high per-trade commissions or a comprehensive asset-based fee that covers a higher level of service. Higher commissions or asset-based fees go largely to cover the wages and overhead costs of the personnel who provide the services. The firm's profit is still largely in your cash balances.

Money Market Fund Accounts

A money market fund account will sweep up cash payments from dividends and interest and from the proceeds of securities sales until you reinvest the cash. When you purchase securities, the money market fund account will be debited to pay for them, and the balance will decline. A few brokers will delay deposits into a money market fund to keep cash uninvested for a brief period of time. This practice is not common because most brokers have learned that it annoys clients and does not generate much additional income for the broker, anyway. The principal source of the income the broker makes from your money market fund balance will typically be from a service fee or from a share of the expense ratio of the money market fund. In most cases, this will be disclosed clearly in an annual or semiannual report the broker sends you on the money market fund(s) used in your account. From that report you will be able to determine at least the money fund's expense ratio, usually expressed as the ratio of expenses to average net assets.

If the money market fund is managed by an entity unaffiliated with your broker, the annual or semiannual fund report will typically indicate that a service fee has been paid by the fund to the brokerage firm for services the broker has provided to the fund in connection with shareholder accounting for the fund and so forth. This service fee (expressed as a percent or in basis points) times your average money fund balance will be a close approximation of the income your broker receives from your balance in the money market fund. To estimate how much the brokerage firm earns from a money market fund that is affiliated with your broker, it is probably safe to assume that the amount available to compensate the broker for the services you consume is equal to the expense ratio of the money market fund less a basic cost of about 30 basis points (0.30 percent). The expense ratio on the money fund my broker uses is 82 basis points or 0.82 percent. Subtracting 30 basis points gives an estimated net revenue of 52 basis points or 0.52 percent on my average money fund balance. Whether this is adequate, inadequate, or overly generous compensation for the broker depends principally on the average money fund balance I keep in the account and the level of service I require.

Cash Deposits

With increasing frequency, brokers are abandoning money market funds as the sweep vehicle for account cash balances and crediting their clients' accounts directly with interest on cash balances. Ordinarily, the interest rate paid will be a low rate on small balances or on all balances in small accounts and higher rates on larger balances. The disclosure that brokerage firms provide on these interest payments is always inadequate, and any linkage of these interest payments to a specific money market rate is usually unstated. If the firm publishes a rate schedule and you can determine that the maximum rate paid on large cash balances is competitive with independent money market funds, you can develop an estimate of the broker's interest income from your cash balances by comparing the return you receive on your average balance to the return you would receive from a comparable money market fund that does not pay a service fee or a marketing fee. The best way to estimate the value of your account to the broker is to check the interest rate available from an independent money market fund. You can calculate how much less you have received under the broker's rate scale. The difference is the broker's fee. You will need to check market rates occasionally because the broker's interest payment structure is designed to make it difficult for you to evaluate the appropriateness of leaving a cash deposit in your brokerage account as an alternative to other short-term cash instruments.[2] You will also want to consider that cash deposits left in your brokerage account are probably not protected by the Federal Deposit Insurance Corporation (FDIC). Unless there is a bank directly involved and you are specifically told that the account has FDIC coverage, the value of any brokerage account insurance protection is usually negligible for cash balances.

Cost versus Value

In general, the rates paid on cash balances are designed to provide the broker with adequate revenue to make the account at least a modestly profitable proposition with a small average cash balance. If you compare your estimate of the broker's revenue to the value of the services you receive and to other choices that might be available to you, you should be able to determine how appropriate the economic side of the relationship is from your perspective. If the calculation reveals that you have been paying the broker too much, a simple solution may be to remove cash balances more quickly and shift them to a low-cost independent money market fund. You should not hesitate to discuss the economics of your account with the individual who services your account or a supervisor. As long as you express a willingness to pay for value received, the conversation should be constructive.

To the extent that a brokerage firm obtains equivalent revenues from a reduction in your yield on money market deposits versus higher commissions that might reduce a long-term capital gain or from a separate asset-based fee for comprehensive account services, the way you pay can have tax and net return consequences. The undesirability of having a higher commission reduce a long-term capital gain or a higher fee reduce a qualified dividend, both of which are taxed nominally at 15 percent, is obvious, but the disadvantage of a separate fee can be even greater for many taxpayers. A separate fee is of limited deductibility for high-tax-bracket investors with large miscellaneous deductions and is not deductible at all for investors subject to the Alternative Minimum Tax. Many investors are best off if their broker gets paid through a reduction in their money market or other taxable interest return. Even if this is a better way to pay the broker, you will still want to monitor the broker's earnings. It is appropriate to transfer cash balances to a higher-earning account if balances are unnecessarily high. It is usually a good idea and a time- and money-saving strategy to let the broker earn a reasonable return without charging you a periodic account maintenance fee. It is also a good idea to vary your cash account's balance over the year. This can reduce the number of cash movements you need to make and lets the broker dream of growth in your cash balance.

Mutual Fund Supermarkets

The fastest-growing mutual fund marketing channel in recent years has been the mutual fund supermarket, now offered by most brokerage firms. The profit that your broker will earn from a fund you purchase through a mutual fund supermarket works much like the service fee paid by an unaffiliated money market fund to a broker using the money market fund to invest customer cash balances. The standard rate paid to the brokerage firm for a "shelf" position as a no transaction fee (NTF) fund has been 35 basis points or 0.35 percent per year, but these fees have been rising as both funds and brokerage firms have discovered that the supermarket format is a very effective way to sell funds. All the selling activity occurs in the first year, but the service fee or 12(b)(1) marketing fee that pays for the fund's place on the supermarket shelf goes to the brokerage firm each year *for as long as you hold the fund shares in the brokerage account.* Even if 12(b)(1) fees are eliminated in the Securities and Exchange Commission (SEC)'s current flurry of reform efforts, fund supermarkets have been so effective that the funds using them will simply raise their management fees and pay a service fee for space on the fund supermarket shelf.

A fund supermarket transaction may not be a bad deal for investors who value convenience and hold small fund positions. In fact, this marketing channel owes its popularity to the fact that it can be an efficient distribution mechanism for many funds. Supermarket operators usually require NTF funds to offer their lowest expense ratio shares through the fund supermarket. In such cases, it will not be possible to buy the shares of a fund at a lower expense ratio than the fund supermarket offers. A limited exception might be **institutional share classes** or other special share classes available to individuals through some 401(k) plans. As is often the case in a free market economy, it was not long before someone developed a way to offer a similar service at a lower fee. In this spirit, E*Trade offers to rebate 50 percent of any 12(b)(1) fee or service fee it receives on shares sold to its fund supermarket clients.[3]

Buying mutual fund shares through a fund supermarket is usually one of the best ways to purchase shares *in the particular funds offered* with no transaction fees. However, you need to be certain that you in fact want to purchase those particular funds. There is a wide range of **no-load funds** offered by fund companies that refuse to pay for NTF shelf space in a fund supermarket. The shares of funds that are not available without a fee are usually available from the broker for a one-time or round-trip transaction fee. Calculating the breakeven fee holding period for a $10,000 position in the ABC fund, which has a 40-basis-point expense ratio and a $100 round-trip commission charge, and the XYZ no-transaction-fee supermarket fund with an 80-basis-point expense ratio is not that difficult. If there is no separate charge for dividend reinvestment, the annual fund expense difference is $40. Assuming the fund price does not change, the breakeven period would be two and a half years. If you are investing $100,000 in a fund, the supermarket and the XYZ fund look a lot more expensive at a fund expense difference of $400 per year.

If a broker is affiliated with a mutual fund company, that company's fund shares might be available without a transaction fee to clients of the brokerage firm affiliate. Favored treatment to in-house funds is available from brokers affiliated with Vanguard, Schwab, Fidelity, and other fund sponsors. Some of the funds that you might want to purchase because of their low expense ratios will probably fall in this category.

One word of warning about supermarket funds to any investor inclined to use them: Many fund companies that restrict trading by market timers have found timers using the supermarket channel to circumvent their antitiming policies. In an attempt to restrict **market timing** through fund supermarkets and retirement accounts, the SEC adopted Rule 22c-2 under the **Investment Company Act of 1940** in March 2005. When the rule becomes effective late in 2006, boards of mutual funds that redeem shares within seven days of purchase must either adopt a redemption fee of up to 2 percent of the value of the shares redeemed or determine that a redemption fee is not necessary or appropriate for the fund. When and if the rule goes into effect, most funds will be required to enter into agreements with intermediaries (specifically broker-dealers and retirement plan administrators) obligating the intermediaries to provide the funds with shareholder trading information to permit the funds to identify shareholders who violate the funds' market timing policies. Funds will also be required to oversee the intermediaries' assessment of redemption fees. (The redemption fees will be paid into the fund.)

Unless and until enforceable redemption fees are in effect with regard to a specific fund and a specific supermarket, market timing is certain to continue, though perhaps at a lower rate than prevailed before the mutual fund shareholder abuse revelations of September 2003. A few funds that make extensive use of futures contracts or impose an earlier cutoff time than 4:00 p.m. Eastern time on most business days can offer reasonable shareholder protection without a redemption fee. For most funds, however, continued availability of fund shares until 4:00 p.m. through fund supermarkets without any redemption fee should be a red flag for investors. A strict redemption fee policy will not eliminate all fund share trading that is costly to ongoing fund shareholders, but it should encourage market timers to use another fund. The importance of using only funds that effectively discourage market timers is discussed at greater length in Chapter 5.

Another area of regulatory ferment is "point of sale" disclosure of sales and marketing fees to be provided to fund share purchasers. Given the cost of providing detailed information to every fund share purchaser, the ultimate disclosure will certainly fall short of perfection. However, the SEC seems determined to improve disclosure, and the result is likely to be a substantial improvement over current practice. Like the disclosure changes that will permit funds to protect shareholders from market timers who use supermarkets, the improved transparency in marketing and sales costs will not be effective before late 2006. An investor should always check a fund's redemption policy carefully and read the marketing cost discussion in the prospectus. At the very least, the cost of using a fund supermarket and the revenue it provides to your broker will be spelled out more clearly by late 2006. When you are evaluating the amount you pay the broker and the services the broker provides, *you will want to include the fees the broker is accumulating each year after the first year from mutual funds you bought through the broker's fund supermarket.*

Minimizing the Nuisance Cost of an Orphan Tax-Deferred Account

Many investors have one or more small tax-deferred accounts that seem to cry for attention. Most of these plans are no longer receiving new money. Some represent one-time deposits into specialized accounts designed, for example, to provide for the future education of a newborn. Such so-called orphan accounts may never see a second contribution. Apart from their small size, a common characteristic of these accounts is that they are more subject to neglect than 401(k) accounts that receive a steady flow of contributions from employees and their employers.

An increase in attention to retirement issues and to investors' neglect of their tax-deferred accounts has stimulated interest in getting these orphan accounts managed and integrated into a financial plan. If a small account is growing from contributions, help from an investment adviser or asset allocator may be in order. The owner of a neglected account may be offered a choice of helpers who will do anything from rebalancing the account's asset allocation annually to integrating the account into a comprehensive family financial plan. A 1 percent fee on a $10,000 orphan account would be $100. The dollar amount is not large, but the percentage certainly is large if the service includes nothing more than providing statements.

If you own an orphan IRA, it is probably best to attempt to find it a permanent home that will provide a minimum level of care without a large fee. If you have a number of accounts at a bank, fund company, or brokerage firm that consolidates accounts for purposes of calculating any account maintenance fees, that firm might be a low-cost home for the account. To reduce everyone's cost and inconvenience, the account might hold a single fund with automatic reinvestment of dividends. In a nurturing (low-cost) environment, the account can grow at a modest pace—until you have to confront integrating it into your mandatory withdrawal plan.

Fund Marketing Fees—How They Should Work

While disclosure of marketing fees is required, it can be very difficult for typical investors to be certain exactly what marketing costs they are paying to buy or hold shares in a fund. Even writing a set of rules requiring disclosure of marketing fees is a challenge, given the variety of payments between and among the various participants in the management, operation, and marketing of funds. The SEC continues to address this challenge under what it calls "point of sale" disclosure.

Stripping out all marketing fees and requiring separately invoiced marketing charges for each fund transaction and for each annual period is certainly not the answer. For one thing, United States tax laws limit the deductibility of such fees for most of the investors who pay them; and for investors subject to the Alternative Minimum Tax, such separately billed fees lose all deductibility. Embedding the fees in expenses charged against a fund's income distributions is appropriate for most investors, but simplification and improved disclosure are still essential.

Directed Brokerage

Until the summer of 2004, it was common practice for many funds to execute trades through the brokerage firms that sold the fund's shares to investors. These transactions were often made at commission rates above the standard level for the difficulty of a specific trade. The quality of execution of some directed trades was below the standard for a simple execution. It is no longer legal for funds to direct brokerage for selling fund shares. Directed brokerage is an example of a hidden marketing cost that should have been disclosed long ago.

Soft Dollars: Commissions May Cover Expenses That Should Be Reflected in a Fund's Expense Ratio

There is nothing wrong with so-called soft-dollar commission pay-ments for research and related services that appropriate disclosure cannot cure. In a soft-dollar arrangement, an investment manager will pay for research and related services by sending trades to a specified brokerage firm for execution. The commissions on these trades have two components: One component is the basic commission appropriate to executing the trade. Typically, in soft-dollar transactions, the trades will be relatively simple and the execution value of the commission will be low.

The second component of a soft-dollar commission is an add-on, which might be five cents per share in additional commission. This add-on is used to pay for research services furnished or paid for by the broker. As long as appropriate rules for the products and services pro-vided are followed, the only objection to this process is that the soft-dollar add-on portion of the commission should be treated as part of the fund's expense ratio.

Many investment management firms have stopped using soft dol-lars. The pressure on managers to abandon this expense payment technique continues to grow. Disclosure in the expense ratio might spell the end of soft dollars because they are, after all, no more than a technique to keep expenses out of the expense ratio.

Trading and Holding Assets Efficiently

The balance of this chapter focuses on the relative economics of differ-ent ways of trading and holding specific assets—separate accounts ver-sus funds.

Bonds versus Bond Funds

If an investor wants to hold a number of different bonds for credit and/or maturity diversification and the account is too small to trade directly with primary dealers in large size, then bond funds or other pooled account structures usually make more sense than direct ownership of separate bond positions. New electronic bond trading systems are reducing the cost of small bond trades, so the portfolio size at which a separate account makes sense will be falling. If a bond fund has a high fee, the probability that the fund manager and the fund strategy can add to net return will be low simply because of the size of the fee. Substantial fees may be justified if sound credit analysis of high yield bonds can add value—in much the same way that an active equity manager might add value with stock selection in an inefficiently priced stock market sector. Unless credit analysis or some other talent of the fund manager can add appreciably to return after deducting the fee, bond fund expenses should be kept low. Most of the indexes used for bond index funds are more inclusive and, hence, more efficient as fund templates than the most popular stock indexes. If an adviser urges you to use a laddering strategy for maturity diversification or even to match your liability schedule, ask for a justification of the costs of such a separate account.

Inflation-Protected Bonds: Treasury Inflation-Protected Securities (TIPS) and Others

Inflation-protected bonds issued by the U.S. Treasury have been justifiably popular in the relatively short period since their initial issuance. Investment-grade corporate bonds with inflation protection will offer additional choices. It is appropriate to question the market's valuation of these bonds if they acquire a significant scarcity value because issuance has not kept up with demand. Apart from the valuation issue, funds holding Treasury bonds and inflation-protected bonds issued by other entities are good candidates for tax-deferred accounts such as 401(k)s and IRAs. Such bonds or funds holding them should be held only in tax-deferred accounts because of the high current federal income tax levied on the bond return. The relatively high cost of trading some of these bonds individually and the complexity of dealing with some tax and cost basis issues in a taxpaying account are important reasons to confine inflation-protected bonds to fund holdings and the funds to tax-deferred accounts. The annual expense ratio on these funds should not exceed 20 basis points (0.20 percent) because the fund adviser is usually providing little more than accounting and administrative services.

Equities

Common stocks, both domestic and foreign, are increasingly held by individual investors inside a fund "wrapper." Aside from the effects of a few unusual tax features described later in this chapter, it is usually more economical to hold a diversified equity position in a fund, particularly in an index fund, than in a portfolio of individual security positions. With careful shopping, the fund wrapper can be inexpensive and the value of greater diversification can more than cover the fund's cost.[4] The total cost (as a percentage of assets) of assembling and maintaining a separate stock portfolio can be surprisingly high unless the portfolio value is more than several million dollars. New technology to support separately managed accounts (SMAs) with large numbers of securities has not reduced SMA costs as rapidly as the cost of the least expensive fund wrappers has declined.

Variable Annuities

Variable annuities based on equity funds have been used to achieve income tax deferral and to structure a stream of payments to match investors' needs for income. However, the current—and likely continuing—preferential tax treatment of qualifying dividends, favorable taxation of long-term capital gains, and deferral of unrealized long-term capital gains in low-fee ETFs make ETFs much more attractive from a tax and expense perspective than variable annuity products. For investors who want the combination of investment and insurance features provided by a variable annuity, a separate term insurance policy combined with ETFs to hold the equities is usually a much lower cost choice. It is hard to imagine a situation where buying a variable annuity would be better than an alternative way to obtain similar after-tax cash flows under current tax rules. If you are tempted to purchase a variable annuity, be sure to read the discussion of variable annuities on the SEC web site at www.sec.gov/investor/pubs/varannty.htm and be certain that you understand any surrender fees you will pay if you close out the annuity investment within a few years.

Choosing Tax-Efficient Fund Positions

Tax efficiency can be a complex issue when it comes to evaluating the wide range of packages and accounts offered for holding and trading securities. The combination of complex tax laws and unusual tax treatment of some packaged products makes definitive statements about tax efficiency difficult in some cases. Separately managed accounts are often advocated on the grounds that an investor can hold separate stock positions indefinitely to defer capital gains taxation yet realize losses on any separate stock position to offset gains realized in other positions. Realizing tax losses on one position to offset taxable gains on another position is called **tax loss harvesting**. If the equity market has not moved significantly in either direction over a period of time, a separate stock portfolio may still have a number of positions with losses and other positions with gains. If the losses are realized, they can be used to offset gains in long-term undiversified holdings that the investor may have elsewhere in the portfolio.

If the same positions with such diverse performance had been held in a single fund, the net asset value of the fund might not have changed materially. The fund might realize losses on some of its holdings and carry them forward for use against gains realized later, but the only way the investor owning the fund shares could realize a loss would be to sell the fund shares and, of course, if the losses had been approximately offset by gains elsewhere in the fund, there would be no net loss associated with selling the fund shares.

Tax management involving tax loss harvesting in separate accounts can be a useful money management and tax management technique. A number of advisers have been successfully using sector ETFs for tax loss harvesting at lower cost than would be possible in a separately managed individual securities account. Because the performance of stocks within a sector tends to be highly correlated and there are significant performance differences across sectors, a portfolio of sector ETFs can be a low-cost way to accomplish many of the tax management objectives of a separate stock account. Unlike a separate account tax loss harvesting program, which will tend to become undiversified as successful positions with embedded capital gains are frozen, the sector fund approach to tax loss harvesting can preserve diversification and minimize broad market index tracking error. ETF sector tax loss harvesting is discussed at length in Chapter 11.

Other Fund Tax Issues

There are a number of obscure tax provisions that fund investors should be alert to if they want to minimize their tax bills. Most funds deal with these issues effectively, but a few fund managers occasionally neglect them—at their shareholders' cost.

Regulated Investment Company (RIC) Diversification Requirements

Under Subchapter M of the Internal Revenue Code, a *registered* investment company (SEC terminology) must qualify as a *regulated* investment company (RIC) (IRS terminology) in order to pass through dividend and interest income and realized capital gains without taxation at the fund level. Regulated investment company requirements consist largely of certain portfolio diversification rules. One key diversification requirement consists of having no single issuer's securities account for more than 25 percent of the assets of the fund. A second requirement provides greater diversification over smaller positions. Specifically, with respect to 50 percent of the assets of the fund, no issuer can account for more than 5 percent of the fund's assets. There are some nuances as to when and how diversification is measured, but they are not significant for most purposes. Occasionally, a fund will fail to qualify as a RIC (IRS terminology) for tax-free pass-through of income, but such failures are extremely rare.

Some ETFs are designed around non-RIC-compliant indexes. Their portfolios are constructed using an optimization process called **representative sampling**.[5] The unacceptable security weightings in the index are simply changed to RIC-compliant weightings in the fund. As a consequence of this change in weightings, these funds do not track their **benchmark index** very closely, making it unnecessarily difficult to evaluate the performance of the fund and the fund manager. You can probably find a comparable index fund with a naturally RIC-compliant index that will be easier to monitor.

Special Income Character Pass-Through Rules for Regulated Investment Companies

The United States tax code has a number of special treatments for pass-through of various kinds of income by regulated investment companies. Most of these special rules affect relatively few funds, but some of them deserve elaboration and comment.

Global funds own both U.S. securities and foreign securities. They can face modestly adverse tax treatment if foreign securities account for less than half the assets of the fund. Shareholders of these funds can usually avoid most double taxation of dividends subject to withholding taxes in a foreign country. However, withholding tax payments come through to U.S. holders of a global fund as a tax deduction rather than as a tax credit unless foreign securities account for more than half the assets of the fund. Since funds holding non-U.S. securities usually have significantly higher expense ratios than domestic funds, global funds of all kinds are usually a bad buy. Get your domestic and foreign equity exposure in separate funds with greater tax efficiency and at a lower average expense ratio.

Municipal bond funds have the ability to pass through municipal interest in its character as municipal interest—exempt from federal income tax—but only if municipal securities account for more than half the assets of the fund.

Treasury interest is, by federal law, exempt from state and local income taxation. Various states have attempted to tax passed-through Treasury interest payments by investment companies, alleging that the character of the interest changes in the pass-through. When this issue has been litigated, the states usually have lost, but the greater the component of Treasury interest in a fund's distribution, the more likely the taxpayer is to receive favorable state tax treatment without taking the state to court.

Passive Foreign Investment Companies (PFICs) are corporations domiciled outside the United States with 75 percent or more of annual gross income from passive investment sources or with 50 percent or more of assets producing passive income. Taxation of PFIC shares held by U.S. entities, including regulated investment companies, is designed to prevent U.S. investors from investing abroad and avoiding U.S. income taxation until the investment is repatriated. Undistributed income of a PFIC may be taxed in the United States, and gains on the sale of PFIC shares are taxed more heavily than gains on other securities. PFICs are particularly common in Japan and, hence, in Japanese stock-based funds, including some index funds. A fund sold to taxable U.S. investors should hold PFICs only if they are significantly undervalued relative to an alternative way to hold a desired position.

Summary

This is a transitional chapter. It deals with the first stage in moving from the big picture risk/reward and asset allocation decisions to the nitty-gritty implementation of a specific investment portfolio. The chapter focus is on the economics of the accounts you will use to implement your investments in funds. The discussion of how your securities broker gets paid is designed to accomplish two things: It provides an open discussion of one of the worst kept, but least understood, secrets of the economics of consumer finance. It also provides an introduction to a process that astute investors must use regularly—the process of determining how much they are paying for something that is nominally free. As the chapter makes clear, there is nothing wrong with the way your broker is paid. In fact, the hidden charge may be more tax-efficient than an explicit fee. The indirect payment mechanism is something that you need to understand. You will confront it for the rest of your financial life. You will want to feel comfortable that you can control the payment mechanism well enough to get your money's worth from a relationship with a financial intermediary.

Supplementary Information

The best way to approach the indirect cost issues raised in this chapter is to remember the TANSTAAFL model and the adage that if something seems too good to be true, it probably is. Consumer-oriented TV reporters and columnists for consumer finance publications may go overboard in claiming to uncover abuses, but keep an open mind. Give their efforts a fair hearing or reading, and be prepared to examine both sides of any controversy. In short, keep your eyes and ears open.

CHAPTER 5

How to Cut Your Fund Costs

Funds incur costs on behalf of their investors. Some of those costs, like the fund's expense ratio, are relatively easy to pin down and evaluate. Others are more complex. This chapter shows how to avoid as many costs as you can without sacrificing performance. A few rules will help you accomplish most of the cost reduction that is possible—unless you are actually running the fund:

- There is strong evidence that the best-performing funds have low expense ratios and minimize trading costs and other expenses that are outside the fund's expense ratio. When choosing among a group of funds, be sure you have a very good reason before you choose a fund that does not have the lowest total expenses of the group.
- It is difficult for an investor to tell how much trading goes on in a fund's portfolio and what causes that trading. All funds report a number called "turnover." As an indicator of transaction costs, turnover can be seriously misleading because it tends to understate the amount of trading in the fund portfolio. If the turnover number is high, much over 100 percent per year, the fund manager may be trading too much. Overtrading may be stimulated by weaknesses in the fund's investment process, or the fund may be used by market timers and short-term fund share traders.
- **Flow** *(the number of fund shares sold to investors plus the number of shares redeemed by investors during a year, all divided by average shares outstanding over the year)* is usually the best indicator of misuse of the fund by active fund share traders. Flow is not regularly reported by any mutual fund service at this time, so you will

have to calculate it yourself from information in a fund's annual report.

■ Fund management companies can reduce or even eliminate the impact of flow on the performance delivered to ongoing shareholders, but they rarely take adequate steps to protect their shareholders from the cost of traders entering and leaving the fund. To minimize the adverse effect of fund share traders on the performance of your portfolios, try to buy a mutual fund that has tight standards for order cutoff prior to the 4:00 p.m. market close and higher redemption fees or longer periods for collecting redemption fees than competitive funds. Unless you are a short-term fund trader, you do not want to own a fund that attracts short-term traders. This simple rule is not enough to protect you from all costs imposed by entering and leaving shareholders, but a fund that has stricter standards than other funds should encourage market timers to use the other funds.

I recommend that all investors read "The Cost of Providing Free Liquidity to Mutual Fund Share Traders," later in this chapter. You will not find this topic addressed in most fund literature, and these costs of providing liquidity to traders can greatly reduce fund performance. Otherwise, browse or study the rest of this chapter as it meets your needs.

In this chapter and the next three chapters, I look at ways investors (and fund advisers) can reduce or avoid various kinds of fund costs. There are numerous places in addition to a fund's expense ratio where investors are hit with costs that reduce their returns. For most investors, the fund's expense ratio is considerably less than half of the annual costs they pay to hold a fund's shares. Even investors who buy low-fee, no-load index funds are usually not avoiding the transaction costs that hurt fund investors most.

Reducing costs at a particular fund is a task for the fund adviser or the fund director, not the investor. As an investor, your role in improving fund efficiency is to insist that the adviser to any fund you own must deliver full value by managing the fund well and protecting you and the fund's other shareholders from unnecessary costs. If most investors are determined to invest efficiently, fund managers will develop funds and fund operating policies that reduce costs and, correspondingly, increase investor returns. My objective is to help you find funds that have succeeded in doing this through sensible cost control efforts. Some of these funds have structures or operating policies that naturally minimize costs.

Frankly, I was surprised at the number and magnitude of the fund cost reduction opportunities that I found when I focused on this issue. However, there are fewer very efficient funds out there than I had hoped to find and there is room for improvement by even the best funds. The improvements need not be so much from reducing management fees and operating expenses as from improved index selection, new policies on early order cutoff times for fund share purchases and redemptions, and various kinds of trading cost reductions. Most operating improvements will show up as improvements in shareholder performance, not as a reduction in the fund's expense ratio. In some cases, a more efficiently structured fund would merit a higher management fee, to the direct benefit of the fund adviser. If an increase in the management fee was more than offset by a greater reduction in unnecessary expenses, the benefit to the fund's shareholders could be substantial.

The 2003–2004 mutual fund scandals convinced many investors that they need to understand the costs of a fund's operations better than they understood them before. They need to understand both costs that are disclosed in fund reports and costs that can only be estimated. The costs that have to be estimated include, for example, transaction costs that are a function of fund share purchases and redemptions—the flow of money into and out of the fund.

The reason for focusing on costs is that costs, even estimated costs, are relatively easy to find, evaluate, and (often) avoid if an investor does the necessary homework to find a fund adviser that looks after shareholder interests. It is usually easier to reduce costs than to find foolproof ways to improve the top-line return from a portfolio. When I examined various ways to avoid costs, I found recurring evidence that cost control is the best single way to increase the probability of good fund performance.

Fund costs fall into three categories. The first category is *costs reflected in the fund's expense ratio.* These costs are the easiest costs to compare in aggregate across funds, but they can be extremely difficult to break down into components in a meaningful way. The best way to think about reported expenses is that they need to cover what the fund management does to manage the portfolio and to ensure the integrity and regulatory compliance of the fund. Some kinds of portfolio management and some kinds of fund operations have inherently higher costs than others. For example, actively managed funds usually have higher expense ratios than index funds, partly because the fund manager is doing more things. But unless the fund's investment process and the specific talents of a portfolio manager are demonstrably worth a premium price, a smart fund shopper will usually get a better net return by being skeptical of high expense ratios.

Apart from the expense ratio, funds and their investors incur two additional types of expenses. These are *marketing expenses* and what I will call *transaction costs* with the understanding that I am defining transaction costs very broadly. Some marketing fees may be included in the expense ratio as 12(b)(1) fees,[1] but other marketing expenses are paid directly by the investor at the time the shares are purchased or at the time they are redeemed. An investor may have some discretion in determining how or even whether to pay marketing fees. It may be most efficient to buy something else—like brokerage firm or financial planning services—with a fund's marketing fees.

For many funds, the largest cost category is what I describe and discuss as transaction costs. The most obvious type of transaction cost includes trading costs associated with the portfolio management process (i.e., with changes in the composition of the portfolio). These transaction costs include costs embedded in the indexing process that will be discussed at length in Chapter 6. Of greater concern and often of much greater magnitude are less obvious transaction costs associated with the flow of money into and out of a conventional mutual fund as the fund's shareholders provide free liquidity to fund share traders. This latter category of transaction costs is largely avoidable if the fund manager is determined to protect the fund's ongoing shareholders. In practice, an investor may have to select a fund very carefully to avoid these costs. The fund scandals have made it clear that a fund investor can enhance performance significantly by choosing funds that protect their ongoing shareholders from the costs of providing free liquidity to entering and leaving fund share traders. Avoiding the most costly of these funds is not that difficult, but it is not something that most fund advisory services will help you accomplish.

Costs Reflected in the Fund's Expense Ratio

It seems appropriate to begin by putting mutual fund management and operating costs in perspective. If I start by looking at the lowest-cost indexed ETFs, the funds that usually have the lowest expense ratios of all types of funds, their base costs should provide a useful frame of reference for evaluating more complex and more expensive funds. Most conventional funds will not be able to operate with costs as low as the lowest-cost exchange-traded index funds, but knowing the costs for simple funds should help you understand what a reasonable cost structure might be for a range of different fund types.

The lowest current annual expense ratios on *pure* ETFs are 9.45 basis points (0.0945 percent) for the iShares S&P 500 Fund and 10 basis points (0.1 percent) for the S&P 500 SPDR Fund.[2] The SPDR is the original ETF in the United States and still the largest. Relative to most other ETFs and even more dramatically relative to the average conventional mutual fund, these are extremely low expense ratios. Both these funds are large (the iShares 500 Fund is the fourth largest U.S.-based exchange-traded fund), giving both funds a lot of *total* revenue to cover their modest fixed operating costs in spite of their low expense ratios. For perspective, 10 basis points in revenue on $1 billion in assets is $1 million per year. The low expense ratios on these funds reflect both intense pricing competition between two comparable ETFs and the low variable operating costs associated with most fund products. Variable operating costs are especially low for ETFs, but they are also low for most conventional mutual funds.[3]

I will not spend much time on fund start-up costs. By the time you purchase a fund's shares, start-up costs will be part of the fund's history. In general, however, essential start-up costs for a fund (including at least a small amount of introductory marketing) can be as much as several million dollars for a single, stand-alone fund or as little as a few hundred thousand dollars for a fund that is launched as one of a group of related funds with a shared legal and marketing structure and shared regulatory and reporting documents. Start-up costs are significant primarily because a new fund has a very small asset base to cover start-up expenses. Regulatory and legal costs associated with start-up and the annual cost of supporting the infrastructure necessary for a family of funds are substantial, but they are largely fixed costs. Legal start-up costs are often highest for ETFs because ETFs do not yet have the semi-automatic regulatory approval process that simplifies the introduction of new conventional funds.

Break-even fund asset levels for ETFs are usually much higher than break-even asset levels for conventional funds because the revenue per dollar of fund assets is lower for most ETFs. An extremely successful fund (of either type) might reach a break-even *operating* level in less than a year, but most funds take several years to gather enough assets to cover ongoing costs. Once a **fund family** (ETF or conventional) is operational, the largest costs tend to be marketing costs. The cost of the marketing effort is set by the manager and may respond slowly, if at all, to changing fund asset levels. Because marketing costs are both highly variable and partly discretionary, there is a limit on how much more deeply an investor can dig into the specifics of their effect on total fund expenses than the brief comments on fund supermarkets in Chapter 4.

The essential variable costs of running an index ETF are small, even relative to low ETF expense ratios, but all fund costs are not fixed and costs do grow as assets grow. Most ETFs have comprehensive or unitary fees that cover all expenses, so the ETF investor usually does not see any effect of asset growth on expense levels.[4] Most conventional funds will have expense ratios that decline very slowly as the fund grows. The marginal cost to a fund adviser of supporting or providing services for an additional dollar of assets consists largely of marketing costs and, for index ETFs, license fees. Once any fund passes breakeven, 50 percent or more of revenue from incremental assets can flow to its issuer's pretax income or to support additional marketing. The *reported* profit or loss of an established ETF or conventional fund adviser will depend more on the level of marketing expenditures covered out of the management fee than on any other variable.

Fund shareholders should keep in mind that a successful fund will have to cover its start-up costs and its annual fixed costs for the enterprise to be considered successful from the point of view of the entrepreneur who launched the fund. The fund's ability to attract incremental assets will not depend on the profitability of the fund, unless a short-term focus on profit affects spending on essential services or leads to a cutback in marketing. The fund's attractiveness to investors is affected by costs, but the marketing value of a fee reduction versus spending the same amount on traditional marketing is impossible to judge from outside and probably not much easier for fund management to evaluate. Before spending more time on marketing expenses, it is useful to take a look at a few of the more readily measurable expense items.

Shareholder Accounting Costs

Conventional mutual funds provide shareholder accounting at the fund level for many of their accounts. For a fund with a large number of small accounts, shareholder accounting can be a significant cost element. Vanguard, which has a policy of trying to assess costs on the shareholders and on the share classes that require its funds to incur specific costs, has estimated that its annual cost of carrying a fund account is $40 to $45, suggesting a breakeven account size of about $25,000 on most of its index fund Investor Shares. See Lucchetti (2001). Vanguard's VIPERs (ETF) and Admiral share classes have lower fees than the firm charges on the Investor Shares purchased by smaller accounts. The difference in the expense ratios suggests that Vanguard's variable cost of shareholder accounting and some other small account-population-related expenses is about 6 basis points (0.06 percent) on assets. Most fund companies appear to spend more than 6 basis points per year for shareholder account-population-related costs for conventional funds.

Shareholder Services

Exchange-traded funds have a modest cost advantage over conventional funds because they do not provide fund-level shareholder accounting. However, like all funds, ETFs have to provide certain shareholder services. Among those services is the legal requirement to provide and pay for distribution of periodic reports to the beneficial owners of the fund's shares. The only direct information ETF portfolio managers have about their shareholders comes from periodic reports from the Depository Trust and Clearing Corporation (DTCC) that list the number of shares held by each of the banks and brokerage firms carrying accounts that hold the ETF's shares and how many copies of the next fund report these intermediaries need to send to beneficial shareholders.

All fund companies provide shareholder support in addition to regular financial statements. This support is typically accessible online or via a toll-free number with some combination of an automated menu and a live person to answer shareholder questions. Most shareholder inquiries relate to a specific account holding, so they fall to the entity carrying the account and into the shareholder accounting category. While I have not seen figures breaking down calls to mutual fund 800 numbers between account inquiries and general inquiries not related to a specific account or transaction, the experience of most ETFs is that the number of general information calls to their 800 numbers is very small. This suggests that most shareholder service costs, except for the mailing of periodic reports, are borne by the intermediary that provides shareholder accounting. Setting up the infrastructure to provide shareholder information on web sites and to ensure that whoever answers the 800 number can answer appropriate questions can be costly; but the variable costs for these shareholder services are small with even the largest families of ETFs reporting very low call volumes.

Differences in Investment Management Costs

The cost of engaging effective portfolio managers, traders, and operations staff varies considerably with the nature of the assets being managed and with the management techniques required. Expecting every ETF to have an expense ratio in the range of 10 basis points and every conventional index mutual fund to have an expense ratio in the vicinity of 20 basis points is not realistic. Nonetheless, an astute fund share buyer should think long and hard about high fees charged by managers of specialty funds.

Stock selection for an actively managed portfolio of small-cap stocks is generally more labor-intensive than actively managing a portfolio of large-cap stocks at a similar level of effectiveness. Competent trading is also a more costly process with small-cap stocks. Whether a fund is indexed or actively managed, the value of trading skill increases as the average stock capitalization in the fund portfolio decreases and as the assets in the fund grow. Active management will be more labor-intensive and more costly than index fund management if both are done conscientiously. Estimating the cost and efficiency of a specific active management process from the outside is difficult and, indeed, *there is no necessary relationship between a fund's actual costs and the expense ratio that investors pay.* The basis for determining a fund's expense ratio is essentially set before the fund has sold a single share to investors. With revenues largely a function of assets under management and most costs (other than marketing) largely fixed from year to year, high operating leverage is inevitable.

Many **fund managers** believe that, within limits, sales of fund shares are not particularly sensitive to the fund's expense ratio. This be-

lief is probably incorrect. There is definite evidence of investor preference for low-cost funds in the growth of indexing and ETFs and in
greater cash flow into low-expense-ratio actively managed funds. However, changing the expense ratio slightly without changing the amount
spent on the investment process might change pretax profit by almost
the entire amount of the fee change in the short run. There is generally
an increase in the amount spent on investment management as the fund
grows and as the expense ratio increases, but solid numbers are hard to
find and the marginal cost of handling an additional dollar of fund assets
is very small. Most costs of handling research and trading that appear in
the expense ratio for a more complex portfolio are fixed/setup costs
rather than asset-level-linked variable costs. The conclusion is inescapable
that the principal determinants of a fund's expense ratio are how large the
management expects the fund to be in a year or two, what marketing expenditures management believes will be necessary, and what fee structure investors (and marketers) will accept for a specific kind of fund.
Management's estimate of fund costs is important only in reaching a determination that a fund with a specific expense ratio and cost structure
can be profitable within a reasonable period. If a fund sells well with a
high expense ratio and low marketing costs, the fund's shareholders are
still not likely to benefit from a fee reduction.

Exhibit 5.1 offers some perspective on the sensitivity of fund investment flows to the expense ratio. The average equity fund *share class* had
an expense ratio of 1.66 percent in 2003, but few of the total fund assets
and almost none of the net new cash flows were associated with funds in

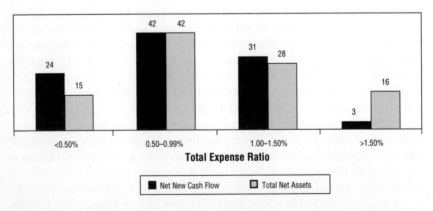

EXHIBIT 5.1   Net New Cash Flow and Total Net Assets of Equity Funds by Total
Expense Ratio,* 2003

*Based on preliminary 2003 expense data.

Data source: Investment Company Institute, *Mutual Fund Fact Book,* May 2004.

that expense range. Investors are obviously sensitive to fund expense ratios when they make new fund purchases. Keep the average expense ratio, cash flow, and net assets relationships of Exhibit 5.1 in mind when you read a fund advertisement stating that the fund's expense ratio is far below the industry or fund category average. The average that the advertisement refers to is almost certainly calculated by weighting each share class equally. As Exhibit 5.1 illustrates, investors have managed to put more of their money in share classes with considerably lower-cost shares.

Look for average fee calculations that are more meaningful. Fund asset-weighted fee calculations are uncommon because the necessary data are not easy to accumulate, but it is not hard to improve on the equal weighting if you want to do so. In its 2004 ads for Spartan Index Funds with reduced fees, Fidelity deliberately excluded the highest-cost funds from its calculation of competitive fund expense ratios.[5]

Expense Ratio Analysis

While it is possible to reject a superior fund by being too cost conscious in evaluating funds, the typical fund investor is probably not cost conscious enough to secure the best possible performance for what he pays. Reducing costs, either those charged directly by the fund manager or those embedded in transactions made on behalf of the fund, is nearly always desirable. Unless the expenses you pay are buying better top-line performance, cutting costs not only increases your return, dollar for dollar, it reduces your annual downside risk, dollar for dollar, because costs are a consistent drag on the fund's investment performance. That is *your* investment performance if you own the shares.

Exhibit 5.2 lists the major categories of expenses that funds incur. You will not find a breakdown like this in any fund annual report. Except for disclosed marketing expenses, a shareholder will find it hard to learn very much about a specific fund's cost structure or the profit margin of the management company.[6] The only way to control your costs is to buy funds with below-average expense ratios and, for conventional funds, with below-average costs from providing liquidity to shareholders entering and leaving the fund. Because expenses penalize performance and because a higher expense ratio does not consistently mean a more effective portfolio management process, funds with lower expenses generally deliver better results. Sharpe (1991) and Chalmers, Edelen, and Kadlec (2001a) found strong links between low expenses and good fund performance, and a more recent study by S&P has confirmed and updated the earlier findings in some detail.

In mid-2004, Standard & Poor's published the results of a study of the relationship between fees (expense ratios) and mutual fund performance. This was the second such study that Standard & Poor's has done, and this

EXHIBIT 5.2   Overview of Fund Expenses

Type of Expenses	Comments
Start-Up/Organization Expenses	Not charged directly to fund shareholders, those expenses must be recovered over time from the management fee.
Legal—Exemptive application	ETFs only—one exemptive order may cover many funds.
Legal—Fund registration	
Legal—Fund counsel	
Legal—Other	
Web site systems	
Fixed Annual Costs	
Legal	Largely prospectus update and fund counsel expense.
Printing	Prospectus and periodic reports (set up).
Auditing	
Web site maintenance and hosting	
Exchange listing fees (ETFs only)	Nominal.
Fund board expenses	
Insurance and fidelity bond	
Fund rating fees	
Distributor and fund transfer agent	
Salaries and other fund staff, office expenses	
Trading, quotations, and fund operating system maintenance costs	
Fund custodian, administration, accounting, daily pricing feed	These may be charged as variable costs by the custodian but they are largely fixed costs to the custodian.
Consultants	
Variable Costs Based on Fund Assets	
Custodian, fund accounting, fund administration	Moderate.
Shareholder reporting	Variable printing and mailing.
Shareholder telephone support	Moderate, significant only for conventional funds with fund level shareholder accounting.
Index license fees	Largest variable cost for most ETFs, usually small and fixed for conventional funds.
SEC fees	Small one-time only fee based on annual incremental additions to fund assets.

EXHIBIT 5.2 *(Continued)*

Type of Expenses	Comments
Discretionary Costs of Fund Marketing Advertising Marketing staff and support Marketing publications and fulfillment	Highly variable and hard to determine. ⎱ Many of these expenses are ⎰ covered by the fund's ⎰ management fee.
Sales charges	Usually expressed and paid for as a sales load.
Transaction-Related Costs	Costs incurred by the fund, but usually not reflected in the expense ratio. Transaction costs may be more a function of shareholder turnover than portfolio turnover in a conventional fund. There should be essentially no cost to ongoing ETF shareholders associated with shareholder turnover.
Commissions	Small
Trading spreads	Moderate
Market impact and missed trades	Highly variable
Trade linked charges by custodian and others	Small

may become an annual undertaking. While the study did not identify specific funds by name, its conclusions are powerful and they are consistent with the results of most other studies that have looked for a link between fund expense ratios and shareholder performance. The S&P analysts simply determined the average expense ratio for the funds in nine domestic fund styles: large, medium and small capitalization funds in growth, blend, and value categories. S&P then sorted the funds into those with an expense ratio below the average for the category and those with an expense ratio above the average for the category. The average annualized net return for each of the two groups was compared over one-, three-, five-, and ten-year periods. With negligible exceptions, the lower-expense-ratio funds won the performance derby.[7] While it would be desirable to know whether there were significant fund size differences in the high-fee and low-fee groups or whether the best-performing funds or worst-performing funds were actively managed or index funds, the significance of the expense ratio difference illustrated in Exhibit 5.3 is clear-cut and, in the aggregate, very dramatic. An investor should be convinced that there is a distinct management quality difference that will be reflected in expected future return before taking a position in a fund with a high expense ratio.

EXHIBIT 5.3 Funds with Low Expense Ratios Generally Outperform Funds with High Expense Ratios

Style Category	1-Year Return(%)	3-Year Return(%)	5-Year Return(%)	10-Year Return(%)	Average Expense Ratio
Large-Cap Growth					
Funds Above-Average Expense Ratio	14.75	−6.97	−5.04	7.19	2.14
Funds Below-Average Expense Ratio	16.07	−5.32	−3.37	8.90	1.09
Large-Cap Blend					
Funds Above-Average Expense Ratio	14.93	−3.89	−2.50	7.93	1.85
Funds Below-Average Expense Ratio	17.27	−2.51	−1.26	10.01	0.75
Large-Cap Value					
Funds Above-Average Expense Ratio	17.74	−1.53	0.84	9.19	1.93
Funds Below-Average Expense Ratio	18.79	0.01	1.81	10.53	0.99
Mid-Cap Growth					
Funds Above-Average Expense Ratio	21.03	−4.45	0.69	6.56	2.39
Funds Below-Average Expense Ratio	22.83	−3.14	2.39	9.47	1.23
Mid-Cap Blend					
Funds Above-Average Expense Ratio	23.35	3.38	8.37[a]	12.13[a]	1.84
Funds Below-Average Expense Ratio	25.47	4.93	7.99	12.12	0.80
Mid-Cap Value					
Funds Above-Average Expense Ratio	25.94	6.89	8.01	11.01	2.02
Funds Below-Average Expense Ratio	26.18	7.29	9.83	12.21	1.16
Small-Cap Growth					
Funds Above-Average Expense Ratio	26.04	−2.58	2.88	6.47	2.38
Funds Below-Average Expense Ratio	27.50	−0.77	5.65	10.29	1.36

EXHIBIT 5.3 *(Continued)*

Style Category	1-Year Return(%)	3-Year Return(%)	5-Year Return(%)	10-Year Return(%)	Average Expense Ratio
Small-Cap Blend					
Funds Above-Average Expense Ratio	30.67	5.60	7.83	10.72	2.03
Funds Below-Average Expense Ratio	31.01	7.33	9.79	11.51	0.96
Small-Cap Value					
Funds Above-Average Expense Ratio	30.73	9.39	12.20	11.36	2.16
Funds Below-Average Expense Ratio	31.78	11.22	13.33	13.40	1.20

[a]Funds in this category with above-average expense ratios outperformed less expensive peers.

Source: Standard & Poor's. Total returns include reinvested dividends. Data as of May 31, 2004.

Five papers—Chalmers, Edelen, and Kadlec (2001a); Elton, Gruber, Das, and Hlavka (1993); Malkiel (1995); Carhart (1997); and Clark (2004b)—collectively resolve any doubt as to the strong negative effect of the expense ratio and other expenses on fund performance.

Sales Charges

Fund sales charges could be the subject of several chapters—or even of several books. Sales charges are levied and disclosed in several ways. A 12(b)(1) fee of up to 1.0 percent (100 basis points) may be levied on shareholders to provide direct or indirect ongoing payments for sales and marketing. The 12(b)(1) fee is included in the expense ratio for the share classes that pay it. A purchasing or selling shareholder may also pay a **front-end load** or a contingent deferred sales charge (**back-end load**) upon redemption. These loads may be funded from a 12(b)(1) fee or they may be in addition to part or all of the 12(b)(1) fee.

The sales charge goes to pay for the sales process, though all of it does not go to the person who sells you the fund. There is a sales management and support structure (including overheads at the firm where the salesperson is employed) that absorbs a substantial fraction of the sales charge. In addition to specific sales and marketing charges, there are no restrictions on how much of the fund's management fee can be spent on sales and marketing.

It is possible—though it has not been easy—for any investor to determine the direct marketing costs he is paying to own shares in a fund. Both direct and indirect marketing costs and marketing expenses paid out of the management **advisory fee** should be easier to pin down after new Securities and Exchange Commission (SEC) point of sale disclosure rules become effective, probably in late 2006.

Because the principal purpose of this book is to help readers locate the best possible funds, it is reasonable to find ways to reduce expenses so money that would otherwise go for expenses goes to increase the investor's return. In this context, it is difficult to justify the sales charges common on certain mutual funds—particularly if you are doing your own research to select the fund or funds that you will buy. Furthermore, aside from getting the fund above a breakeven asset level, it is hard to attribute any positive marketing contribution to fund performance.

However, there are marketers of funds of vastly different capability and vastly different usefulness to investors. For example, if you are reading this book because a fund salesperson suggested to you that it might help you decide what funds you want to use, and if that salesperson has provided you with comprehensive cost comparisons and clear, risk-adjusted performance comparisons that you would not be able to develop on your own or obtain as readily elsewhere, that salesperson merits some compensation. To the extent that he has been candid about fund costs and his compensation, he deserves your consideration. However, the mutual fund sales process does not ordinarily proceed along this line.

If the material a salesperson has presented to you is not designed with your interests in mind, you will not feel much obligation to pay for the salesperson's effort. While certain funds are difficult or impossible for the average investor to purchase without some sales costs, there are often comparable funds with lower fees that will probably show a better net return than the higher-cost funds simply because of lower fees. You may have to do some of your own research to find these funds, but they do exist among the more than 18,000 fund share classes available in the United States. To the extent that you are convinced that a specific high-sales-cost fund has merit, Chapter 4's discussion of fund supermarkets may give you some ideas about how you can channel unavoidable marketing costs to productive use.

Given the uncertainty associated with any investment process, it is hard to believe that investors will be at a serious or systematic disadvantage if they exclude **load funds** or funds with large 12(b)(1) fees entirely from their fund selection process.

Transaction Costs

In a typical fund, it is very difficult—but very important—to estimate the magnitude of the transaction costs that penalize shareholder performance. Other things being equal, transaction costs are usually greater in less liquid market segments than in more liquid segments. Funds with less liquid portfolios usually have smaller asset bases, more complex portfolio management processes, and, paradoxically, higher portfolio turnover. A number of funds of all types have high transaction costs because they have been used aggressively by market timers or, simply, by frequent traders of fund shares. Many funds—some of those that have been in the news and some that have not—continue to be used by fund share traders. In many of these funds, the transaction costs from furnishing liquidity for fund share traders are much greater than the fund's expense ratio. In this chapter, I look at portfolio composition changes partly reflected in a fund statistic called turnover and at flow or **churn**, which reflect purchases and sales of fund shares by traders and investors. I will save the transaction costs embedded in the benchmark index fund composition change process for discussion in Chapter 6.

Portfolio Composition Changes—Turnover

Most fund portfolio managers are conscientious. They change a fund portfolio's composition only when they believe a trade will improve the performance of the portfolio. There is considerable, though not always compelling, evidence that the stocks portfolio managers buy do better than the stocks they sell. There have been numerous studies designed to determine whether various groups of investors—ranging from online traders to institutional portfolio managers—add value to their portfolios when they trade. The typical test centers on whether securities purchased do better than securities sold, and if they do, whether they do enough better to cover the transaction costs associated with the portfolio composition change.

The principal agreement among *most* of these studies is that, before transaction costs, professional portfolio managers have tended to add value. When all of the costs of the transactions and the expenses of engaging a portfolio manager are added in, the value of the typical active manager is less clear and varies considerably by portfolio type and market segment. Charles Ellis (2002, 19n) cites a number of studies that show net performance penalties associated with portfolio transactions. Grossman (1976), Grossman and Stiglitz (1980), Edelen (1999), and Chalmers, Edelen, and Kadlec (2001a) find substantial evidence that even if portfolio managers do not add value with their trades, the information content of their investment process neutralizes *some* of the transaction costs directly associated with those trades. Portfolio composition trading may not always improve performance; but it is usually less damaging to portfolio performance than trading done to provide liquidity to traders and investors entering and leaving the fund.

Part of the controversy over the net cost of portfolio composition transactions stems from changes in transaction costs over time. The recent trend has been an increase in institutional trading costs as the reduction in the tick size in equity markets from eighths ($0.125) and sixteenths ($0.0625) to pennies ($0.01) has reduced the willingness of market makers to offer as much liquidity to large institutional traders as they have offered in the past. The result has been a significant transaction cost increase for larger trades.

The best estimates of institutional transaction costs probably come from the Plexus Group, a wholly owned subsidiary of J. P. Morgan Chase. Based on its institutional customer database that covers approximately 25 percent of worldwide listed stock exchange volume, Plexus estimates that the average institutional cost of trading a $30 stock is $0.47 or 1.57 percent (157 basis points). This breaks down as:

Commissions	17 bps	$0.05
Market impact	34 bps	$0.10
Delay	77 bps	$0.23
Missed trades	29 bps	$0.09
Total	157 bps	$0.47

The expected cost of a round-trip trade (a purchase and a sale) to change the composition of a portfolio is double this amount, or over 3 percent of the assets involved in the trade.

Wayne Wagner, chairman of the Plexus Group, has observed that "total transaction cost is the largest cost borne by investors over time, in most cases being a larger drag on performance than management and administrative fees. Yet these figures are never disclosed, and often are dismissed by a manager as merely 'part of the process.' "[8] Pending changes in equity trading rules may slightly reduce institutional trading costs from these levels, but any change is likely to be small.

As required by the SEC, a number intended to measure portfolio composition changes is reported as turnover in every fund's annual and periodic reports. The turnover calculation is expressed as a percentage, and it is picked up and republished by most fund advisory services. It is an easy number to find and to compare across funds.

Unfortunately, the SEC definition of turnover does not produce a very useful number to serve as a proxy for the trading costs associated with changes in portfolio composition. The instructions from the SEC for the turnover calculation in a fund's annual or semiannual report runs to six paragraphs,[9] but a simple paraphrase is *the lesser of a fund's securities purchases or securities sales divided by average fund assets over the period, expressed as a percentage.* If a fund buys $30 million and sells $50 million worth of securities on average assets of $100 million, its SEC-defined turnover is 30 percent. Unless the fund report specifically states otherwise, the reported turnover percentage for a semiannual report is not annualized. Transactions in any security with a remaining life of less than one year (which would include most options and futures contracts) are excluded from the calculation.[10] This provision means that the turnover number will tend to understate changes in fund portfolio composition.[11]

Because it is readily available, analysts often try to use turnover to guesstimate the cost of flow trading in and out of the fund, but the turnover statistic does not reflect the volume and cost of flow trading in the fund's shares.[12] In the range of turnover percentages reported by most funds—the average equity fund turnover in 2004 was 50 percent (Investment Company Institute 2005, 15)—the net cost of portfolio composition trading was probably modest. This conclusion is based partly on the limited evidence that trades in actively managed funds add value before transaction costs. If a fund's turnover exceeds 100 percent per year, caution is appropriate, but the turnover calculation has so many weaknesses that it is best ignored unless it is unusually high.

Cost of Providing Free Liquidity to Mutual Fund Share Traders

The transaction costs that most often and most significantly reduce a fund's performance are costs associated with giving free liquidity to fund share traders.[13] To understand these costs, we need to examine the way money moves in and out of mutual funds and how the mutual fund scandals of 2003 and 2004 have highlighted this major cost obstacle to good fund performance.

Fund share buy orders frequently arrive in large size on days when the market is strong near the close. A trader cannot buy the stock positions held by a typical equity fund at 4:00 p.m. closing prices by entering stock buy orders at 3:59 p.m. Orders to be executed at the close must be entered earlier. The trader can, however, buy shares in most funds a few seconds before 4:00 p.m. Just as a trader cannot execute stock trades at the closing price seconds before the net asset value (NAV) calculation, the fund cannot make an immediate trade for its portfolio to invest the new cash at closing prices. Whether they intend to get in and out quickly or to stay for years, many buyers of fund shares make last-minute purchases on days with a strong market at the close. If they capture market momentum (buy fund shares at an NAV based partly on prices that were not updated by a closing rally) their trades are particularly costly to their fellow fund share-holders. The fund usually will have to buy stocks at even higher prices on the next trading day to invest the cash inflow. Correspondingly, if a share-holder redeeming fund shares with an order entered near 4:00 p.m. cap-tures momentum, the fund usually will have to sell portfolio securities the next trading day, at lower prices, to cover the redemption. The fund is thus providing free liquidity for entering and departing investors—and the fund's ongoing shareholders pay the cost of that liquidity.

If the portfolio manager knows that the fund share purchase is a tem-porary investment designed to capture market momentum, she may not equitize (invest) the cash. When the fund shares are redeemed the next day or within a few days, momentum will often have driven the fund share NAV higher. The fund share price of the redemption will be higher than the share price at which the shares were purchased. The cash that entered the fund earned modest money market rates for fund sharehold-ers and earned those rates for only a few days. The appreciation in the fund share price that the trader captured came from the increased value of the equity portfolio and it came at the expense of the ongoing share-holders of the fund. Because the fund had proportionally more cash and less stock as a result of the timing trade, the performance of the fund's equity positions was diluted by the cash invested temporarily by the fund share trader. The value of some of the stock portfolio appreciation was transferred from the long-term shareholders to the temporary sharehold-ers who traded the fund shares. Market timing trades in some of the more abusive stories that came out in 2003 and 2004 accounted for flow trading of hundreds of percent per year at times. If the appreciation taken from the fund was, say, 2 percent for each side of the average market timer's trade, purchases and sales by market timers equal in value to a fund's av-erage assets would reduce the fund's performance for ongoing sharehold-ers by about 4 percent per year. With allowance for a greater market impact effect when a trader is not paying the cost of the impact, this esti-mate is consistent with the Plexus Group trading cost figures cited earlier in this chapter. Studies of the impact of fund share trading offer com-pelling evidence that the costs of this trading to ongoing (nontrading) shareholders are substantial.[14]

Providing free liquidity to entering and leaving shareholders is costly to ongoing shareholders even if the buyers and sellers of fund shares are not market timers. In a study to measure the cost to ongoing shareholders of providing liquidity to entering and leaving shareholders, Roger M. Ede-len (1999), then a Wharton School (University of Pennsylvania) professor, quantified the adverse effect of shareholder entry and exit costs on fund performance. Using a sample of 166 conventional funds ranging in type from "small cap" to "income," Edelen investigated the cost to the fund of providing liquidity to investors who enter and leave the fund. His study examined all purchases and sales of securities by the funds over a series of six-month periods. The six-month interval was determined by the standard portfolio reporting interval for mutual funds at the time of the study.[15] Edelen was able to break down each fund's trading into flow (fund share trading) and nonflow (portfolio composition changes) components. He measured how much of the flow-related portfolio trading was incremental trading from having to purchase and sell portfolio securities in response to the entry and exit of shareholders. His methodology revealed the cost of the fund share trading, not the motives of buying and selling fund shareholders. To phrase that point in a different way, his analysis did not reveal whether a fund share buyer or seller was an ordinary investor or a market timer. Some reports have suggested that market timers are unique in costing fund shareholders lost performance, but it is not clear that market timing trades are materially worse than other kinds of fund share trades that rely on the free liquidity offered by most conventional mutual funds. The modest 70 percent flow trading in Edelen's sample notwithstanding, the trading costs he attributed to the liquidity offered to entering and exiting shareholders accounted for an average *net* reduction in *annual investor return* of about 1.43 percent. With annual net (one-sided) flow at 70 percent, Edelen's result is essentially the same as the 4 percent flow cost for 100 percent *fund share* turnover (200 percent flow) suggested in the preceding paragraph.

As a practical matter, an individual investor will find it difficult to determine how much portfolio turnover in a large number of funds might be due to intended portfolio composition changes and how much comes from providing liquidity to entering and leaving shareholders. Exhibit 5.4 compiles and compares data on (portfolio) turnover and flow from fund shares issued and redeemed for a few funds. Of the two types of trading, fund share flow is not only more costly than turnover from intentional portfolio composition changes; it is also a little harder for an investor to determine how much flow a fund has experienced.

Exhibit 5.4 deserves careful attention because it reveals some of the different characteristics of fund share flow from entering and leaving shareholders and the portfolio turnover that is in the hands of the fund's portfolio manager. The number that I call fund share flow and which appears in the column with that label in Exhibit 5.4 is not a standard or reported number, but I define it as Edelen (1999) defined it. Flow for a year is equal to fund shares issued plus fund shares redeemed, divided by average fund shares outstanding. (The flow calculation counts the purchase and sale separately because they occur at different times and each has a clearly separate market impact cost.) The calculation of flow is not required by the SEC and, to the best of my knowledge, it is not calculated or published by any fund service whose data are readily available to the investing public. As logical as its significance appears to be, aside from

EXHIBIT 5.4   Fund Share Flow and Portfolio Turnover for Selected Funds During Selected Periods

Fund (Period Ending)	Shares Outstanding	Shares Issued[a]	Shares Redeemed	Fund Share Flow[b]	Portfolio Turnover
Vanguard 500 (12/31/03)[c]	733,805	146,182	115,745	37%	2%
Vanguard Total Market (12/31/03)[c]	925,632	324,147	120,340	54%	2%
Fidelity Mid-Cap Stock (4/30/04)	389,735	122,333	61,953	51%	137%
Fidelity Technology (2/29/04)	41,960	14,603	11,248	64%	127%
PBHG Growth Fund (3/31/02)[d]	101,665	760,668	791,641	1,325%	171%
PBHG Growth Fund (3/31/03)[d]	80,513	10,894	32,046	47%	168%
PBHG Growth Fund (3/31/04)[d]	53,810	8,149	37,279	68%	164%
Invesco Technology 2003 (3/31/03)[c]	63,039	224,764	235,590	673%	107%
Invesco Technology 2004 (3/31/04)[c]	55,023	38,943	46,959	146%	141%

[a]Usually excludes shares issued in dividend reinvestment.
[b](Shares issued + Shares redeemed)/(Average shares outstanding during period).
[c]Investor class shares only.
[d]PBHG class shares only.
Source: Fund reports and SEC filings.

Edelen's work, I have not seen the calculation made, described, or defined elsewhere. The closest published equivalent is Lipper's "churn" measurement (described later).

When I began the analysis that led to the calculations in Exhibit 5.4, I expected that there would be a high correlation between (unreported) flow and (reported) turnover. I expected that funds where market timers and other traders had engaged in active fund share trading—as illustrated in several of the figures in the flow column of Exhibit 5.4—would also show extraordinarily high turnover for the same period(s). My expectation that turnover would be highly correlated with flow was incorrect. Apparently, some combination of knowledge by the fund manager that certain fund share purchases were temporary and the common practice of equitizing fund share purchases with futures contracts or other short-term instruments eliminated the link I had expected to find between turnover and flow. If the portfolio manager had believed that the fund share purchases that were part of this extremely high flow were being made by ordinary investors, I would have expected her to buy and sell stocks. If she had, the reported turnover would have increased to about one-half of the flow number. Chalmers, Edelen, and Kadlec (2001a), using a much larger sample, found no correlation between performance and turnover but a strong negative relationship between fund returns and trading expenses. Don Cassidy of Lipper finds only a weak relationship between his measure (churn), and turnover. (Churn is captured in a combination of two ratios. It is measured as high redemptions as a percentage of average net assets accompanied by a redemptions-to-sales ratio that is close to 100 percent. Churn would be approximately one-half the value of flow for the funds with flow over 400 percent during the same period.)[16]

The PBHG Growth Fund and the Invesco Technology Fund featured in Exhibit 5.4 are two of the funds often cited as having been used by market timers during part of the period for which data are displayed. The reason for the association of these funds with market timing trades is apparent in the fund share flow calculations, which show extremely high fund share trading volume.

As noted, flow is simply the sum of shares issued and shares redeemed divided by the average of shares outstanding at the beginning of the year and shares outstanding at the end of the year, expressed as a percentage. This percentage should give a very clear picture of the dilution experienced by a fund's ongoing shareholders when the fund is accommodating traders. During the period of highest flow, the turnover numbers for the PBHG Growth Fund and the Invesco Technology Fund were not materially different from the reported turnover in other periods or from the turnover in several Fidelity funds with similar investment objectives. In contrast to the PBHG and Invesco funds, the Fidelity funds saw only modest flow, probably because they have some protective features in place to discourage their use by market timers.

Flow is easy to calculate, but the data for the calculation may be hard to find if you do not have a copy of a fund's annual report. The effort to find the data can be worthwhile because, as described in the next section, flow is the best measure of the largest cost element most fund investors pay.

Flow—A Measure of the Largest Cost Most Fund Shareholders Pay

Flow is a measure of the money entering and leaving a conventional mutual fund through the purchase of new shares and the redemption of outstanding shares. Flow for equity mutual funds in the aggregate was 64 percent for 2003 and 51 percent for 2004 using the calculation methodology described earlier and industry figures published by the Investment

Company Institute (2005, 61, 77). As Exhibit 5.5 indicates, the flow value for 2004 was the lowest rate of flow trading for any year in more than a decade. Flow was probably reduced for both 2003 and 2004 as a result of the Eliot Spitzer mutual fund scandal revelations, which began in September 2003.

The reason for adding sales and redemptions in the flow calculation rather than using the lesser of the two as is done in the official portfolio turnover calculation is that purchases and redemptions of shares in a fund tend to have separate cost effects on the fund's ongoing shareholders—and they affect costs even if they do not represent timing trades. Flow is costly if it represents predominantly purchases in a growing fund or predominantly redemptions in a shrinking fund or even if it balances out on average but occurs at different times.[17] If a fund share purchase transaction is equitized by the portfolio manager or if a redemption results in the sale of portfolio securities, the cost of the underlying securities transaction will be paid by all the shareholders of the fund. If a purchase followed by a quick redemption does not lead to a portfolio transaction, but the fund share trader profits from capturing market momentum, this entry and exit will still be costly to ongoing shareholders in most cases, though they may lose a bit less because no securities were traded in the portfolio. All types of fund share transactions, whether a fund is growing on balance or suffering net redemptions, can lead to costly transactions that dilute shareholder performance with unwanted changes in the fund's cash balance.

The cost of these transactions will not show up in the fund's ex-

EXHIBIT 5.5   Fund Share Flow in U.S. Domestic Equity Funds

Year	Purchases	Redemptions	Sum of Purchases and Redemptions	Average Assets	Fund Share Flow
1994	366,659	252,134	620,788	796,720	78%
1995	433,853	309,461	745,310	1,050,920	71%
1996	674,323	457,386	1,133,706	1,487,550	76%
1997	880,286	653,180	1,535,464	2,047,020	75%
1998	1,065,455	908,422	1,975,876	2,673,130	74%
1999	1,411,013	1,223,347	2,636,360	3,510,060	75%
2000	1,975,880	1,666,515	3,644,396	4,001,910	91%
2001	1,330,685	1,298,720	2,631,406	3,690,040	71%
2002	1,220,214	1,247,880	2,470,096	3,040,590	81%
2003	1,086,421	934,143	2,022,568	3,173,910	64%
2004	1,125,378	947,527	2,072,905	4,034,120	51%

Data Source: Investment Company Institute, *Mutual Fund Fact Book*, May 2005.

pense ratio, but Chalmers, Edelen, and Kadlec (2001a) found a strong correlation between fund expense ratios and transaction costs. Transaction costs come directly off the investors' bottom line as a penalty to fund performance.

The management of a fund can do a number of things to reduce the effect of fund share flow on its shareholders. Redemption fees greater in size or applicable for a longer period than industry average will discourage many short-term traders from using a particular fund. But the remaining fund share turnover from ordinary fund share traders (nontimers) is likely to be almost as costly to ongoing shareholders as market timing trades, unless the fund actually succeeds in collecting a lot of redemption fees on behalf of its shareholders—an unlikely outcome. *Investors should expect any fund share flow to be costly, unless the portfolio manager knows about it early enough in the day to incorporate it into her trading plans before the next NAV calculation.* The only way a fund can protect ongoing shareholders from a substantial performance penalty associated with flow is to implement early trade cutoff times as described briefly in the next section of this chapter.

Until most funds take the step of implementing early trade cutoff times and additional research develops more precise flow cost estimates, I suggest that investors use each fund's flow record and a rough estimate of the cost of the flow to handicap funds that they are considering for purchase. This measure may discourage the use of smaller and newer funds and encourage the use of older, larger-cap funds, where opportunities for superior portfolio management may be less exciting. In some cases, this effect on fund choice may seem unfair to some good funds, but aggressive, smaller funds have been used most extensively by timers and the costs of flow are real costs. As far as fairness is concerned, a fund management that is determined to do so can neutralize the cost of flow to ongoing shareholders. If they do not take steps to neutralize the cost of the flow to ongoing shareholders, you do not want to be one of their shareholders.

Until a fund advisory service begins publishing fund share flow for each fund as a regular feature, you can calculate it yourself for the most recent fund reporting period from data in a fund's financial reports. The fund share purchases and redemptions are usually reported in a footnote to the financial statements. A fund that provides dividend or capital gains reinvestment services will usually report the issuance of reinvestment shares separately. The fund should know the timing of its dividend receipts and the percentage of any distribution that will be automatically reinvested. Consequently, the fund should be able to manage these cash flows in much the same way that it would manage cash flows if it knew a day's fund share purchases and sales early in the trading day. I exclude share issuance for such reinvestments from the total for share purchases in flow calculations.

The denominator in the flow calculation is equal to the average of shares outstanding at the end of the year and shares outstanding at the beginning of the year. Shares outstanding at the end of the year will be reported prominently in the annual report. If shares outstanding at the beginning of the year are not reported, the same footnote that provides information on share purchases and redemptions will show a net increase or decrease in shares for the period, and that can be subtracted from or added to the end-of-period shares to get the beginning share figure.[18] It will usually be adequate to make the calculation for the dominant share class in a fund rather than to compute an average value for all share classes.

I am not prepared to argue that you should automatically reject a fund on the basis of a specific fund share flow figure. Nonetheless, I would find it very difficult to justify purchasing the shares of any fund that was more than a few years old and had a flow of more than 100 percent per year unless the fund had *effective* early trade cutoff times in place to neutralize the cost of flow to shareholders.

A fund manager cannot be expected to stop fund share flow by refusing to accept fund share orders. But the fund manager can discourage short-term trades with strict redemption fee policies. Furthermore, with appropriate early order cutoff times for entering and leaving shareholders, the manager can largely eliminate the cost of such flow to the fund. If the cost to ongoing shareholders is eliminated, the incentives for in-and-out market timers to use this specific fund disappear, and market timers will abuse the shareholders of another fund instead. Allowing for portfolio capitalization differences and some uncertainty as to the source of fund share trading, Edelen's estimate of 1.43 percent per year in performance costs associated with an average rate of about 70 percent flow or 2.0 percent for 100 percent flow is a reasonable estimate of the cost an average fund incurs by providing liquidity to fund share traders. If the fund is a large-cap index fund that can equitize cash flow with futures, the expense might be much less, probably under 0.5 percent for 100 percent flow. If the fund is an actively managed small-cap fund, 3 percent to 4 percent for 100 percent flow is a better estimate.[19] If the fund share traders are deliberate market timers, the costs will probably tend to be higher.

High flow usually indicates that the fund manager (the management company, not necessarily the portfolio manager herself) is not taking adequate steps to discourage costly orders that arrive late in the trading day. Any cost from flow that exceeds 200 percent per year is highly likely to be associated with a fund management that is openly providing free liquidity to shareholders who are entering and leaving the fund at substantial cost to ongoing shareholders.

Two questions that come up frequently in discussions of fund share trading are: "Can the fund manager know that a specific fund share purchase is likely to be reversed quickly?" and "Could the fund manager have protected shareholders by rejecting a purchase transaction?" The answer to the first question is probably yes. Exhibit 5.4 shows that the flow trades in the PBHG Growth Fund in the year ending 3/31/02 and in the Invesco Technology Fund in the year ending 3/31/03 were not equitized with stock transactions (note the stable turnover rate in both funds over the period in the face of huge changes in flows), suggesting that the manager probably knew that incoming cash would go out quickly. While this behavior is suspicious, it does not necessarily indicate a major conspiracy between fund personnel and timers. Johnson (2004) found that certain types of fund share accounts and certain types of purchases are much more likely than others to place liquidity demands (and costs) on a fund's shareholders. Most of the characteristics of the accounts that redeem relatively quickly are not surprising. Johnson found that older shareholders (who have more free time to trade), larger accounts, accounts that wired money for a purchase, requested telephone redemption privileges, or came in through **Fund/SERV** (i.e., from a third-party marketer) were more likely to demand liquidity in closing the account relatively soon. Johnson's methodology did not give clear results on the liquidity cost of fund supermarket (omnibus-type) accounts. If a fund manager had performed an analysis of the liquidity demands of various account types along the line of Johnson's work, the fund might have appropriately delayed equitizing some fund share purchases.[20]

The answer to the second question—can the fund reject a transaction?—is harder to answer definitively, but it seems clear that active fund share traders would be encouraged to use other funds by a stronger redemption fee policy than the industry standard. Furthermore, one high flow cost short-term round trip should make an account ineligible for additional trades unless the commitment for any subsequent trade comes in early in the trading day, giving the portfolio manager time to neutralize the cost to ongoing shareholders. Market timers enter orders near 4:00 p.m. precisely to profit from free liquidity.

Try to avoid funds that incur excessive transaction costs *at least* as aggressively as you would avoid costs reflected in a high fund expense ratio or in high marketing fees. Flow has the same *kind* of adverse effect on investor performance as any other cost, but the *magnitude* of the effect of flow on performance is often greater because flow can be very large. In the light of at least scattered investor outrage at the mutual fund scandals, a few investor-oriented fund managers may adopt policies against fund share trading designed to protect ongoing shareholders from the costs of providing liquidity to traders. The fund reforms that the SEC has implemented so far do remarkably little to reduce the cost of market timing trades or to reduce the cost of flow from fund share traders who do not have timing motives.

Effective flow cost reduction depends on individual fund policies in light of the SEC's failure to act effectively. In the past, fund managers have announced policies designed to discourage fund share trading and to reduce the impact of trading on ongoing shareholders. As the events of 2003 and 2004 have illustrated, these policies were not always implemented effectively. Many funds' practices were very different from their stated policies. There is certainly scope for a few fund companies to appeal to sophisticated investors by requiring an earlier cutoff of fund share orders than the 4:00 p.m. standard.

A Simple Solution

A simple solution to the free liquidity problem is based on three fund policy changes that implement an early cutoff time for fund share transactions:[21]

1. For domestic equity or balanced funds, any open[22] mutual fund would accept purchase orders and all redeemable funds would accept redemption orders delivered to the adviser until 2:30 p.m. on any normal business day[23] for pricing at that day's NAV. No order cancellations would be permitted after 2:30 p.m. and the fund could trade to adjust its portfolio for these investor orders before the market close.
2. After 2:30 p.m., market makers unaffiliated with the fund adviser would be able to provide liquidity to investors who want to enter an order for execution at a share price based on that day's NAV.
3. For funds holding more than 3 percent of their assets in stocks traded on one or more primary markets outside the United States, orders would be accepted until 4:00 p.m. on any U.S. business day for pricing at the NAV next determined for the fund after a full trading day in the primary markets for stocks accounting for 97 percent of the fund's equity portfolio.

If a firm steps forward with such a policy, any performance-seeking investor should consider its fund offerings seriously. Even if this fund company's managers are not the most skilled, they will start off with a cost advantage over the average manager at funds that do not adopt similar policies. Edelen's study suggests—and the extraordinarily high flow revealed by many funds implicated in the market timing scandals illustrates—that a fund's cost of providing free liquidity to fund share traders can be a greater penalty to fund performance than a high expense ratio. Astute investors will try to avoid unnecessary costs whenever and wherever they can.

How Bad Does Fund Share Churn Get?

At the request of *Fortune* magazine, Don Cassidy of Lipper compiled a list of funds with share sales roughly equal to redemptions and with a level of redemptions that exceeded average net assets. The table in Exhibit 5.6 shows part of the list that *Fortune* published (Stires 2003). The article appropriately interpreted the redemptions column (with totals ranging above 800 percent of average net assets) as an indicator of the cost of transactions associated with providing liquidity to fund share traders. Any reasonable estimate of the performance impact of this fund share turnover suggests a staggering cost to the shareholders of the funds listed. Translating these numbers to the flow measure would approximately double the percentages.

A legendary investor, the late Philip Caret, has been quoted as saying, "Turnover usually indicates a failure of judgment" (Ellis 2002, 19n). High fund share turnover, whether measured as flow or churn, almost certainly indicates a failure to provide adequate shareholder protection and often indicates shareholder abuse.

EXHIBIT 5.6 Some Funds with Extreme Purchase and Redemption Activity

Fund Name (Ticker)	Average Net Assets 2002 ($ Billions)	Redemptions as Percent of Average Net Assets
AllianceBernstein Technology (ALTFX)	$1.49	837%
PBHG Growth (PBHGX)	$2.52	701%
MFS Emerging Growth (MFEGX)	$3.44	518%
AllianceBernstein Premier Growth (APGAX)	$2.71	348%
Invesco Technology (ITYAX)	$2.10	219%

Source: Lipper, as published in Stires (2003). Cassidy (2005) has a much more comprehensive listing.

Summary

This chapter provides a comprehensive look at fund costs ranging from the explicit costs reflected in the fund's expense ratio to marketing expenses and broadly defined transaction costs. Since the evidence is strong that expenses—in the broad sense—are the primary enemy of fund performance, the investor needs to be certain that expenses are held to a minimum. When there is little choice but to pay, marketing expenses may sometimes be used to cover other costs.

Here, as with the earlier discussion of tax efficiency in Chapter 3, I suggest a more comprehensive approach to costs than the common measures used by advisory services. The key lessons of the chapter are that, unless there is a compelling reason to do otherwise,

- Look for a fund expense ratio among the lowest available for the type of fund you are considering.
- If possible, use marketing fees to get something of value.
- Take great care to avoid investing in funds with flow measures greater than 100 percent. Such funds are probably providing free liquidity to last-minute fund share traders and market timers whose investment objectives are antithetical to your own. Even if those trades are not made by timers, avoid the fund unless you are confident it has an effective early order cutoff time.
- Once the SEC's redemption fee rule becomes effective, do not even consider a conventional mutual fund that does not adopt and enforce a strict redemption fee policy.[24]
- Do not consider buying a fund that uses the supermarket channel unless the fund has a strict redemption fee policy that applies to supermarket transactions. A strict redemption fee is your *only* protection from exposure to market timing trades in funds that use the supermarket channel. A stricter-than-average redemption policy encourages market timers to use other funds.

Supplementary Information

The best way to stay on top of what is going on in the fund industry is to read the better financial columns that cover funds. Most fund topics of importance will be discussed at least once by each of the major financial publications.

The text describes how the flow calculation is made, but getting data for the calculation may not be easy. If fund reports are available on the fund web site, they will usually provide a more user-friendly format than filings on the SEC web site. If you have no choice but the SEC web site, go to: www.sec.gov/edgar/searchedgar/webusers.htm. If you encounter a problem, you can direct an inquiry to the SEC staff by going to: https://tts.sec.gov/acts-ics/do/question. They are prompt in responding to e-mail messages and will help you locate information on a particular fund. It will be helpful if your Internet browser has a good search feature, because fund families typically consolidate information from many funds in a single filing. Data on the fund you are looking for may be interspersed with data from other fund family members.[25]

Read fund prospectuses with particular attention to order cutoff requirements. Look for a hard 2:30 p.m. order cutoff as evidence of an appropriate protective attitude toward long-term shareholders. (You will not find many of these early cutoffs yet.)

CHAPTER 6

Reducing Costs with Index Funds

Some of the costs embedded in index funds differ in both significant and subtle ways from the costs incurred by actively managed mutual funds. Index funds based on popular indexes are subject to different kinds of transaction costs than an active manager might incur in changing a fund's portfolio composition, but the fact that a high level of trading is associated with index composition changes may lead to index fund trading costs as great as the trading costs at many actively managed funds.

There is a longer list of dos and don'ts for index fund selection at the end of the chapter, but the most significant points are:

- Avoid popular equity indexes, especially the Russell 2000 and the Standard & Poor's 500. Other Russell and Standard & Poor's indexes are also widely used and impose embedded transaction costs on the shareholders of funds benchmarked to them.
- Use as few funds as possible. The best diversification values relative to fund expense ratios and trading costs are total U.S. market funds and U.S. extended market funds. These funds include small capitalization stocks in their portfolios, but their expense ratios are usually similar to the expense ratios of funds with all large capitalization stocks.
- Consider the lowest-cost conventional index funds as well as exchange-traded funds (ETFs) for positions in your tax-deferred accounts.
- Use *only* ETFs in your taxable accounts for long-term tax efficiency.
- Use specialized funds only for special needs—to realize tax losses that will offset gains in other positions or to diversify the overall portfolio in the presence of one or a small number of very large low-cost positions.

- Foreign stocks are an unnecessary luxury for most U.S. investors.
- With the exception of funds benchmarked to indexes that are inherently inefficient because they are too widely used, the best measure of an index fund manager's performance is usually the **tracking error** between the fund and the index. Be certain that both the fund return and the index return used to calculate tracking error are total returns (fully adjusted for dividends and interest).

I suggest most readers read the following section to get a balanced view of the advantages and disadvantages of indexing, the section "Evaluating Index Mutual Funds and ETFs" (pp. 132–137) and the text box "Evaluating the Performance of an Investment Manager" (pp. 132–137). Other than that material, feel free to scan your way to the end-of-chapter material and the beginning of Chapter 7.

A Realistic Approach to Indexing

A great deal has been written about how to choose an index fund or a portfolio of index funds to accomplish various investor objectives. The best examples of this genre of investment literature focus on the trade-off between risk and reward, on diversification, and on the importance of minimizing expenses.[1] This chapter attempts to combine a number of the analyses that have been offered by others with new observations to provide a synthesis that an investor can use to build an effective and efficient portfolio that considers both personal investment objectives and the economics of implementing those objectives. This chapter is *not* an unqualified endorsement of index fund investing *as it is practiced today.*[2]

An investor who commits to an incremental index fund cost reduction and performance improvement process should expect an average improvement in risk-adjusted return of at least 2 percent annually over the typical actively managed equity mutual fund portfolio. Investors who are already doing some of the things I suggest or using index funds might have less scope for improvement, but most investors should find substantial opportunities to reduce expenses, including some expenses that relatively few investors think about when they make investment choices. Most of my examples come from equity indexes and equity funds, partly because the savings possibilities tend to be larger, but indexing cost savings and transaction cost reductions from using a more efficient index and a more efficiently managed fund can be important in fixed-income funds as well.

At several points in the general cost reduction discussion in Chapter 5, I tried to quantify, at least approximately, some of the performance improvements available to investors from specific kinds of cost reduction. I continue and expand on that process in this chapter. While the opportunities for return improvement through cost reduction are not always additive, an average or expected return improvement of 1 percent should be easy for most investors who are using index funds now. A return improvement of 1 percent can come just from learning where to look for cost reduction opportunities. An aggressive approach to cost reduction should put a 2 percent return improvement within the reach of most mutual fund investors.

My focus in this chapter will be on how to build a largely indexed portfolio or set of portfolios designed to implement an investment plan as efficiently and effectively as possible. I look first at the reasons why index funds should be at the core of most investors' portfolios. This will be familiar material to many readers and I will not restate arguments made elsewhere at great length. Taking the usefulness of indexing as established, I emphasize choosing better indexes to serve as templates for mutual funds or ETFs. The differences between and among indexes offer significant opportunities for reductions in embedded costs and corresponding improvements in returns.

Index fund manager skills are not evaluated by most fund analysts or fund evaluation services, but a good index fund manager can add materially to an investor's results. There are useful ways to evaluate the performance of index fund managers, many of whom use similar indexes but return very different levels of performance. Using effective index fund manager evaluation as a guide in fund selection can help improve investor performance significantly. This is not the same process as choosing a fund based on past returns, on a magazine profile of the fund's manager, or on counting stars received from a fund advisory service. Choosing last year's performance leader or picking a fund on the basis of the number of stars it receives is not a reliable winning strategy. With a little work, an investor should be able to improve the chances of selecting an index fund where the manager uses sound management practices and regularly succeeds in adding value for investors.

Just as all index fund managers are not created equal, all indexes covering the same part of the market are not equivalent. Choosing the right index can add materially to your return. The index selection process proceeds from a discussion of index composition, transaction efficiency, index popularity and tax efficiency. Silent index funds—described later in this chapter—use proprietary indexes that do not announce index changes publicly until after the portfolio change has been made. This procedure is intended to protect the fund's shareholders from traders who often reduce an index fund's performance by front-running the fund's trading.

There is nothing in this chapter about how to find the next hot fund or hot manager. (Actually, I will tackle that task in Chapter 9.) The attentive reader who makes an effort to implement the lessons of this chapter will enjoy the performance advantage suggested by Joe's expected results described in the Introduction. This approach offers the advantage of a much higher probability of success than any process for finding a hot manager could ever offer.

A Brief History of Equity Index Funds

Peter Bernstein's history of the development and application of the great ideas of finance, *Capital Ideas* (1992), makes it clear that index funds were part of a broader plan. The unifying objective among the index fund pioneers seems to have been to replace the traditional trust department dog-walking (personal service) and stock-picking (active portfolio management) process with portfolios that had more diversification and a more scientific construction. Eliminating the adverse cost impact of active trading on performance and increasing portfolio diversification were as important as lower operating costs in the minds of many early practitioners of what has come to be known as Modern Portfolio Theory, but cost reduction was foremost on the minds of *all* the early indexing advocates.[3]

The first indexed portfolio, launched in 1971 by Wells Fargo, was created for a single pension fund client. In 1973, Wells Fargo organized a commingled fund for trust accounts. In 1976, the funds were combined and the capitalization-weighted S&P 500 index was used as the template for the combined portfolios. By 1977, Wells Fargo had commissioned a study of the feasibility of moving beyond the S&P 500 to the Wilshire 5000. They wanted the investable U.S. market in a single fund.

Theoretically, it should be easy to persuade pension funds to adopt indexing. Sophisticated decision-makers on the pension plans' boards of trustees would evaluate the economic argument rationally and approach the choice with a full understanding of the facts. Introducing the idea to individual investors was a more daunting proposition. In fact, the idea of indexing caught on with both institutional and individual investors thanks to some influential advocates. For example, in the first edition of his best seller, *A Random Walk Down Wall Street* in 1973, Burton Malkiel called for "A New Investment Instrument." He said, "What we need is a no-load, minimum-management-fee mutual fund that simply buys the hundreds of stocks making up the broad stock-market averages and does no trading from security to security in an attempt to catch the winners."

Paul Samuelson (1974) set down some arguments he had been making among the investment community in the *Journal of Portfolio Management.* He noted, "The only honest conclusion is to agree that a loose version of the 'efficient market' or 'random walk' hypothesis accords with the facts of life." Samuelson questioned why no money management organization offered an unmanaged diversified fund to the public. He believed that this could be done at relatively modest cost and that the fund would probably be a better repository for his savings than most actively managed funds.

Less than a year later, Charles D. Ellis (1975), in one of the most widely cited papers in the literature of both finance and tennis, marshaled some simple facts illustrating that the institutionalization of the equity markets in the 1960s and early 1970s had made it probable that the *average* institutional investment manager would typically underperform the market as measured by a representative index. The costs of trading actively managed institutional portfolios and paying administrative expenses and management fees—combined with the increased institutional share of the market—leave too little stock in the hands of nonprofessional investors to let amateurs fill the ranks of underperformers. Average active institutional investors are inevitably going to underperform the unmanaged market indexes over time.

With the implicit or explicit support of Malkiel, Samuelson, Ellis, and others, John Bogle of Vanguard launched the first broad-market stock index fund for retail investors in 1975. Bogle was as motivated by the desire to reduce investor costs at that time as he is today. Neither Bogle nor his supporters could have anticipated the success of indexing—or, ironically, the high costs that the index management and publication process would impose on many of today's index fund investors. It is time to consider the cost of indexing's success to today's index fund investors.

The Newly Profitable Role of the Index Publisher

One cost-saving feature of indexing that clearly attracted the pioneers who found fault with traditional active investment is rarely discussed. Using established market indexes as fund templates gave indexers access to the work of index publishers at very low cost. An index fund manager did not need a research department or conventional Wall Street research. Most of the information necessary to manage an index fund was available at low cost from index publishers.

The earliest market indexes were developed as market benchmarks or performance measurement gauges. No equity index creator or publisher had index fund applications in mind until after 1980. Any revenue from a license sold to an index fund before 1990 was pure gravy for the index publisher. Furthermore, the fund's implied endorsement of the index was helpful in making other licensing deals and in selling index data. The limited information available on early index fund licensing fees (which were typically confidential) makes it clear that the index providers were not paid high rates to provide an index fund's database and portfolio template. See the text box for an account of how index licensing fees have changed with the development of ETFs.

Index Publishing Revenues and Exchange-Traded Funds

In 2001, litigation between Vanguard and Standard & Poor's over Vanguard's claim that it had the right to issue an exchange-traded fund share class of its Vanguard 500 Index Fund led to the revelation that Vanguard pays Standard & Poor's $50,000 per year to license Standard & Poor's indexes.* Partly as a result of the unfavorable outcome of this litigation (from Vanguard's perspective), Vanguard changed the indexes on most of its funds from the S&P and Russell families to new indexes provided by Morgan Stanley Capital International (MSCI). Yet Vanguard still has as much as $150 billion in assets benchmarked to Standard & Poor's indexes, largely the S&P 500. Expressing Vanguard's S&P index license fee in basis points can be awkward, but to put the fee in a useful perspective, it works out to approximately $0.33 per year for every million dollars of Vanguard assets benchmarked to an S&P index.

It is interesting to contrast this license fee to index license fees common for ETFs. In some cases, ETF index license fees are expressed as a fixed number of basis points on assets; in others, they are a percentage of the fund's stated expense ratio. Defining an index license fee as any payment made to an entity that claims intellectual property rights over an index name or has a contractual right to receive payments in connection with the index calculation methodology, index license revenues range from under 10 percent to more than 30 percent of the expense ratio of various ETFs. A good rule of thumb is to assume that the average holder of an ETF pays (indirectly) a license fee of approximately 6 basis points (0.06 percent) per year on assets.

In contrast to the $0.33 annual index license fee for Vanguard funds per million dollars, the average annual ETF index license cost works out to $600 per million dollars under management—almost 2,000 times as much as Vanguard pays to S&P. The proliferation of equity and other indexes, primarily to provide indexes for the ETF market, is leading to the development of indexes in response to economic forces that are unrelated to any effort to find a better fund index. When U.S.-based ETF assets passed $200 billion, index licensing revenues for ETFs were around $120 million per year, with additional license fees associated with trading ETFs and derivative products—largely options—on these funds.

*The trial court decision, Hellerstein (2001), in the *McGraw-Hill vs. Vanguard* litigation (U.S. District Court, Southern District of New York, 00 Civ. 4247 (AKH)) on introduction of exchange-traded share classes, indicates that the license fee Vanguard pays S&P is capped at $5,000 per year. This figure is more correctly stated as $50,000 per year in Lucchetti and Lauricella (2001).

The index publisher performs some important portfolio calculations for an index fund manager. The index rules determine when and how the index and, hence, when and how the fund portfolio will be modified. In the early years when all index funds combined held a small fraction of 1 percent of the capitalization of each stock in an index, there was little reason to be concerned about competition for a limited supply of shares when a change was made in the index. As index funds grew, investors and analysts began to pay attention to index membership effects. It became clear that index membership carried implications for a company's stock performance.[4]

Low turnover of the index's constituent companies was an inherent part of the indexing strategy. Tracking a low-turnover index with a fund that was growing meant that the fund was buying stock relatively consistently and selling a few positions completely from time to time when stocks were dropped from the index. Index fund portfolio turnover and its associated costs were low, and tax efficiency was much better than active managers were achieving because the index funds typically sold relatively few low-cost positions. If a stock experienced problems, its weight in the portfolio was its weight in the index, and no individual was blamed for the stock's adverse impact on fund performance.

The index fund pioneers had achieved a number of things at once: relatively objective portfolio selection criteria, cost savings in fund operations, the limited portfolio management direction they needed to achieve a high degree of diversification, low trading costs from low portfolio turnover, and a high degree of natural tax efficiency. I have found nothing in the early indexing literature to indicate that the relative tax efficiency of index funds was anything other than serendipitous, suggesting that it is possible to be smart and lucky at the same time.

It is not possible to calculate the total assets of indexed portfolios in the United States today with any degree of precision. If a manager does not announce that a portfolio is tracking an index, there is no basis for the index publisher to collect a license fee. This simple statement suggests that most estimates of indexed assets are likely to be low. Morgenson (1997) cites an S&P estimate that 8 percent of the U.S. stock market's capitalization was indexed, presumably as of the end of 1996. Given the S&P 500's dominant share of U.S. large-capitalization index funds and the continuing growth in the Vanguard S&P 500 fund, the SPDRs, and other S&P 500 indexed portfolios, it is a safe assumption that *at least* 10 percent of the shares of any stock in the S&P 500 index is now held in an S&P 500 indexed portfolio. Wiandt (2004) cites a more recent S&P study finding that more than $1.2 trillion was "directly indexed to S&P's U.S. indexes," largely the S&P 500. This confirms both the continuing growth of indexing and the popularity of the S&P 500. There are higher estimates for the market share of indexing. Peter Bernstein (1992), for example, used a 30 percent share for indexed institutional portfolios.[5] The precise figure is not critical for our purpose because some passive portfolio managers take their time adjusting portfolio composition to changes in index composition. The important point is that at least 10 percent of the shares of any stock in the S&P 500 are held by committed indexers who change their portfolios at approximately the same time that the index changes. These hard-core indexers are part of the problem of growing transaction costs in index funds.

Recognition of Index Fund Transaction Costs

Enough has been said and written about the turmoil frequently associated with constituent changes in the S&P 500 and the Russell 2000 indexes that there is no need to reprise the stories here.[6] Several general comments are in order, however. Most observers agree that market roiling episodes associated with index changes were at their worst in 1999 and 2000 and that some of the most serious incidents involved S&P 500 additions with restricted floats. The appropriate way to analyze and evaluate the effect of these index changes on indexing portfolios is to view them as transactions and to try to measure their costs as one would measure the transaction costs incurred by an active portfolio manager.

I have encountered two different reactions to discussions of the transaction costs indexed portfolios incur when they trade to match changes in the index. The first reaction is that there are no transaction costs. The argument for the absence of transaction costs goes something like this: If an index fund manager modifies an S&P 500 portfolio with **market-on-close (MOC) orders** on the day the index change is effective, the portfolio can track the index perfectly. Unless the fund pays a commission or makes its transactions at some time other than at the market close on the day the index changes, fund performance in terms of index tracking will not be adversely affected by any transaction costs. One weakness in this argument is that there are predictable opportunities to transact at significantly better prices during a period starting before the announcement of an index change and ending a month or two after the index change becomes effective. These opportunities demonstrate the effect of index changes on the performance of the index itself.

As evidence that there are transaction costs associated with an index change, some indexers—Vanguard being the most widely discussed—regularly outperform the S&P 500 by trading at different times than the moment of the official index change.[7] These indexers capture some of the transaction costs embedded in the index reconstitution process and improve on the index return for their shareholders. A number of institutional managers indicate privately that they have captured an average of 100 basis points per year in incremental performance in the annual Russell 2000 reconstitution. The resulting favorable tracking error adds to the fund's performance and increases the popularity of the Russell 2000. Indexers as well as active managers prefer the Russell 2000 as a small-cap benchmark because the embedded transaction costs make it an easy benchmark to beat.[8]

Using a measure called **tracking error** (the fund return minus the index return) we can evaluate the index fund manager. (See the text box "Evaluating the Performance of an Investment Manager," pp. 137–139, for more on the meaning of tracking error.) Investors have varying attitudes toward any tracking error experienced by an index fund. A few managers and their clients match the formal index changes slavishly. Most passive investors are willing to live with substantial tracking error as long as it is highly likely to be positive tracking error. (This kind of tracking error is positive when the fund beats the index.) Aggressive index fund managers may deliberately trade at times other than the moment of an official index change to capture some of the trading costs embedded in the index and improve their fund's performance. They may evaluate blocks of stock that are bid for and offered in the market and buy or sell only when their measured transaction cost is small or even negative. They are providing liquidity for an anxious party on the other side of the trade. Being a seller of liquidity can help them outperform their benchmark index. Patient trading and providing liquidity can be particularly effective in improving portfolio performance with smaller stocks.[9] For marketing and (rarely) for legal reasons, some index fund managers are constrained in their ability to deviate from precise index replication. These managers tend to trade at the exact moment of an official index change.

The most common reaction to the notion of index fund transition/transaction costs is agreement that transaction costs are present in an index change, and that they should be measured by taking the difference between prices just before the index change announcement or determination and closing prices on the day of the official index change. This is a sensible approach, but it does not work very well for some indexes. It is easy to illustrate some of the problems with an example based on the way the S&P 500 index is modified.

The most widely used measures of transaction costs start the cost measurement clock running when the decision is made to trade. In their simplest form, these measures incorporate the net price change and any commissions in the trading cost calculation. The indexer's decision to trade is made when the index change is announced or, for some indexes, determined by the index composition model. While the first opportunity to trade is usually at the next day's market opening, a better case can be made for using the price just before the announcement or determination of the index change as the starting point.

The greatest problem with either of these starting points for an index composition transaction cost calculation is the growth of a cottage industry that attempts to anticipate changes in the indexes before they are announced.[10] At any time a company is scheduled to leave the S&P 500, there are probably 10 to 20 serious candidates to replace it. Some of these candidates can be set aside or moved higher on the list for one reason or another. If a candidate is in the same industry as the departing company or in what the S&P Index Committee considers to be an underweighted industry, it is more likely to be chosen than another company of similar size that S&P has not used in its smaller-cap indexes. If a company is in the S&P 400 (MidCap) index, it is more likely to be chosen for an opening in the S&P 500 than a similar company that S&P has not used in its indexes before. If a company is a recent initial public offering (IPO), it is less likely to be added to the S&P 500 than a company with a longer trading history unless its capitalization is too large to ignore. S&P also avoids adding companies without current reported earnings to the principal S&P indexes.

The effort to predict the next addition to some indexes can lead to unusual transactions and to price impact on the new index member's shares well ahead of the index change announcement, creating a situation that does not fit easily into a transaction cost analysis framework for any of several reasons:

- The preannouncement anticipatory trading has no determinable starting date or price.
- S&P MidCap 400 index stocks have lower apparent transition/transaction costs when they move to the S&P 500 than stocks not in the MidCap 400. MidCap 400 membership is more likely to lead to selection for the S&P 500 than lack of prior membership in an S&P index. Consequently, there is likely to be more preannouncement purchasing of S&P 400 stocks. In addition, the transaction cost impact will be reduced by the fact that MidCap 400 indexed portfolios will sell the shares when the company leaves that index for the S&P 500.
- It is impossible to separate these transition/transaction costs from the traditional S&P 500 membership effect[11]—and it is not clear that one should try to separate them.

Outlook for Index Transition/Transaction Costs

The dominant portion of the transaction costs that S&P 500 and Russell 2000 index funds experience is attributable to all the competition that the funds indexed to these benchmarks have whenever they need to transact in connection with an index change. From the time index funds were introduced until the early 1990s, market impact costs from index modifications were a nonissue for most index fund managers. The success of indexing and consequent trading in competition with other index fund reconstitution traders is the direct cause of the magnitude of these transaction costs in most recent years. Only the end of growth in equity fund indexation or a radical change in the indexes used (and how they are used) will keep the benchmark index fund internal portfolio transaction costs illustrated in Gastineau (2002b) and Chen, Noronha, and Singal (2004) from growing when merger and acquisition activity picks up.[12]

The indexing process must change. The index fund manager needs an index that has modification rules (or committee policies) that are as independent as possible from the rules used by other indexers operating in the same general market space (e.g., large-cap, small-cap, sector, or style). The new operating format for index funds should be funds based on silent indexes—indexes with disclosure of composition changes delayed until after the single fund using the index as a template has had an opportunity to implement the change. I expand on the silent index idea in a later section.

Setting aside the difficulty of estimating the transaction costs of index transitions with precision, there clearly are incremental transaction costs. Looking at stock price changes in other ways demonstrates that there are very real trading costs associated with an S&P 500 index change.[13] It is best to focus on the probable size of these transaction costs relative to the total expenses of a fund, accepting the principle that a rough estimate is better than no estimate at all. The problem of measuring these costs usefully and consistently needs more attention, including attention to the cost of trading stocks that stay in the index but are reweighted as a result of index changes. I estimate the average embedded transaction costs in the S&P 500 at 50 to 100 basis points (0.5 percent to 1.0 percent) per year and the embedded transaction costs in the Russell 2000 at 100 to 300 basis points (1.0 percent to 3.0 percent) per year, but the variation from year to year in both indexes is dramatic.[14]

It is a safe generalization that the more popular an index is as a template for index funds, the less likely its funds are to deliver good performance relative to a similar fund portfolio not directly affected by these transaction costs. This point gives full recognition to the modest increases in portfolio investment efficiency that can come from being able to trade the basket of securities represented in an index more cheaply as a basket when the index becomes popular. The conclusion is inescapable that a long-term investor whose interests are in the return on a long-term holding in the basket will want to minimize the ongoing transaction costs associated with indexing basket changes, reconstitutions, and rebalancings. The less popular its index is as a fund template, the more attractive a fund should be to a long-term investor. A suitable fund index should be "fund friendly" to investors rather than indiscriminately popular (i.e., widely used).

Essential Characteristics of a Fund-Friendly Index

The index universe for a **fund-friendly index** should encompass a market that investors want to buy. This relatively simple principle should be easy to accommodate in an index design. Without it, the best-structured index will not attract investors to a fund. The market covered by the index must be large enough to permit construction of a viable fund, and the securities in the fund's universe, (i.e., the population of companies from which members of the index will be selected) should consist of acceptably liquid securities.

To the extent that the index is capitalization-weighted[15]—or, even better, float-weighted[16]—the smaller companies in the index need not have a great deal of individual liquidity because their positions in the fund will be quite small. There will be some pricing and index tracking issues if there is not reasonably regular trading in the shares of each index member. Exhibit 6.1 lists some important characteristics of fund-friendly indexes.

EXHIBIT 6.1   Some Desirable Characteristics of Fund-Friendly Indexes

1. The index meets IRS regulated investment company (RIC) requirements for a U.S. fund or Undertakings for the Collective Investment of Transferable Securities (UCITS) requirements for a fund distributed in Europe either (1) naturally, (2) by special weighting rules, (3) with custom structured instruments, or (4) by representative sampling. (1) and (2) are vastly preferable to (3) and (4).
2. Rebalancing and replacement rules minimize portfolio turnover.
3. Style indexes (growth/value) should not cover all the companies in the corresponding broad market aggregate index because many companies lack distinct growth or value characteristics.
4. The index creates a fund that makes investment sense and appeals to investors.
5. The resulting fund has many uses and useful derivatives. Fund derivatives are usually more useful than index derivatives.
6. The index is rules based. A backup decision-making entity is used only for emergencies not anticipated by the rules. The rules need not be publicly disclosed and may include randomizing elements. A silent index is always more fund friendly than an index with changes published before the fund can trade. Actively managed indexes, following the S&P model, will enjoy increased popularity until truly actively managed ETFs are approved by the SEC.
7. The fund is inherently tax-efficient.
   - It has low turnover, but some stocks may be completely removed from the index each year.
   - There is no loss of the foreign withholding tax credit or other pass-through benefits due to structure or portfolio composition.
8. Index license fees are modest relative to benchmark index licensing fees unless the licensed name or other features promise to bring in enough assets to lower total fund costs.

Other Issues

Handling of float: Float is rarely an issue for a fund-friendly index that is designed for a single fund. It can be very important if an index is designed for use by a number of funds. A minimum capitalization percentage requirement on float or a delay on IPO entry into an index past the lockup period is okay, but staged additions to weighting as float increases should be avoided unless they can be integrated into a plan that reduces reweighting costs.

    Modularity: It is harder to create and redeem in kind if the index has a large number of issues, so funds of funds can be useful in creation and redemption of funds with a large number of issues.

Silence Is Golden

The most fund-friendly index is a silent index. The silent index fund is the solution to index congestion, embedded transaction costs and fund-*un*-friendly indexes. Unfortunately, there are no silent index funds today. The SEC requires that fund indexes be transparent. Front-running and embedded transaction costs are the inevitable result of this regulatory requirement. A silent index is an index developed and maintained for the use of a single exchange-traded fund or a single traditional mutual fund. It is not designed to serve as a performance benchmark, as an underlying index for multiple funds, or for stand-alone derivative instrument trading. The fund itself may have derivatives or there may be derivatives on a licensed index developed from the fund's sequence of net asset value calculations, but the template index for the fund portfolio is used exclusively as a template index for that single fund. The silent index has no licensing value beyond that application. Changes in the silent index are not made public until after its fund has had an opportunity to act on the index changes (i.e., to change the composition of the fund portfolio).

    The silent index fund's performance should be superior to an index fund based on a benchmark index because of the benchmark index fund's unnecessary transaction costs. Multiple licensees of benchmark indexes, together with speculators and other investors who easily acquire knowledge of benchmark index changes, impose a transaction cost penalty on funds using benchmark indexes. Benchmark index funds are forced to make portfolio changes amid a flurry of market activity caused by the announcement of changes to their index—and are often forced to buy high and sell low during the blizzard of rebalancing and related speculation. The problem with this trading activity is that transaction costs associated with index changes are increasingly embedded in the benchmark index's performance, reducing returns measured by the index and returns from funds using it as a template.

A silent index is based on the same kinds of rules as a good bench-mark index—but the specific silent index rules are not subject to use by multiple funds or by speculators attempting to front-run trades by the fund using the index. As a result of the delayed disclosure of index changes, the silent index fund should outperform a comparable benchmark index fund by a few basis points to a few hundred basis points per year depending on the benchmark index's rules, capitalization range, and popularity. The silent index will be less well known than similar benchmark indexes and, consequently, it may have a fund marketing penalty associated with it. In many cases, however, the performance of comparable benchmark indexes is so adversely affected by embedded transaction costs that the silent index (and its fund) are relatively certain to outperform the benchmark over any reasonable time interval. A small but consistent performance advantage based on the easily understood principle of confidential treatment of planned fund transactions should overwhelm any cachet attached to a branded index fund.

Someone immersed in the minutiae of today's benchmark index funds may be shocked by the suggestion that a silent index could be cre-ated and managed by the same organization that advised the fund. Yet who has the interests of the fund more in mind than the fund manager? Indeed, with actively managed funds, a single organization or even a sin-gle individual is responsible for the whole investment process. Anyone who suggests that index management is inherently different from active portfolio management is not familiar with the operation of the Standard & Poor's Index Committee.

The manager of a benchmark index fund is not permitted to know about changes in the index or to implement changes in the portfolio be-fore the changes are known to the world.[17] The benchmark index fund is the only type of fund in the world that operates under such an information disclosure handicap. No one seems able to explain why such publication of a fund's trading plans makes sense for investors. Indeed, full advance disclosure exposes long-term index fund investors to profiteering by short-term traders. Common sense dictates that fund management should adjust procedures to better serve the investor rather than simply continue with a flawed tradition. Market impact costs are hurting benchmark index fund investors—and the more assets that are invested in funds tracking a given benchmark index, the greater the transaction cost penalty associated with using that index. One reason equity indexes and equity index funds are so widely criticized today is that when indexing was in its infancy, the market impact of index funds trying to match index changes was not significant. These market impact costs have risen significantly but without much fan-fare until recently. While the best solution—a silent index—is not available today, an investor can choose a less prominent index than the S&P and

Russell indexes. Choosing a less prominent index should be the cardinal rule in selecting an index fund today.

Other Index and Index Fund Issues

RIC Compliance

The fund-friendly index should be regulated investment company (RIC) compliant (or UCITS compliant for European investors). The template index for a fund serves as just that—a template. There should be no need for an index fund manager to take a non-RIC-compliant index, change its composition in any of several ways, and manage the index to create a fund that may show little or no tendency to track the theoretically underlying index because of changes the manager had to make to achieve RIC-compliant diversification.[18] If RIC compliance is obtained at the index provider level rather than at the fund level, there is a clearer basis for evaluating the performance of both the index structure methodology and the index fund portfolio manager's trading skills.

Tax Efficiency

The index rules should ensure that the fund is inherently tax-efficient. Here "tax efficiency" is a measure of the extent to which capital gains are not realized by the fund's shareholders until they sell their fund shares. Obviously, this kind of tax efficiency means little or nothing to the short-term trader or to tax-exempt investors, but it can be extremely valuable to taxable long-term buy-and-hold investors. This kind of tax efficiency is one of the reasons index funds have become so popular with long-term investors and investment advisers in recent years. An index can help ensure the tax efficiency of the fund through reductions in unnecessary portfolio turnover. Intelligent handling of stocks that depart the index is important in maintaining a tax-efficient fund. The timing of periodic rebalancing or reconstitution of the index and implementation of rules designed to ensure RIC diversification compliance are also important in ensuring the tax efficiency of a silent index fund.

Float Weighting for Liquidity and Other Non–Market Value Index Structures

Given the importance of portfolio component liquidity in keeping transaction costs for any fund as low as possible, the gold standard for index construction is float weighting on top of capitalization-based stock selection as the best readily available proxy for underlying market liquidity. While definitions of float are not always consistent, a conscientious effort to incorporate float will have a desirable effect on the liquidity of a fund index and the likely cost and performance of its fund.

Equal-weighted and tier-weighted indexes have enjoyed some recent popularity. Portfolios based on these indexes are not consistent with the mean variance efficiency criterion of modern portfolio theory, but they can compensate by offering greater risk/return improvement from diversification if the companies in an index vary greatly in capitalization or float. A fund with composition changes inversely linked to share price changes (e.g., an equal-weighted index) can incur higher rebalancing costs than a float-weighted index fund. Because an equal-weighted index fund will have to reduce its weighting in the best-performing stocks when it rebalances, tax efficiency will be harder to achieve.

Indexes weighted by variables unrelated to market value or stock prices have been attracting increased attention. Introduced by Ken Safian and Ken Smilen in the 1960 as Dual Market Principle Averages (Safian, Dillon, and Corbett 2005), indexes weighted by fundamentals like sales, book value, cash flow, or payroll have been offered as the criticism of benchmark indexes has become more vocal. Arnott, Hsu, and Moore (2005) brings new credibility to the argument that the traditional benchmark index portfolio replication model is outdated. Innovations in index weighting will be an important factor in fund development in the years ahead.

Index Rules Designed to Minimize Turnover

There are many ways indexes can be constructed and reconstituted to minimize portfolio turnover costs in a fund based on the index. If, for example, an index is based on mid-cap stocks or small-cap stocks, turnover can be reduced by putting a buffer range above or below—or possibly at both ends of the capitalization range—to limit changes in the membership of the index that are likely to be reversed on the next rebalancing date. If a stock gets far enough outside the index's desired company size range, a quick reversal is unlikely and the stock can be dropped from the index with little likelihood of its reentering the index at the next rebalancing.

Turnover in growth/value-style indexes can be controlled by rules that require a specific degree of change in measured style characteristics before a stock moves from one classification to another. Changing an index on the basis of small changes in size or style characteristics can lead to extremely high rates of turnover. The resulting indexes may be truer reflections of the size and style features the index is designed to reflect, but the transaction costs a fund will incur making the changes are likely to offset the advantage of size or stylistic purity. A truly fund-friendly set of growth and value indexes has not yet been offered. A fruitful approach might be a combination of buffers and exclusion of stocks that lack distinct growth or value characteristics from each pair of indexes.

Indexes Should Be Integrated Whenever Possible to Reduce Fund Transaction Costs

Perhaps the best example of this principle is to consider how the major Russell indexes might have worked if the value of the portfolios using the Russell 1000 as an index portfolio template was between seven and eight times the portfolios using the Russell 2000. The annual Russell rebalancing—which has become chaotic in recent years—would be an almost tranquil event. With a seven- or eight-to-one portfolio size relationship, the changes in composition in the Russell 2000 and the Russell 1000 across the interface between the two funds/indexes would be easy and cost-efficient to execute. Russell 1000 funds would need to sell approximately the same number of shares of stocks dropping into the Russell 2000 as Russell 2000 funds would need to buy.

Correspondingly, Russell 1000 funds would need to buy approximately the same number of shares of stocks graduating from the Russell 2000 as Russell 2000 funds needed to sell. There would still be some dislocations on the lower end of the Russell 2000, but the total transaction cost penalty to shareholders using these indexes, particularly the Russell 2000, would be substantially reduced by balanced use of the indexes as fund templates. Unfortunately, Russell has not succeeded in marketing index portfolio usage of the 1000 extensively enough to achieve this cost damping effect. The result is a high annual reconstitution cost for the Russell 2000.

What Kinds of Indexes Cannot Qualify as Fund-Friendly Indexes?

Benchmark indexes do not qualify as fund-friendly indexes because changes in the composition of the index are always public before the fund can act. The best index for a fund, while it may lack the benchmark brand, will always be a silent index. Funds using silent indexes will benefit from the lack of publication of the fund's need to trade. The only investment manager of any kind who cannot trade until after her trading plans are broadcast to the world is the manager of a benchmark index fund. When stated this way, the pretrade publication of index template changes is obviously unacceptable.

Global indexes rarely make good fund indexes. Apart from some multicountry clearing, settlement, and custody issues, a tax problem with global indexes for U.S. investors highlights another feature of funds that should be considered in any fund index adoption. The Internal Revenue Code has a number of notable features with respect to regulated investment company diversification rules. The diversification requirements for equity funds are relatively well known. Less widely known is the rule that a fund with less than half its assets invested in foreign securities cannot pass through credits for the dividend withholding taxes it pays on foreign stocks as tax credits to its U.S. shareholders. It must pass them through as a tax deduction, which is often less valuable to its shareholders.

Multi-asset class funds can present problems similar to global funds. Similar provisions to the foreign securities weighting provision can affect the pass-through of the tax-exempt nature of municipal bond interest and even, in some states, the ability to deduct the Treasury interest component of fund dividends from state taxes without a hassle with state taxing authorities.

Evaluating Index Mutual Funds and ETFs

Most individual investors using indexed mutual funds and ETFs have limited access to good quality information that helps them:

- Distinguish among the indexes used as templates for the funds.
- Evaluate the quality of index fund management provided by fund issuers.
- Choose between conventional mutual funds and ETFs.

In general, the best information published on ETFs is available from major investment banking firms, like Morgan Stanley and Smith Barney, and, to a certain extent, on indexing-oriented web sites. The fund services available to most ETF investors do not provide very useful or comprehensive coverage of indexing or ETFs. Some brokerage firms do a better job of covering ETFs than the fund services. A small factor in this coverage might be that the brokerage firms are more likely to be involved in an ETF transaction (which is executed in the securities market) than in a conventional fund transaction (which is often executed directly with the fund issuer or through a nonbrokerage intermediary—such as a 401(k) or other retirement plan provider—with direct links to the mutual fund issuer). The growth of advisers that use ETFs extensively in clients' accounts—as described in Chapter 11—is another stimulus to brokerage firm research coverage. Several brokerage firms also publish excellent material on changes in the major indexes.

Exhibit 6.2 shows the median tracking errors and ranges of tracking errors for most major U.S.-based ETFs for 2002 through 2004. The median tracking errors and the ranges of tracking errors are often large. The magnitude and the negative signs of the median tracking errors are evidence that these funds have not been managed aggressively. The dominant ETF performance determinant appears to have been fund cash balances. An ETF manager does not have to maintain a cash balance in

EXHIBIT 6.2   Comparison of U.S.-Based ETF Tracking Errors, 2002–2004

Fund Type	Symbol		Tracking Error 2002	Tracking Error 2003	Tracking Error 2004
Large-Cap Broad Market					
S&P 500 SPDR	SPY		1	−30	−14
iShares S&P 500	IVV		−6	−17	−10
Fortune 500	FFF		−12	−38	−29
iShares Russell 1000	IWB		−7	−25	−12
Vanguard Total Market VIPERs	VTI		−10	−21	−5
iShares Russell 3000	IWV		−9	−29	−19
iShares DJ US Total Market	IYY		−9	−33	−23
Nasdaq-100 Index Tracking Stock	QQQQ		−12	−34	−28
DJIA DIAMONDS	DIA		−11	−30	−20
iShares S&P 100 Index Fund	OEF		−13	−27	−19
		Median	**−9**	**−30**	**−19**
Mid-Cap Broad Market					
S&P 400 MidCap SPDR	MDY		−5	−46	−34
iShares S&P MidCap 400	IJH		−21	−25	−19
iShares Russell MidCap	IWR		2	−33	−29
		Median	**−5**	**−33**	**−29**
Small-Cap Broad Market					
iShares Russell 2000	IWM		−4	−31	−17
iShares S&P SmallCap 600	IJR		−11	−20	−20
Vanguard Extended Market VIPERs	VXF		−24	−29	−21
		Median	**−11**	**−29**	**−20**
Growth Style					
iShares S&P 500/BARRA Growth	IVW		−9	−24	−21
iShares Russell 1000 Growth	IWF		−11	−29	−21
streetTRACKS Dow Jones US Large Cap Growth	ELG		−7	−33	−26
iShares S&P MidCap 400/BARRA Growth	IJK		−24	−19	−29
iShares Russell MidCap Growth	IWP		−14	−32	−33
iShares S&P SmallCap 600/BARRA Growth	IJT		−19	−26	−39
iShares Russell 2000 Growth	IWO		−3	−35	−18
streetTRACKS Dow Jones US Small Cap Growth	DSG		−5	−43	−29
iShares Russell 3000 Growth	IWZ		−12	−31	−27
		Median	**−11**	**−31**	**−27**

(Continued)

EXHIBIT 6.2   *(Continued)*

Fund Type	Symbol	Tracking Error 2002	Tracking Error 2003	Tracking Error 2004
Value Style				
iShares S&P 500/BARRA Value	IVE	−13	−28	−21
iShares Russell 1000 Value	IWD	−16	−32	−21
streetTRACKS Dow Jones US Large Cap Value	ELV	−19	−35	−29
iShares S&P MidCap 400/BARRA Value	IJJ	−26	−51	−28
iShares Russell MidCap Value	IWS	−4	−37	−45
iShares S&P SmallCap 600/BARRA Value	IJS	−17	−28	−28
iShares Russell 2000 Value	IWN	−9	−41	−22
streetTRACKS Dow Jones US Small Cap Value	DSV	−35	−72	−41
iShares Russell 3000 Value	IWW	−17	−38	−29
	Median	**−17**	**−37**	**−28**
Foreign Single-Country				
iShares MSCI-Australia	EWA	20	36	−52
iShares MSCI-Austria	EWO	−77	−150	−59
iShares MSCI-Belgium	EWK	−82	573	−39
iShares MSCI-Brazil	EWZ	−269	−198	−132
iShares MSCI-Canada	EWC	−46	−126	−25
iShares MSCI-France	EWQ	−10	−60	−2
iShares MSCI-Germany	EWG	13	−71	−35
iShares MSCI-Hong Kong	EWH	−225	−128	−97
iShares MSCI-Italy	EWI	16	102	−32
iShares MSCI-Japan	EWJ	−16	−203	−108
iShares S&P/TOPIX 150	ITF	19	−203	−100
iShares MSCI-Malaysia	EWM	−145	−154	−79
iShares MSCI-Mexico	EWW	55	343	−3
iShares MSCI-Netherlands	EWN	−10	−238	−125
iShares MSCI-Singapore	EWS	−119	210	−35
iShares MSCI-South Korea	EWY	−223	−128	−384
iShares MSCI-Spain	EWP	193	−168	−52
iShares MSCI-Sweden	EWD	55	−29	−57
iShares MSCI-Switzerland	EWL	−137	−88	−70
iShares MSCI-Taiwan	EWT	−73	−199	−43
iShares MSCI-U.K.	EWU	−33	−132	−98
	Median	**−33**	**−128**	**−57**
Foreign Multicountry				
iShares MSCI-EAFE	EFA	3	−14	−49
iShares MSCI-EMU	EZU	−17	−76	−34
iShares MSCI-Pacific ex-Japan	EPP	−5	−5	−22

EXHIBIT 6.2 *(Continued)*

Fund Type	Symbol		Tracking Error 2002	Tracking Error 2003	Tracking Error 2004
iShares S&P Europe 350 Index	IEV		−21	−102	−177
iShares S&P Latin America 40	ILF		136	−358	−17
streetTRACKS Dow Jones Global Titans	DGT		−42	−33	−60
		Median	-11	-54	-41
Sector					
Select Sector SPDR-Technology	XLK		−15	−46	−28
iShares DJ US Technology	IYW		−36	−90	−61
iShares DJ US Telecommunications	IYZ		−358	552	−57
iShares Goldman Sachs Technology Index	IGM		−31	−61	−68
iShares Goldman Sachs Networking Index	IGN		−4	−91	−52
iShares Goldman Sachs Natural Resources	IGE		0	−77	−36
iShares Goldman Sachs Semiconductor Index	IGW		−21	−79	47
iShares Goldman Sachs Software Index	IGV		−23	−67	−65
streetTRACKS Morgan Stanley High Tech 35	MTK		−3	−92	−50
Select Sector SPDR-Financial	XLF		−19	−53	−26
iShares DJ US Financial Sector	IYF		−46	−86	−66
iShares DJ US Financial Services	IYG		−49	−87	−64
Select Sector SPDR-Energy	XLE		−19	−49	−52
iShares DJ US Energy	IYE		−196	138	−72
Select Sector SPDR-Health Care	XLV		−26	−36	−28
iShares DJ US Healthcare	IYH		−39	−73	−64
iShares Nasdaq Biotech	IBB		−11	−16	−175
Select Sector SPDR-Consumer Discretionary	XLY		−21	−44	−38
iShares DJ US Consumer Cyclical	IYC		−42	−77	−67
Select Sector SPDR-Consumer Staples	XLP		−16	−35	−30
iShares DJ US Non-Consumer Cyclical	IYK		−58	−73	−66
Select Sector SPDR-Industrial	XLI		−22	−59	−36
iShares DJ US Industrial	IYJ		57	−84	−84
Select Sector SPDR-Materials	XLB		−18	−71	−40
iShares DJ US Basic Materials	IYM		−48	−85	−72

(Continued)

EXHIBIT 6.2   *(Continued)*

Fund Type	Symbol	Tracking Error 2002	Tracking Error 2003	Tracking Error 2004
Select Sector SPDR-Utilities	XLU	−21	−51	−45
iShares DJ US Utilities	IDU	−43	−80	−78
iShares DJ US Real Estate	IYR	−59	−115	−85
iShares Cohen & Steers Realty Majors	ICF	−29	−66	−74
streetTRACKS Wilshire REIT	RWR	−34	−68	−45
iShares S&P Global Energy	IXC	80	35	−69
iShares S&P Global Financials	IXG	−59	−93	−85
iShares S&P Global Healthcare	IXJ	−14	−65	−74
iShares S&P Global Information Technology	IXN	−79	−44	−96
iShares S&P Global Telecommunications	IXP	−21	−63	−49
	Median	−23	−67	−64

Sources: Morgan Stanley, Barclays Global Investors, State Street Global Advisors, Thomson, Bloomberg. All calculations are fund return minus index return.

the fund portfolio to meet redemptions. The manager can invest virtually all the fund's cash. In 2002, a very weak year in many equity markets, the median negative tracking error was relatively modest. The performance in 2003 suggests that the reasonably good results for ETFs in 2002 probably came from holding cash in a weak market environment. Strong evidence that cash balances were a boon in 2002 is the fact that tracking errors became larger and increasingly negative across the board in 2003, a year in which a strong market environment made holding cash balances a bad idea. In 2004, most indexes turned in modest positive performances, making the impact of cash balances modest with a few conspicuous exceptions where funds based on strongly performing indexes lagged their index badly. The next text box should answer any questions about using tracking error to evaluate an index fund's management.

Evaluating an index fund manager is complicated by the fact that some of the indexes underlying ETFs are not inherently compliant with the RIC diversification requirements for pass-through of income to investors in the United States and the UCITS diversification requirements in Europe. A fund that has to be either RIC or UCITS compliant may be based on an index that is not designed to meet the applicable diversification requirements.[19] If diversification requirements prevent the fund from using the same stock weights as the index, tracking error analysis will not reveal the effect of a specific fund's expense ratio on the one hand and the effectiveness with which the manager is matching or beating the index on the other hand. The use of noncompliant indexes will affect the range of tracking errors, but it usually will not affect the median tracking error in a fund category. The use of a noncompliant index makes evaluation of a particular fund's performance more difficult and is one reason for investors to avoid ETFs based on indexes that do not automatically meet their home country's fund diversification requirements.

Analysis of conventional index fund and ETF performance will become a much more significant activity than these simple examples suggest. If one or more of the conventional fund services begin to provide good ETF data and analysis, individual investors will be better able to evaluate ETFs for themselves.

Evaluating the Performance of an Investment Manager

Fund performance evaluation can be a complex topic. Many consultants to institutional investors make their living by studying and reporting on the nuances of portfolio performance. Most investors only want to know if a fund had good, bad, or indifferent performance for a specific time period. We want a simple measure of performance and we are not interested in why a performance shortfall might have been beyond the investment manager's control.

Fund managers are characterized as either **passive managers** or **active managers**. Reduced to its essentials, passive investment management is usually the same thing as indexed investing. Active investment management includes a number of techniques, most of which involve specific securities selection (stock picking) or other methods to construct a portfolio that the manager hopes will beat a performance benchmark. There are gradations of passive and active investment management ranging from strict adherence to an index to a totally free-form, unstructured, multi-asset class active portfolio. Regardless of the flexibility of the mandate stated in a fund's investment objective, all investment managers are evaluated relative to standard benchmark indexes, and the indexes used are the same indexes whether the fund is passively managed or actively managed—equity indexes in the case of equity funds, and fixed-income indexes in the case of fixed-income funds. In a few cases, the benchmark will be a weighted combination

(Continued)

Evaluating the Performance (Continued)

of several standard indexes, but the most common technique is to evaluate performance relative to a single index.

Passive management is typically highly structured, and the performance of a fund will follow the index very closely. Most active portfolios also have structure, but an active manager may make selected bets on particular securities or on market segments that she believes will perform better than the benchmark. While the term is rarely heard in connection with passive management, an active investment manager is trying to capture **alpha (α)**. Alpha is an incremental return over the benchmark index return at a specified level of risk. Positive alpha (a superior risk-adjusted return) is a reward for taking the risk of active management—and taking it successfully. In most respects, alpha is the principal measure of an active manager's skill (see the Glossary for a more comprehensive definition of alpha and a diagram that shows positive alpha as a superior return at a specified level of risk). Index fund managers are not ordinarily expected to earn alpha, but both passive and active managers are often evaluated using a simple calculation that is closely linked to the concept of alpha, called **tracking error.**

Tracking error means a number of things in different contexts. In discussing fund performance, I use tracking error in a way that is closely related to the idea of alpha. I use it simply as a measure of the difference between (1) the performance of the fund and (2) the performance of the benchmark index selected as a template for an index fund or as a benchmark for performance comparisons in an actively managed fund. If the fund is up 3.8 percent for the year and the index is up 3.9 percent, the tracking error is –0.1 percent or minus 10 basis points. In this sense, tracking error is an approximate but useful proxy for the alpha the fund manager has created (positive alpha or positive tracking error) or dissipated (negative alpha or negative tracking error).

When the measure of tracking error is positive, the fund has done better than the index. When the measure of tracking error is negative, the fund has underperformed the index. All funds have expenses, so a portfolio that tracks the index perfectly will have a negative tracking error equal to the expense ratio. Good index fund managers who manage funds based on popular but inefficient indexes regularly add value by trading at a different time than the official time of the index change. If a fund is based on an index with substantial embedded transaction costs, a capable portfolio manager will be able to recapture some of those transaction costs and reduce the size of any negative tracking error. In a Russell 2000 fund, the magnitude of the trading costs embedded in the annual index reconstitution is so great that a competent portfolio manager should be able to more than cover the fund's expense ratio and achieve a positive tracking error in a typical year. The same can be said with slightly less confidence for index portfolios based on the S&P 500 and a few other indexes.

A number of ETFs are based on indexes that are not RIC compliant. These funds include some of the iShares MSCI Series country funds and some of the iShares Dow Jones sector funds. Because these funds cannot hold the precise index portfolio, the fund will not track the index closely. The tracking errors on funds with non-RIC-compliant indexes can be highly erratic. A large positive tracking error or a large negative tracking error for these funds is simply evidence that the portfolio manager has to deal with an index that the fund cannot track. For these funds, a large positive or negative value for tracking error is not necessarily an indication of skill or lack of skill by the portfolio manager. But not being able to use tracking error to evaluate performance might be a reason to avoid a fund. For most index funds and for actively managed funds, a positive tracking error relative to the fund's benchmark usually indicates good decision making by the manager in deviating from the benchmark—even if the only deviations are in timing the implementation of index changes.

Subject to this explanation and these qualifications, a positive tracking error or a negative tracking error that is smaller than a fund's expense ratio is probably the best single measurement of the skill a fund manager has brought to the job.

Other definitions of tracking error that are *not* used in this book include (1) a measure of the planned risk taken by an active portfolio manager in an attempt to provide a better return than the benchmark and (2) a relatively obscure definition that focuses on the difference between the closing market price of an ETF and the per-share net asset value of the ETF at the end of a trading day. In every discussion of tracking error in this book, tracking error means simply the difference between a fund or portfolio's total return for a specified period and the total return on an index for that same period.

Changing Role of the Index Fund Manager with Better Indexes

Most of the fun of being a benchmark index mutual fund manager has come from meeting the challenge of outperforming your fund's benchmark index. Index funds have attracted some excellent managers who demonstrate their skill by consistently beating the benchmark before the fund's costs and occasionally beating it after costs. This has been possible because the definition of a good benchmark index fund manager has *become* the ability to trade better than the other market participants who attempt to profit from index changes. These good managers simply recapture some of the transaction costs embedded in the benchmark index.

Competitive traders will not have advance notice of silent index changes. Consequently, there will not be a competitive trading frenzy surrounding silent index changes. It will be harder for silent index fund managers to beat their indexes. Managers of funds based on silent indexes may beat or lag their indexes occasionally for reasons unrelated to trading competition to make index changes. Their funds should perform better than comparable benchmark index funds—even if the manager simply matches the silent index—because most of the embedded competitive transaction costs of the benchmark index can be avoided. In fact, simply matching the index was one of the fundamental principles the pioneers of indexing advocated. If the goal again becomes matching the silent index return, the criterion for evaluating an index fund manager will change to ability to choose or develop an efficient index that beats traditional benchmarks. This will be possible not because the new index is much different, but because the new index is less popular.

Getting Better Returns from Index Funds by Reducing Costs

The only virtue I can think of for a benchmark index as a fund template is that it provides an objective standard against which to evaluate the fund manager's performance. Since I would expect most silent indexes to be developed and maintained by the same organization that manages the fund, the appropriate criterion for evaluating the performance of a silent index fund should be a standardized benchmark index based on an approximately equivalent security universe. Since the benchmark index was almost certainly designed to serve as a benchmark rather than as a fund template, the challenge for the designer of a silent index should be to develop an index that will outperform the benchmark on average. There may be a remaining question of whether to attribute the superior or inferior performance of a silent index fund to the silent index design or to the execution of the design by the fund's portfolio manager and trader. That will typically be an issue calling for evaluation of a single organization, the fund management company.

Given that a silent index fund is not permitted in the current regulatory environment, the next-best choice is a benchmark index with (1) desirable rules to limit composition turnover and (2) very little index money using it as a fund template.

Exhibit 6.3 lists some usually older, relatively inefficient benchmark indexes on the left-hand side and some usually newer, less popular indexes on the right-hand side in some categories that an investor might consider using. This list is deliberately far from comprehensive. It covers only broad market and capitalization range indexes. Style and sector index funds tend to be used more for trading and for specialized diversification and tax management applications. They should be of limited interest to most long-term investors.

In shifts of stocks between members of an index family, the effects of different relative portfolio commitments to the three S&P indexes are more modest than differences between the two major Russell indexes. The most popular index in the S&P family, both absolutely and relatively, is the S&P 500. The greatest market impact occurs when a new name is added to the S&P family, especially to the S&P 500, from outside. S&P's long-awaited movement to float-adjusted weightings will have a modest negative effect on these indexes and the funds using them as templates through September 2005.

The Russell 3000 is a better choice than a combination of the Russell 2000 and the 1000, but the greater relative popularity of the Russell 2000 makes the annual turnover during the Russell reconstitution extraordinarily costly among stocks being added to or deleted from the Russell 2000 at the

EXHIBIT 6.3 Transaction Cost Inefficient and Efficient Selected U.S. Total Market and Capitalization Range Indexes

Total U.S. Market Indexes Inefficient	Efficient
Russell 3000	DJ Wilshire 5000
S&P 1500	Dow Jones Total Market
	MSCI U.S. Investable Market 2500

U.S. Capitalization Range Indexes Inefficient	Relatively Efficient[a]
S&P standard family	Dow Jones indexes
Russell 2000	MSCI U.S. index family
	S&P Citigroup (formerly Salomon) indexes

[a]Relative *only* to their competition because few indexed assets are in funds using these indexes. Their appearance on the right-hand side of the table is not an unqualified table-pounding endorsement of these indexes as fund templates.

bottom of its capitalization range and, hence, at the bottom of the Russell 3000 capitalization range as well. Far better index choices would be the more comprehensive DJ Wilshire 5000, the Dow Jones Total Market index, or the MSCI U.S. Investable Market 2500 index. They are preferable largely because they are designed for lower turnover and, especially in the cases of the Dow Jones Total Market and MSCI U.S. Investable Market 2500 indexes, they are less widely used.

Fidelity, Vanguard, and the Great Index Fund Price War

At the end of August 2004, Fidelity Investments announced a reduction in the expense ratios for some of its Spartan index funds to 10 basis points (0.1 percent). The reduction was originally implemented through a fee waiver that could have been rescinded whenever Fidelity wanted to increase the fees. In early March of 2005, Fidelity announced that future increases in the domestic funds' fees would require a shareholder vote and that any increase above 20 basis points in the Spartan International index fund would also require a shareholder vote.[20]

Fidelity has long considered its Spartan S&P 500 fund a loss leader at an expense ratio of 19 basis points. Fidelity clearly does not expect to earn a profit on any of these index funds by offering them at 10 basis points. Most observers agree that Fidelity's index fund fee cut was designed to make its index fund offerings more attractive to investors than Vanguard's; see Gabriel (2004) and Wiener and Lowell (2004). If these low-cost index funds are selected for 401(k) and other tax-deferred accounts, Fidelity apparently expects its other funds to be chosen as well.

The same month, Vanguard made a dramatic change in its ETF pricing strategy. In response to Fidelity's decision to become the low-cost provider of conventional mutual funds tracking broad market indexes and in recognition that the Vanguard Index Participation Equity Receipts (VIPERs) structure was not attracting taxable investors in large numbers, Vanguard apparently decided to become the low-cost provider of broad market index ETF *share classes*. The VIPERs now have expense ratios at least as low as the expense ratios of any comparable ETF or conventional fund share class. The range of effects these price cuts will have on ETF and mutual fund cash flows will be interesting to watch.

Under the prior price structure, the VIPERs offered little or no incentive to taxable investors to favor the hybrid VIPERs over pure ETFs. A small ETF share class of a fund dominated by conventional mutual fund shares is unlikely to do much to make the overall fund more tax-efficient. Any tax benefits of the ETF share redemption process are shared proportionately by all the Vanguard fund share classes. If the ETF share class is inconsequential, the key ETF advantages of shareholder protection and tax efficiency will not be available to *either* conventional or ETF shareholders in these hybrid funds. Growth in most VIPERs share classes since their introduction can charitably be characterized as "modest." However, Vanguard's new ETF share class pricing policy changes the outlook for some of the VIPERs. Some VIPERs will appeal to tax-deferred accounts, like 401(k)s and IRAs, on the basis of their low expense ratios.[21] Most taxable investors should be cautious, but all investors should compare the total costs of buying and holding VIPERs with the economics of competitive ETFs and conventional funds. The fee-saving possibilities from choosing the VIPERs over the best alternative may be zero or as much as 45 basis points, depending on how one defines a comparable fund. A 10-basis-point expense reduction on a $100,000 fund position is worth $100 per year, but this is simply an illustrative cost calculation to put possible savings in perspective. The economics of choosing VIPERs versus an alternative fund or share class vary greatly across the fund spectrum and involve more than just an annual fee comparison.

Vanguard has used some aggressive cost accounting in setting the new VIPERs expense ratios. In the past, Admiral Shares have cost Vanguard about the same amount to support as VIPERs; but Vanguard has reduced the investment requirement for its Admiral Shares from $250,000 to $100,000. This change will slightly increase Vanguards's relative costs for the typical Admiral Shares account. It will also increase the incentive to hold Admiral Shares rather than VIPERs for investors who invest between $100,000 and $250,000 in a single Vanguard fund. Most of the new VIPERs expense ratios are very close to the same fund's Admiral Shares expense ratio. However, the Large Cap Index Admiral Shares have an expense ratio of 12 basis points versus 7 basis points for the VIPERs version of the fund under Vanguard's new fee schedule. The Extended Market Index Admiral Shares have an expense ratio of 15 basis points versus 8 basis points for the VIPERs shares. These discrepancies may reflect an effort by Vanguard to encourage holders of Admiral Shares in these funds to convert to VIPERs. Even if Admiral Shares expense ratios are more than a basis point or two above the VIPERs expense ratios, there seems to be no reason to make a change unless the fee difference seems likely to persist for a long period *and* an investor has no plans to sell the shares for at least several years. Admiral shares can eventually be sold at net asset value. In evaluating a decision, however, keep in mind that conventional share classes of the Vanguard international funds and sector funds have redemption fees on sales within two months and one year of purchase, respectively. A seller of the VIPERs share classes will pay some transaction costs, but they are likely to be less than a 2 percent redemption fee in most cases.

Large holders of Investor Shares in Vanguard's index funds who plan to hold their positions for a number of years might reduce their annual costs by paying Vanguard's $50 conversion fee to exchange their conventional shares for VIPERs.[22] These new VIPERs shareholders are unlikely to improve a fund's tax efficiency because one premise behind the conversion is the absence of an intention to redeem the shares anytime soon. Anyone who plans to be a seller/redeemer over the next few years should stay in the conventional shares.

Major increases in VIPERs shares outstanding will have to come from new investors. The question then becomes: How do VIPERs look to new investors now, relative to other funds? There are three issues:

1. Permanence of the fee reductions.
2. Expected fund performance.
3. Tax efficiency.

Fidelity's late 2004 expense ratio cuts originally led to concern over the permanence of the fee reductions. Fidelity responded by making most of the cuts permanent. A few of the recently lowered VIPERs fees might rise slightly if the VIPERs do not attract substantial new assets, but any increase is likely to be small. Investors can safely assume that these fee cuts will be permanent.[23]

From the perspective of performance, Vanguard has generally done a better job of managing index funds for retail investors than its ETF competitors.[24] Vanguard also generally uses more efficient indexes than its competitors. The MSCI indexes that Vanguard uses for the VIPERs have a slightly larger capitalization bias relative to the offerings of some other index publishers, so comparing performance will not be easy in future years.[25] One result of Vanguard's adoption of the MSCI indexes will be to reduce its relative portfolio management, trading, and even printing costs slightly because most of its funds will hold fewer stock positions with larger average capitalizations than most funds that use Dow Jones Wilshire or Russell indexes. An exception to this pattern will be sector VIPERs, which hold more positions in small-cap stocks and which will continue to have a hard time competing with the sector SPDRs. See Chapter 11, pp. 211–220. Investors and their advisers should understand the likely effect of this capitalization bias on performance and focus on tracking error as the best measure of a fund manager's performance. On balance, tax-deferred accounts that can hold ETFs will probably choose the broad market index VIPERs over other broad market ETFs or conventional funds.

Taxable investors will probably want to proceed with caution until the VIPERs share classes hold a substantial fraction of the Vanguard index funds' assets. For investors who cannot wait, the Total Stock Market VIPERs, the Extended Market VIPERs, and the international VIPERs offer the best prospects for asset growth, ETF share class dominance, and corresponding tax efficiency.

An examination of the Total Stock Market VIPERs illustrates what Vanguard needs to accomplish. The ETF share class of the Vanguard Total Market Fund (the first to offer VIPERs class shares) is the only Vanguard fund to attract significant VIPERs assets. This VIPERs share class had assets of slightly less than $4.3 billion at the end of 2004, making it the 12th largest ETF share class listed in the United States.[26] The total assets of the entire Vanguard Total Market Fund as of December 31, 2004, were $57.0 billion, making the ETF share class about 7.5 percent of the fund's total capitalization. The capital gains overhang for the fund was 13.5 percent. In calendar year 2004, 600,000 of the VIPERs shares were redeemed. At this rate, VIPERs share class redemptions in 2004 accounted for less than 0.12 percent of the fund's total assets at year-end. It is hard to imagine in-kind redemptions in this ETF share class contributing materially to the tax efficiency of the entire Vanguard Total Market Fund until it becomes much larger relative to the conventional share class.[27]

The Vanguard Total Market Fund has relatively few composition changes each year, so tax efficiency is not likely to be a major near-term issue for this fund. So far, the small ETF share class has contributed little to improved tax efficiency, but Vanguard has time to increase the size of the VIPERs share class—and the lower VIPERs fees will help. I will return to the implications of this price war in Chapter 7—with a strategy suggestion for Vanguard. (See "Uncertainties in Fund Selections," p. 163.)

Fifteen Rules for Selection and Location of Index Funds

1. *Recognize that your commitment to an equity fund in a taxable account may be a very long-term commitment.* Assuming no massive changes in U.S. tax law, if the fund performs well, you may want to keep it in your portfolio for the rest of your life. It can be advantageous to pass the fund shares to your heirs 50 years or more in the future. In this long-term context, tax efficiency and a commitment by the fund issuer to low expenses can be very important. Funds used in tax-deferred retirement accounts do not have to be tax efficient and you can feel freer to experiment in these accounts because there will be no immediate tax impact if you decide to sell a fund position.

2. *Their combination of low expense ratios, effective investor protection, and tax efficiency makes ETFs the clear index fund choice for taxable accounts.* This rule is a corollary to Rule 1.

3. *Hybrid ETFs like Vanguard's VIPERs ETF share classes are unlikely to be as tax-efficient as funds where all redemption is through an ETF share class.*

4. *A low expense ratio is extremely important.* In ETFs, in particular, the popularity of unitary fees means that funds with comparable investment objectives will tend to have similar and competitive expense ratios. A small fund may reduce the issuer's profitability, but as long as the expense ratio is competitive and the fund's index is efficient, a small fund should be fine.

5. *As of mid-2005, available fixed-income index ETFs offer no significant advantages over some of the better low-cost conventional fixed-income funds.* Most investors' principal holdings in tax-deferred accounts will be taxable fixed-income securities or funds holding these securities. Vanguard has typically done a better job of both equity and fixed-income index portfolio management (with an occasional slip) than its competitors have done with ETFs. Vanguard's shareholder protection is not as good as it once was, but as long as you stick to Vanguard funds with more than $5 billion in assets (this covers the major funds), most Vanguard fixed-income funds provide excellent value in tax-deferred accounts.

6. *Subject to your overall asset allocation between fixed-income and equities, tax-deferred accounts are also a great place to experiment with actively managed small-cap and sector-rotation funds where tax efficiency in conventional funds cannot be assumed.* If an attractive actively managed ETF becomes available in the future, it can be purchased in either a tax-deferred or a taxable account.

7. *Avoid popular and high-turnover equity indexes.* Embedded transaction costs in the two most popular index fund templates,[28] the Russell 2000 and the Standard & Poor's 500, make them very undesirable choices for index funds. Through September 2005, the entire Standard & Poor's index family will be affected in various ways by S&P's movement to float weighting. On balance, I would expect these indexes to underperform very slightly before September 2005 as funds based on them reduce their holdings in some less liquid securities where float weighting dictates sales and increase their holdings in more liquid securities with larger floats. The net effect of these transactions will certainly be a net increase in transaction costs and probably net pressure on the prices of the securities held in S&P index funds.

Beyond September 2005, the Standard & Poor's MidCap 400 and SmallCap 600 are significantly less objectionable than the S&P 500, in part because they may benefit when a stock is promoted up the capitalization scale to the S&P 500. However, the reasoning behind the "avoid popular indexes" rule applies to all popular benchmark indexes including the entire Standard & Poor's and Russell index families. Among the other index families, your primary basis for selection should generally be unpopularity followed closely by the lowest expected rate of turnover in index composition. As a broad generalization, the composition turnover in various index types, barring the specific introduction of buffer zones or other rules to reduce turnover, is reflected in the following list:

Relative Index Turnover

Lowest Turnover:	Total U.S. market indexes
	Large-cap indexes
	Sector indexes
	Mid-cap indexes
	Small-cap indexes
Highest Turnover:	Style (growth/value) indexes

Exhibit 6.4 shows representative turnover figures for some popular index ETFs that generally reflect this hierarchy. The various index families have signature methodologies, and there are variations in each firm's product line. I am reluctant to hazard a sweeping general statement about transaction cost efficiency, except to note that Russell does not use any buffering or do anything else to reduce turnover. Indexes without buffering are probably more useful as performance benchmarks, but the fact that the Russell benchmarks are used as portfolio templates *causes* their indexes to underperform the market universes they are designed to measure. This makes the Russell indexes, particularly the 2000, easy benchmarks for a manager to beat.

8. *Use as few funds as possible.* The greatest cost and diversification value available through index funds is a total U.S. market fund. Even if the capitalization- or float-weighted index does overweight large-cap stocks from a pure diversification perspective, the investor gets exposure to all parts of the market at very low cost in terms of both expense ratios and transaction costs embedded in index composition changes. If an investor adds a small-cap actively managed fund to the total market fund, the small-cap fund will modestly increase overall diversification. The ideal single index fund position should offer broad exposure and be float-weighted with, perhaps, a cap on percentage exposure to the largest-capitalization stocks.

9. *Use specialized funds only for special needs such as tax loss harvesting or diversifying the overall portfolio in the presence of one or a small number of very large, low-cost positions.*

10. *Foreign stocks are an unnecessary luxury for most U.S. investors.* With the growth of globalization, financial markets throughout the world have become increasingly correlated, particularly in times of market adversity. The higher correlations of foreign markets with the U.S. market in recent years and the convergence in national

EXHIBIT 6.4   Annual or Annualized Turnover in Selected Exchange-Traded
Index Funds[a]

Fund	Turnover
Large Cap or Total Market	
iShares S&P 500 Index Fund	3%
iShares Dow Jones US Total Market Index Fund	5%
Diversified Mid Cap	
iShares S&P MidCap 400 Index Fund	11%
Diversified Small Cap	
iShares S&P SmallCap 600 Index Fund	11%
iShares Russell 2000 Index Fund	26%
Style[b]	
iShares S&P 500/BARRA Growth Index Fund	14%
iShares S&P 500/BARRA Value Index Fund	5%
iShares S&P MidCap 400/BARRA Growth Index Fund	37%
iShares S&P MidCap 400/BARRA Value Index Fund	11%
iShares S&P SmallCap 600/BARRA Growth Index Fund	37%
iShares S&P SmallCap 600/BARRA Value Index Fund	12%
iShares Russell 2000 Growth Index Fund	37%
iShares Russell 2000 Value Index Fund	16%
Sector	
iShares Dow Jones US Basic Materials Sector Index Fund	7%
iShares Dow Jones US Consumer Cyclical Sector Index Fund	6%
iShares Dow Jones US Consumer Non-Cyclical Sector Index Fund	5%
iShares Dow Jones US Energy Sector Index Fund	2%
iShares Dow Jones US Financial Sector Index Fund	7%
iShares Dow Jones US Health Care Sector Index Fund	4%
iShares Dow Jones US Industrial Sector Index Fund	3%
iShares Dow Jones US Technology Sector Index fund	5%
iShares Dow Jones US Telecommunications Sector Index Fund	22%
iShares Dow Jones US Utilities Sector Index Fund	7%
Consumer Discretionary Select Sector SPDR Fund	2%
Consumer Staples Select Sector SPDR Fund	4%
Energy Select Sector SPDR Fund	9%
Financial Select Sector SPDR Fund	6%
Health Care Select Sector SPDR Fund	7%
Industrial Select Sector SPDR Fund	3%
Materials Select Sector SPDR Fund	5%
Technology Select Sector SPDR Fund	3%
Utilities Select Sector SPDR Fund	4%

[a]All Select Sector SPDRs and iShares S&P figures are for periods ending March 31, 2004. All iShares Dow Jones US fund figures are for periods ending April 30, 2004. The reported semiannual turnover for the Sector SPDRs funds was doubled to annualize it.

[b]Differences between growth and value funds in the same capitalization range are due to the peculiarities of the turnover calculation in a specific instance, not to differences in real turnover between the growth and style splits of a specific cap range index. These differences illustrate the inappropriateness of the turnover measure. In most cases, the turnover appears low because the fund grew substantially after the growth and value reallocation for the index was made.

economic growth rates reduce the diversification effect of foreign equity investment. Any remaining cross-border diversification effect is probably largely due to currency fluctuations. Cross-border investing is inherently more costly than domestic investing for most investors.[29] U.S. corporations are better equipped to create and manage affiliates in foreign countries than U.S. investors are to invest in foreign stocks.

Unless your net worth exceeds, say, $5 million, it usually makes sense to ignore foreign securities markets. At the $5 million level, you might begin to add diversified international funds with the objective of reaching a 10 percent position in foreign equities at a substantially higher net worth. Although the cost impact is not great, the ETF structure is not as operationally efficient as conventional funds when many foreign markets are involved.[30] This cost disadvantage for multicountry ETFs will diminish over time. Shareholder protection is particularly important in conventional international funds. Any conventional international fund you purchase should use **fair value pricing** regularly or, even better, defer pricing by one trading day for share purchases and redemptions. As with domestic ETFs, the cost of providing liquidity to fund share traders is not an issue with international ETFs.

11. *Ignore fund share trading volume as a criterion for choosing an ETF—with the minor exception of sector funds to be used in a tax loss harvesting/diversification strategy.* Even the size of the bid-asked spread is not particularly important in a position that you might hold for as long as 50 years. Over that time frame, the expense ratio and the efficiency of the index are far more important.

12. *In most cases, a large short interest indicates only that an ETF trades efficiently and is useful in some risk management applications.* While short interest may be correlated with recent market trends or even with someone's expectation for future trends, ETF short interest is not a reliable market forecaster. Occasionally, a large short interest may indicate that a fund is poorly managed. Check the fund's tracking error for a quick measure of performance.

13. *Consider enhanced index funds benchmarked to efficient indexes when they are available.* An enhanced index fund will typically be based on a standard benchmark index, but the manager will depart from the index in ways expected to add value for investors. If the benchmark is an inefficient index, like the S&P 500 or Russell 2000, a manager who recaptures some of the embedded index trading costs in the fund is certainly better than a manager who replicates the index precisely. However, the best choice will usually be to choose an efficient index. Even the best enhanced index fund manager cannot recapture all the embedded transaction costs in an

inefficient index. An unpopular index or a silent index will be a far better choice than an effort to recapture embedded transaction costs with an inefficient index.

14. *Look for funds with improved structures for shareholder protection and for funds designed to achieve better performance.* The best example of an improved structure in a conventional fund would be an early cutoff for purchase and sale of the fund shares.[31] Also, look for silent indexes at some future date.

15. *Tracking error is the single most appropriate basis for evaluating the job an index fund manager is doing.* To the extent a popular benchmark index is used, any negative tracking error should be significantly less than the fund's expense ratio. For an S&P 500 or Russell 2000 fund and for (growth and value) style splits based on these funds, a small positive tracking error is possible. Sector funds are unlikely to have consistent positive tracking errors, but any negative tracking error should be less than the expense ratio. Tracking error should be relatively consistent from year to year with deviations largely associated with different levels of index composition turnover. Any tendency to lag the index in up markets and beat it in down markets probably indicates that the fund is not fully invested in stocks. An index ETF should never have a significant cash position. The manager was hired to invest the portfolio in the securities in the index. It does not take a great deal of effort on the manager's part to keep the portfolio fully invested.

Summary

This is not the typical "indexing is the greatest thing ever" chapter. As it is practiced today, indexing needs a great deal of improvement. A useful approach to indexing is summarized in the "Fifteen Rules for Selection and Location of Index Funds." The most important lessons from this chapter are: avoid funds based on the most popular indexes, and look for major reforms in the way index funds are run and index information is published.

Supplementary Information

There are a number of excellent books on indexes and indexing available. My favorites are:

Baer, Gregory A., and Gary Gensler, *The Great Mutual Fund Trap*, Broadway Books, 2002.

Bogle, John C., *Common Sense on Mutual Funds*, John Wiley & Sons, 1999.

Bogle, John C., *John Bogle on Investing—The First 50 Years*, McGraw-Hill, 2001.

Schoenfeld, Steven A., *Active Index Investing, Maximizing Portfolio Performance and Minimizing Risk Through Global Index Strategies*, John Wiley & Sons, 2004.

The weakness of these four books, though, is that their authors are cheerleaders for indexing. They do not offer adequate discussions of the weaknesses of indexing and of specific index products. The same is true of some otherwise excellent web sites:

www.vanguard.com/bogle_site/bogle_home.html
www.journalofindexes.com/
www.indexuniverse.com/TheBook/outlineAndSummary.php

For balance, I offer, in addition to the present volume, my book *The Exchange-Traded Funds Manual* (John Wiley & Sons, 2002) and my own web site, www.etfconsultants.com, where I post papers on various subjects related to indexes and indexing and, of course, exchange-traded funds. I try to provide balanced material, but the citations above will give you plenty of exposure to unexpurgated indexing enthusiasm if you need it.

CHAPTER 7

Fund Advisory Services— or Do-It-Yourself?

The time has come to begin assembling and applying the fund tax, cost, and performance information described in Chapters 3 through 6 in order to pick the best available funds. Starting from the premise that reducing costs is the easiest way to increase an investor's expected return from a fund, the logical next step is comparative evaluation of funds that are candidates for investment. Without a high-quality, comprehensive database, assembling the appropriate data for more than a small number of funds is a frustrating exercise. To make the task manageable, I focused on funds with very low expense ratios to reduce the data requirements. I went directly to prospectuses and fund reports on the fund managers' web sites or to hard copies of these documents when I could get them by snail mail. When no more user-friendly alternative was available for some older data, I consulted the Securities and Exchange Commission (SEC) web site (www.sec.gov).

I have not made much use of the fund databases available without charge or at modest cost on some mutual fund advisory web sites. The data that I have examined on these web sites are inadequate and, candidly, not reliable. Firms with good reputations for data accuracy, like Bloomberg and Lipper, do not offer basic fund data free or at low cost.[1]

I am not inclined to attempt a comprehensive evaluation of all the sources of mutual fund information and advice that investors can find in libraries, in magazines, or on the Internet. In this chapter and others, I describe some of my experiences with a few of these sources while working on this book. My language will be too polite to do full justice to the frustrations I felt in trying to find a reliable, free, or low-cost fund database. Conversations with other users of the Morningstar database and some bad

EXHIBIT 7.1   Data That Is Frequently Inaccurate, Stale, or Missing from Fund Service Reports

---

Single Fund Data Available from Fund Annual Reports
Index and fund total return calculations[a]
Capital gains tax overhang (see p. 44 and note 6 (Chapter 3))
Flow (see pp. 105–110 (Chapter 5))
Expense ratios (Chapter 5, pp. 88–97)

Aggregate Industry or Fund Type Data (Read definitions carefully)
Average expense ratios (see pp. 92–93)
Tax efficiency (see pp. 42–49)

---

[a]Returns are often understated by the amount of reinvested dividends for both funds and indexes. The problem is most common for indexes because some index providers do not calculate a total return version of their index—or do the calculation badly. The best single source I have found for checking or calculating index total returns is Bloomberg.

press confirm that I am not alone in my frustration with Morningstar's inadequacies and inaccuracies. See Sharpe (1998), Stein (2004), Urbanowicz (2004), Dale (2005), and Mansueto (2005).

My experience with the free and low-cost mutual fund services has been so unsatisfactory that I would advise an investor looking for any of the key information listed in Exhibit 7.1 to consult someone with access to Bloomberg or Lipper databases, or to use index provider and fund issuer web sites. With that sad preamble, I offer some comments on what you will find when you examine free or low-cost fund databases and fund ratings—and why you will not be pleased with what you find.

I would advise any reader who plans to play an active role in fund selection to try to read this relatively short chapter in its entirety. Parts of the "Fund Ratings" section may be heavy going but the implications of that section for the concluding section of the chapter justify the effort.

Fund Databases

For the most part, fund services are dependent on fund managers to provide them with fund financial and operating data. The fund management organization fills out a questionnaire for fund advisory services each time reports are sent to shareholders and the SEC. The fund service takes in the data from the questionnaires, makes a few calculations, and publishes the output in hard copy and/or electronic versions. Answering a fund advisory service questionnaire seems to be a casual and informal process at some fund companies. Responsibility for responding to fund advisory service data inquiries is often assigned to relatively untrained people. Data consistency problems might be caused in part by fund personnel turnover in the data compilation assignment. Comments from several fund database publishers suggest that a small fraction of the data is spot-checked against published fund reports for accuracy. Some of the data that the fund databases compile are not in reports sent to fund shareholders. The need to consolidate multiple sources of data limits the scope of any data checking process, but it is hard to excuse inaccuracies in advisory service data items that appear accurately in fund reports.

Data checking is expensive. I suspect that the more carefully fund data is checked and corrected, the less likely an individual investor is to see the corrected data on a free web site. Stale data on some fund service web sites suggest that if a fund service does not receive a fund report for the most recent period, the published data are simply not updated until the next comparable report arrives three months to a year later. Intuitively, reports on small funds and small fund companies should be less reliable than those from the major fund issuers. However, I have found egregious data errors for some major funds on fund advisory sites. Exchange-traded fund (ETF) data are a relatively recent addition to most fund service databases, and errors and omissions in ETF data seem to be particularly common.

Part of the problem behind the data inaccuracy seems to be that fund services apparently believe few fund investors or their advisers care about specific data items. Fund services see their offering as value-added processing of the basic data, interpretations based on interviews with fund managers, and insights into industry developments. Fund ratings and recommendations for purchase or sale are based on a very small number of data items, and the data items used in the fund ratings are often not the most relevant indicators of future fund performance.

To minimize data problems, my recommendation is to narrow your search to a small number of funds on the basis of expense ratios, shareholder protection policies, and portfolio management quality (tracking error) and obtain the latest annual reports for that small group of funds for your final analysis. I will be more specific on this process later in the chapter.

Fund Ratings

Most of the major fund services offer free and "objective" fund ratings based on their processing of fund data. The most widely used fund ratings are published by Morningstar and Lipper. Morningstar's star ratings are based on a risk-adjusted return analysis that leads to the issuance of one to five stars for standard reporting periods. Five stars go to the most highly rated funds. A fund's star allotment is based on its performance relative to

other funds in its Morningstar fund category. Thanks in part to the public-
ity given to the **Morningstar ratings** by fund managers that pay Morningstar a license fee for the right to use its star ratings in their advertising,
the Morningstar ratings have achieved an almost iconic status.

In contrast to the Morningstar ratings that are based entirely on risk-
adjusted return calculations for specific past periods, Lipper rates funds on
five elements. The **Lipper Leaders ratings** rank funds within investment
categories broadly similar to the Morningstar categories on three performance criteria—total return, consistent return, and preservation—as well
as on expenses and tax efficiency. Lipper's top rating is a checkmark ($\sqrt{}$),
which designates the top 20 percent of the category's funds as Lipper
Leaders in terms of that measure. The other funds are rated 2 through 5,
with 5 as the lowest rating on Lipper's scale covering the bottom 20 percent of funds by that measure. The Morningstar and Lipper competitive
ranking systems are by far the most frequently cited and widely used.
They are worth a few comments because they illustrate some of the problems of fund ratings construction and the pitfalls of using such ratings for
selecting mutual funds.

By far the most extensive analysis of the Morningstar rating system
was undertaken by Nobel laureate William Sharpe of Stanford University.
Sharpe is also a founder of the Financial Engines organization, which provides one of the widely used retirement planning software packages described in Chapter 2. Sharpe devoted a great deal of attention to the
Morningstar performance ratings because Morningstar made the mistake of
using a variant on the **Sharpe ratio** inappropriately as its measure of risk-
adjusted performance.

At the beginning of his analysis, Sharpe offers the common and valid
criticism of using past performance as the sole or principal fund selection
criterion, noting that "measures of average or cumulative return are, at
best, highly imperfect predictors of expected future return." But Sharpe
goes a great deal deeper into the Morningstar ratings than that. He notes
that while "Morningstar's approach and the simpler excess-return Sharpe
ratio do give similar results in times of relatively high returns for U.S. equity funds," there are other problems with Morningstar's approach that
make the ranking of funds, particularly within peer groups, less useful
when this technique is used. He argues that "using any procedure to rank
funds within peer groups and then using the rankings to select one or
more funds from each of several peer groups is likely to be sub-optimal. In
some cases, the process will be highly sub-optimal."[2]

Sharpe's point is that you have to pick the best fund in the context of
the risks and returns of your *entire portfolio*, not the fund that has done
best of the funds in a narrowly defined but not homogeneous category. In
combination with other funds, a five-star specialized fund might reduce
your diversification and, hence, reduce the expected risk-adjusted return

of your total portfolio. The fund portfolios developed by Financial Engines and Advisor Software, Inc. overcome this problem by looking through the fund to the individual portfolio positions and optimizing the investor's holdings by aggregating the individual positions in each fund into a combined portfolio.[3] This is not something that an individual investor can duplicate by using back-of-the-envelope calculations to adjust for the shortcomings of best-in-category fund ratings. This capability is one of the significant features of some of these retirement planning programs. In contrast, the Morningstar retirement planning calculator, Advice Online, apparently has not been upgraded to look through the funds to their underlying positions.[4] Ironically, investors selecting from among Morningstar five-star rated funds may be more likely to get a suboptimal overall portfolio than if they picked funds in another way. Funds with unusual portfolios for their categories are more likely to have extreme (good or bad) performance for any short period and, correspondingly, are more likely to provide less diversification when combined with other funds that were highly rated during the same time period or market environment.

Sharpe concludes his evaluation of the Morningstar rating system with a devastating statement: "If the only choice for a measure by which to select funds is between Morningstar's RAR [risk-adjusted return] measure and the excess-return Sharpe ratio, the evidence favors selecting the Sharpe ratio. The more appropriate choice, however, is to use a different performance measure or *none at all*." (Italics added; all quotes from Sharpe (1998)). Sharpe also suggests that a different version of the Sharpe ratio is more appropriate than the excess-return version most comparable to the Morningstar technique for risk adjustment. But Sharpe's most important message is clear: in Sharpe's view, the Morningstar ratings are fatally flawed and best ignored.

Sharpe is the most frequently cited critic of the Morningstar ratings, but he is not alone. Blume (1998) and Morey (2002) find Morningstar ratings subject to distortions stemming from averaging and survivorship effects. Morey (2005) identifies a kind of "winner's curse" on funds receiving their first five-star Morningstar ratings: they often perform badly after they get the five-star rating.

The Lipper Leaders ratings rank funds by five characteristics, three related to performance over different periods and in different market environments, plus tax efficiency and expenses. The Lipper Leaders technique is less dramatically flawed in the aggregate than the Morningstar stars, but it still falls short of the comprehensive risk/return aggregate portfolio analysis that Sharpe and most finance professionals advocate. The Lipper ratings avoid the misleading universality of the Morningstar single performance measure. Lipper also leaves the weightings to be assigned to near-term, long-term, and weak market performance—and expenses and tax efficiency—up to the investor.

It is not clear that the Lipper performance ratings are more likely to lead an investor to an optimal portfolio of funds than the Morningstar ratings. The Lipper tax efficiency ratings overlook the significance of capital gains overhang in assessing the likely long-term tax efficiency of a fund because they focus almost entirely on the SEC-mandated preliquidation after-tax return calculation.[5] The Lipper expense ratings are appropriate as far as they go, but the precise value of each fund's expense ratio would be far more useful to an investor than a √ through 5 category rating. The range of expense ratios and of other values for funds with the same numerical rating is too wide to be truly useful. The specific data underlying the Lipper ratings are not offered to individual investors. Morningstar does offer underlying numerical data, but I have not found their database to be reliable.

The absence of a readily available and accurate comparative mutual fund database is surprising, given the size of the mutual fund industry. In contrast to the dearth of detailed analysis of open-end, conventional mutual funds, some of the brokerage firms that provide analysis and evaluation of exchange-traded funds do a good job of assembling comparative data, particularly on expense ratios and tracking error.[6] As I noted in Chapter 6, tracking error (fund performance minus index performance) is the most important single measure of an index fund manager's skill. It is hard to find multiperiod tracking error comparisons in conventional fund reports or databases. Most fund shareholder reports do provide fund-to-benchmark index performance comparisons for the most recent periods, but assembling a spreadsheet with useful fund-to-index performance comparisons for a group of funds over a period of time can be a labor-intensive task if you are relying on the fund services.

Closed-end funds are also well covered by brokerage firm analysts. Many closed-end fund analysts do an excellent job of analyzing the relative values of closed-end funds based on a combination of factors including the fund's price premium or discount from net asset value, fund performance, and the capital gains tax overhang.[7] The weakest analyst coverage is the coverage of conventional mutual funds.

What's an Investor to Do?

I can offer only one suggestion to investors who want useful fund comparisons: Do it yourself. Begin by assembling financial data for the funds you are considering. You cannot compile data on every fund and there is no reason to try to include them all. You can stick to funds that Lipper gives a √ for expenses and apply some of the other criteria suggested in earlier chapters to reduce the number of funds even further. For the funds you will examine in detail, pull the data from printed fund reports or from the funds' own web sites. The data you will find on the fund web site are subject to regulatory standards similar to the standards for SEC filings and printed shareholder reports. If the data are not highly reliable, the fund manager will have far more serious problems than any complaint you might make. If a fund portfolio is less comprehensive than a total U.S. market fund, examine the fund relative to its peers' portfolio composition by comparing size, style, industry, and other appropriate defining characteristics. Either the Lipper or Morningstar fund categories should be adequate for a first-pass comparison. Look at the expense ratio and the fund's tracking error relative to its benchmark index over a number of years.

I take a reasonable performance record for granted, but picking a fund on the basis of a spectacular record for last year will often give you what you should expect: the ideal portfolio for *last year's* market. Another good and simple screen for performance is a √ Lipper Leaders rating for three-year total return. If a fund meets that standard, you have learned as much as you should expect to learn from past performance.[8]

For index funds, follow the rules at the end of Chapter 6. In the case of actively managed funds, be skeptical—and consider the discussion of active management in Chapter 9. Look at the size of the portfolio manager's total asset management responsibility.[9] Check a fund company's policies on fund growth, fund cloning, and fund size capping.[10] Look skeptically at a turnover ratio greater than 100 percent and, more importantly, at flow measures. Consider the fund's policy on late-arriving orders and on redemption fees. If you have any doubt that the fund follows its stated policies on market timing and fund share trading, you can try to circumvent them and see what kind of reaction you get. In the wake of the 2003–2004 fund scandals, I would expect most firms to follow their stated policies on fund share trading very closely. The only exception is likely to be trading through a fund supermarket. Supermarket proprietors are not yet cooperating fully with some funds' attempts to exclude market timers. If there is nothing in a fund's trading policies that makes them stricter than average, the fund is not doing enough to encourage short-term traders to go elsewhere. If traders are welcome, you will want to go elsewhere. You want a fund manager that insists on offering the best possible shareholder protection.

If any of the data that you assemble come from a fund service database, check the data carefully against hard-copy shareholder reports or fund web sites for any funds you are inclined to use to be sure the data are accurate. The accessibility of data on a wide range of funds from Morningstar is enticing because it is a great deal easier to get some of the relevant data from Morningstar's web site or its disc-based data archive than to go to fund reports, but my experience suggests that it is worth checking original sources on the best and second-best funds you find. This is particularly important for the data items listed in Exhibit 7.1.

Building a Structure for the Analysis of Funds

The rather free-form structure of the suggestions for fund selection in the previous section was intended primarily to convey a sense of the range of issues an investor should consider in fund evaluation. The purpose of the current section is to draw attention to five essential elements of fund selection in a more systematic way. If the work I have done in fund evaluation in preparing this book has taught me nothing else, it has helped me discover that no single overall rating system or even an unweighted fund evaluation based on specific fund characteristics will meet the needs of all fund investors. While certain fund features like shareholder protection are important for all investors (except, perhaps, market timers), other features like tax efficiency are important only to investors who plan to hold fund shares in a taxable account. The defining feature of conventional mutual funds—entry and exit from the fund at net asset value, regardless of the size of the transaction—is important to small investors and should be almost irrelevant to large investors, whose fund selections should be based on an appropriate mixture of shareholder protection, tax efficiency, and a low expense ratio. For reasons that will be clear by the end of this chapter, this discussion focuses on indexed mutual funds and indexed exchange-traded funds.[11] Furthermore, the conventional mutual funds considered specifically here and in Chapter 8 are confined to the offerings of two issuers, Fidelity and Vanguard. These firms' funds were chosen because I am more familiar with them than with the offerings of other fund managers. Fidelity and Vanguard offer some very low expense ratio funds, and both firms are above average in their shareholder protection policies.

Shareholder Protection

In the aftermath of the mutual fund scandals of 2003–2004, investors have seen evidence of substantial performance penalties associated with the ownership of funds that do not afford adequate shareholder protection from late trading and market timing. In Chapter 5, I argued that protection from the costs of ordinary shareholders buying and selling fund shares at net asset value was nearly as important as protection from market timers. If a fund offers free liquidity to traders at the expense of the fund's ongoing shareholders, you do not want to be one of those shareholders. Shareholder protection should be an essential feature of any fund that investors consider for their portfolios. The exchange-traded fund in-kind creation and redemption process provides a high degree of semiautomatic shareholder protection from entry and exit costs associated with trading in the fund's shares.

Among conventional mutual funds, firms vary greatly in the degree to which they implement policies designed to protect their shareholders, and the extent to which the structure of their funds provide a high degree of automatic protection. Fidelity and, to a lesser extent, Vanguard have made extensive use of redemption fees to compensate ongoing shareholders for the cost of any short-term trades made by other shareholders. The scope for significant shareholder abuse through market timing or other fund share trades is significantly reduced because all the funds I have evaluated are index funds and most are relatively large funds. Smaller funds and actively managed funds are more vulnerable to the costs of in-and-out trading. The issuer's shareholder protection policies are more significant for smaller and actively managed funds.

Trading Costs

Most of the costs associated with the failure of a shareholder protection policy are trading costs. To measure a fund's shareholder turnover trading costs, do not rely on the widely published turnover statistic as a proxy for trading activity. Turnover invariably understates the amount of trading that affects the cost of holding a fund. The best single measure of shareholder-related trading costs is flow, which is easy to calculate from a fund's annual report.

A second kind of trading cost that will affect some investors' choice of funds is the cost of buying and selling ETFs in the secondary market place. Conventional mutual fund transactions, regardless of the size of the trade, are generally done at net asset value. ETF share purchases and sales usually involve transaction costs that can be analyzed as part of the fund choice decision-making process. In general, the larger, more actively traded ETFs will usually have slightly lower transaction costs for investors than smaller, less actively traded ETFs.

The embedded transaction costs in the index composition change process should also be considered in fund selection as a third kind of transaction cost. Somewhat perversely, the most actively traded ETFs are based on popular indexes and have substantial embedded transaction costs associated with index composition changes. The funds discussed in Chapter 8 are all based on less popular and/or generally efficient indexes.

Expense Ratios

As a very approximate trade-off for the higher trading costs of taking and liquidating a position in ETFs relative to conventional funds, ETFs generally have lower expense ratios for comparable funds. At the expense levels common among large index funds, the differences in expense ratios are often small. Nonetheless, the calculations necessary to compare the transaction costs of share trading and expense ratios across funds are relatively simple and should be part of any fund evaluation and choice process. In general, a *long-term* shareholder will find the low expense ratio ETF a better buy, even after higher costs to buy and sell the shares.

Portfolio Manager Quality

Whole libraries could be filled with books and articles describing techniques to rate and evaluate individual portfolio managers, teams of portfolio managers, and the organization of the investment process followed by investment management organizations. There is no perfect or foolproof system and any evaluation based on the past record of a fund or a manager has no necessary implications for the future results that someone who invests with that portfolio management organization will obtain. There is a simple measure of past performance that is inherently fair (with only modest qualifications) and can be used with equal applicability for index managers and active managers. The measure is one I have discussed at length: tracking error.

Every fund, whether an index fund or an actively managed fund, has a benchmark index. As long as that benchmark is not an unacceptably inefficient index, calculating a fund's tracking error by subtracting the total return on the benchmark index from the fund return is a simple, elegant, and generally effective measure of the portfolio manager's skill. As suggested earlier, certain indexes with high embedded transaction costs—the S&P family, especially the S&P 500, and the Russell family, especially the Russell 2000—have had substantial embedded index composition trading costs in most years.

With the exception of the S&P 500 and the Russell 2000, where portfolio managers should be expected to beat the index after expenses in most years, giving a positive tracking error, comparing funds by comparing their tracking errors should take into account most shareholder protection and expense ratio comparison issues, whether the fund is an index fund or an actively managed fund. The only caveat of consequence in this approach—aside from the warning to be wary of benchmarks with embedded transaction costs—is that some active managers run portfolios that depart substantially in nature and risk from the benchmark index the fund uses in its comparative valuations.

Tax Efficiency

Tax efficiency is an issue only for funds held in taxable accounts; but for those accounts, tax efficiency should be a make-or-break element in the decision-making process for any long-term investor. Unless you are more than 100 years old and in poor health, the tax efficiency offered by ETFs should be the dominant choice criterion in your selection process for any fund to be used in a taxable account. If you are over 100 and in poor health, you should have enough respect for your doctors to avoid a significant capital gains overhang in any conventional mutual fund you select. *The tax efficiency criterion for fund selection is the reason no actively managed conventional mutual funds are on my list of attractive funds for taxable accounts.* The estimated 0.5 percent to 2.5 percent annual value of tax deferral from ETFs excludes inherently tax-inefficient conventional actively managed funds from consideration for taxable accounts (see p. 54). Unless you have a compelling reason to believe that an actively managed fund will first introduce an ETF share class and then permit all its conventional holders to convert their shares to the actively managed ETF share class, which will then be spun off as a separate fund, avoid today's actively managed mutual funds in taxable accounts.

Since no one can be sure what form the first active ETFs will take or whether conversion to the ETF format will be feasible for today's actively managed funds, any actively managed fund position should be considered only for your tax-deferred accounts. Actively managed funds will be discussed and evaluated at length in Chapters 9 and 10. They should have a role in investor portfolios, but they have some weaknesses in the conventional fund format that they can overcome as actively managed ETFs.

Uncertainties in Fund Selection

I am more than slightly amazed that Vanguard continues to pursue a strategy of introducing ETF share classes tied to conventional funds. A better business strategy for Vanguard and a much more effective investment strategy for its taxable shareholders would be to spin off the VIPERs ETF share classes as separate funds. There is a kind of catch-22 element in Vanguard's current product structure. Investors looking at these funds for use in a taxable account will continue to be uncertain of the ultimate success of the ETF share class and, hence, uncertain of the fund's ultimate tax efficiency. Unless Vanguard's 2005 expense ratio cuts in VIPERs attract large numbers of investors and increase trading volume, the funds' overall tax efficiency will continue to be doubtful.

The only certain way to break out of this dilemma and overcome the concern any rational investor would have about the tax efficiency of these funds would be for Vanguard to give investors the option to convert to the ETF share class at no charge and, after a designated date, to divide each fund into two funds: one conventional and the other a pure ETF. Chapter 10's discussion of an improved fund structure will illustrate the advantage of making the ETF share class the dominant share class—and the only way to add or remove assets from a fund. Vanguard has tried to add the advantages of an ETF share class the wrong way around.

Summary

The combination of generally lower expense ratios and highly probable tax efficiency makes ETFs the dominant choice for fund investment in taxable accounts. Tax-deferred accounts have more flexibility. Fund selection should be based on five criteria: shareholder protection, trading costs, expense ratios, portfolio manager quality, and tax efficiency. The importance of each of these criteria varies across funds and across the range of taxable and tax-deferred accounts available to investors. There is no single criterion or weighting scheme that will select an all-purpose, all-investors fund from the choices available today.

CHAPTER 8

Some Winning Funds— and Why They Win

There are fewer funds listed in Exhibit 8.1 than I would have liked to include. However, I believe the list includes a number of highly satisfactory index fund offerings. It includes all fund types that most investors will want to use except for actively managed funds, which will be the subject of Chapters 9 and 10.[1] I am not opposed to actively managed funds, but the investment industry needs to markedly improve their structure. In the meantime, I believe this short list will satisfy most investors' requirements. With a few reservations with respect to some of the ETFs, the quality of their managers and the level of fund costs (both expense ratios and transaction costs) are excellent.

Funds for Tax-Deferred Accounts

Looking first at the choices for tax-deferred accounts in Exhibit 8.1, I used three primary criteria: low operating costs (low expense ratio), the efficiency of the index used as a portfolio template, and the commitment of the management firm to turning away market timers and other short-term traders. With a 10-basis-point expense ratio on a number of its funds, Fidelity has taken the lead in aggressive expense ratio reduction in conventional indexed mutual funds.[2] Of the funds listed, only the expense ratio on the Vanguard Total Market Fund and Vanguard Extended Market Fund VIPERs share classes are lower than Fidelity's 10 basis points on a comparable fund. Most tax-deferred accounts are characterized by small periodic additions or withdrawals. This investment and withdrawal pattern does not work well with ETFs without a special trading process for small orders.

EXHIBIT 8.1 Funds to Consider

	Tax-Deferred Accounts[a]	Expense Ratio[a] (bps)	Taxable Accounts	Expense Ratio[b] (bps)
Broad Capitalization	Fidelity Spartan Total Market Index Fund[c] (FSTMX)	10	iShares DJ U.S. Total Market Index ETF (IYY)	20
	Vanguard Total Market Fund (VTSMX) (VTSAX) (VTI)[d]	19–15–7	streetTRACKS Total Market ETF (TMW)	20
			Vanguard Total Stock Market (VTI)	7
Large Cap	Use broad capitalization		Use broad capitalization	
	Vanguard Large Cap (VLACX) (VLCAX) (VV)	20–12–7	Vanguard Large Cap VIPERs (VXF)	7
Mid/Small Cap	Fidelity Spartan Extended Market Index Fund[c] (FSEMX)	10	No fully satisfactory funds available	
	Vanguard Extended Market (VEXMX) (VEXAX) (VXF)[d]	26–20–8	Vanguard Extended Market VIPERs (VXF)	8
	Vanguard Small Cap Index (NAESX) (VSMAX) (VB)[d]	27–18–10	Vanguard Small Cap VIPERs (VB)	10
	Vanguard Mid Cap Index Fund (VIMSX) (VIMAX) (VO)[d]	22–13–13	Vanguard Mid Cap VIPERs (VO)	13
U.S. Sectors	See text		Select Sector SPDRs ETFs (various)	26
Non-U.S. Stocks	Fidelity Spartan International Index Fund[c] (FSIIX)	10	iShares MSCI EAFE Index ETF (EFA)	35
	Vanguard Emerging Market Index Fund[e] (VEIEX) (VWO)[d]	48–30	iShares MSCI Emerging Markets ETF (EEM)	75
			Vanguard Pacific VIPERs (VPL)	18
			Vanguard European VIPERs (VGK)	18
			Vanguard Emerging Markets VIPERs (VWO)	30
Fixed Income	Vanguard Fixed Income Funds (various)	11–28	See text	

[a]For Vanguard funds the expense ratios and symbols are listed in the order (Investor Shares) (Admiral Shares) (VIPERs).

[b]All ETF shares or share classes. See text.

[c]These funds impose redemption fees on sales within 90 days of purchase for ongoing shareholder protection.

[d]ETF share classes are not currently available to most 401(k) accounts.

[e]The conventional share classes of this fund impose a redemption fee on sales within two months of purchase for ongoing shareholder protection.

Most 401(k) providers do not yet offer such a trading process in support of ETF shares.

Fidelity has imposed redemption fees for the funds listed in Exhibit 8.1, and the firm has been aggressive in attempting to require third-party intermediaries in retirement plans and fund supermarkets to apply its redemption fees at the account level to all redemptions within 90 days of purchase. Fidelity's unrelenting push for enforceable redemption fees on shares held through third-party intermediaries has been a major factor in the planned implementation of redemption fees by the Securities and Exchange Commission (SEC) for late 2006.[3] For tax-deferred accounts that neither invest additional funds frequently nor face frequent small withdrawals, the Vanguard Total Market VIPERs share class with a 7-basis-point expense ratio has a slightly lower ongoing cost.

Every long-term investor would do well to take maximum advantage of broad market capitalization index funds that have inherently less turnover than large-cap, mid-cap, or small-cap funds. With broad market index funds, it is possible to have your entire portfolio managed at a low expense ratio typical of large-cap funds. Why spread your investment over a number of different funds and managers when the resulting index (portfolio) turnover will only add costs and the small-cap funds will carry a higher expense ratio? A broad market index fund also eliminates any concern about the adequacy of overall portfolio diversification.

One result of the ubiquity of large-cap index funds, particularly funds benchmarked to the S&P 500, is that many investors already have more representation in the large-cap sector than they need. In all cases, the broad market funds offer more diversification and lower costs than a set of separate capitalization range funds. In the large-cap category of Exhibit 8.1 under tax-deferred accounts, I suggest use of a broad capitalization fund as a preferred choice over a large-cap fund. If, for some reason, an investor feels the need for large-cap exposure, the Vanguard Large Cap Fund VIPERs share class is available at 7 basis points and it is based on a relatively efficient index.

For investors who already have enough large-cap exposure, the most efficient way to get mid-cap and small-cap exposure in a tax-deferred account is to use the Fidelity Spartan Extended Market Index Fund based on the Dow Jones Wilshire Extended Market Index, which is the Dow Jones Wilshire 5000 less the securities held in the S&P 500. While there may be more turnover in this index than in the Dow Jones Wilshire 5000, it represents an inherently more efficient way of taking small-cap and mid-cap positions than separate small-cap and mid-cap funds. The higher-fee Vanguard Extended Market Fund, apparently, will soon use an S&P index with similar characteristics. Vanguard's Small Cap and Mid Cap Index Funds are at the bottom of the list, because they are distinctly inferior choices relative to the Extended Market funds listed above them. The

MSCI U.S. Small Cap Index is based on U.S. companies that are capitalization-ranked from 751 to 2,500, giving it an almost mid-cap flavor. A substantial portion of this float-weighted MSCI index overlaps other mid-cap and even large-cap index ranges with relatively less exposure in the truly small-cap market segment. This feature and a higher expense ratio on the Vanguard Small Cap Index Fund makes the Fidelity DJ Wilshire 4500 fund a more diversified and lower-total-cost way to obtain mid-cap and small-cap exposure in any tax-deferred account.

There is no listing for U.S. sector funds on the tax-deferred account list because most sector fund applications are tax-oriented. An actively managed sector rotation portfolio in a tax-deferred account could certainly use the Sector SPDRs.

The Fidelity Spartan International MSCI EAFE Index Fund is an extraordinary bargain for foreign exposure in tax-deferred accounts at a 10-basis-point expense ratio. Fidelity is committed to a maximum 20-basis-point fee for that fund in the long term. Even a 20-basis-point fee for this market segment is excellent. The operating process for a multicountry conventional mutual fund is far more mature (and efficient) than the ETF process for such funds. However, international funds are usually most dividend tax-efficient in a taxable account because of the tax credit pass-through mentioned on page 82. But if international exposure is to be taken in a taxable account, then the long-term tax efficiency requirement would disqualify the Fidelity Spartan International Index Fund.

Vanguard's fixed-income funds have traditionally offered the best fee structure and, usually, some of the better portfolio management available in the taxable fixed-income sector.

Funds for Taxable Accounts

For taxable accounts, my top broad-cap choices for domestic equities are two of the smaller ETFs. The iShares Dow Jones U.S. Total Market Fund uses an efficient index, and all entry and exit from the fund is by the traditional ETF in-kind creation and redemption process. This fund's position as the only pure ETF based on an efficient broad market index has been overlooked by investors—and even by the fund issuer's marketing staff for years. The second small, broad market pure ETF is a renamed and reconstituted fund. The streetTRACKS Total Market Index Fund was created out of a discontinued Fortune 500 ETF in June of 2005. Its benchmark index is the Dow Jones Wilshire 5000. The Dow Jones Wilshire 5000 Index has deeper coverage of the U.S. stock market than the Dow Jones Total Market Index. Although this fund is listed second because of its newness and small size, I would go for the broader coverage of the Dow Jones Wilshire 5000.

The iShares Dow Jones Total Market Index Fund and the street-TRACKS Total Market Fund rank ahead of the Vanguard VIPERs Total Market Fund ETF share class for two reasons. First, they are pure ETFs, so their tax efficiency should be assured for the long run. Unless an investor is confident that the ETF share class will ultimately dominate the Vanguard Total Stock Market Fund or that Vanguard will spin off the ETF share class into a separate fund, the pure ETFs should be the choice. I am more confident that the iShares Dow Jones U.S. Total Market Fund and the streetTRACKS Total Market Index Fund will be able to avoid capital gains distributions than I am that the VIPERs Share Class will be tax-efficient if it remains linked to its conventional mutual fund share classes. Second, the Dow Jones Wilshire 5000 index provides a deeper cut into the small cap universe than the MSCI U.S. Total Market Index used by Vanguard.

While there is no fully satisfactory (i.e., pure) ETF fund available across the mid-cap and small-cap categories, the Vanguard Extended Market Mid Cap and Small Cap VIPERs offer the prospect of better tax efficiency to come. Even better would be a pure ETF version of the Dow Jones Wilshire 4500 or, secondarily, pure ETF versions of the Vanguard Mid Cap or Small Cap funds.

The clear choices for sector funds are the Sector SPDRs, with their combination of low expense ratios, low trading costs, slightly higher volatility, and tax efficiency unchallenged among current ETF sector offerings. The reasons for choosing the Sector SPDRs over competitive sector funds are discussed at length in Chapter 11. There is room for a challenge to Sector SPDRs but State Street Global Advisors seems to be doing a more aggressive job of managing the Sector SPDRs portfolios relative to their indexes.

In Exhibit 8.1 the iShares MSCI EAFE Index Fund and Emerging Markets Fund are the top choices on the taxable accounts list for intermediate funds. They are pure ETFs with non-U.S. stock portfolios. Any reluctance to include them would be based on a combination of high expense ratios for index funds (35 basis points for the EAFE ETF and 75 basis points for the Emerging Markets ETF) and the cumbersome and costly process by which the ETF model has been adapted to deal with multiple foreign markets in a single fund. Nonetheless, an investor determined to take non-U.S. stock exposure in a tax-efficient manner should use these funds, expecting that some of the costs will be reduced as multicountry investing in an ETF format becomes increasingly efficient and as competition puts pressure on the high expense ratios.

Three of the Vanguard VIPERs share classes are listed among the non-U.S. funds. The conventional share classes of these Vanguard funds are not nearly as large as the conventional share class for the Vanguard Total

Market Fund, but the conventional share class still represents a significant tax efficiency drain, making a position in the VIPERs in a taxable account a speculation on how Vanguard might assure the long-term tax efficiency of these funds.

I have not listed specific fixed-income funds for taxable accounts. An investor planning to hold fixed-income funds in a taxable account might consider Treasury funds (Treasury interest is exempt from state and local income taxes). Even better for most taxpayers, a number of excellent analysts follow closed-end tax-exempt funds. The evaluations of these analysts are worth consideration by anyone who wants to carry tax-exempt fixed-income securities in a taxable account. Some of these funds are designed for investors resident in specific states. Analyst reports will generally consider and highlight that feature in their recommendations. Tax-exempt securities in an ETF look closer than they have looked before.

How Much Better Are These Funds?

How much better these fund choices might be than the funds the reader is using today depends on a number of things. First, in terms of index efficiency, the Dow Jones Wilshire 5000 and the Dow Jones Wilshire 4500 indexes are hard to beat in terms of the kind of low turnover that leads to index efficiency. Expense ratios as low as 7–10 basis points offered by fund companies with excellent reputations represent extraordinary value. When we take into consideration six facts, the performance advantage of these funds over the typical fund is probably about 200 basis points (2 percent) per year, with considerable variation around that average:

1. These index funds have very low absolute and relative expense ratios.
2. They track relatively efficient indexes.
3. Most index funds track one of two inefficient indexes, the S&P 500 or the Russell 2000.
4. Most efficient index funds usually provide better investor returns than the typical actively managed fund because they have lower transaction costs and lower expenses.
5. Most fund investors use higher-cost actively managed funds and do not have a significant position in index funds.
6. The pure ETFs should be much more tax-efficient than any conventional mutual fund is likely to be in the long run.

Additional choices, if the choices make sense, are always desirable. The short list in Exhibit 8.1 is a good start.

Summary

A cost reduction approach to fund analysis produces a short list of today's best fund choices for a variety of account types and asset levels. Structural changes and investor-oriented innovation should increase the range of choices in the future. In the next two chapters, we look at actively managed funds. Actively managed funds represent a much larger segment of the mutual fund industry than index funds, yet they face significant obstacles to tax efficiency. Some structural changes, among them the development of actively managed ETFs, are essential if actively managed funds are to play a role in a well-structured taxable investment portfolio.

CHAPTER 9

Active Investment Management: Can You Find a Manager Who Can Beat the Market?

One question occupies more investors' minds, is the subject of more reports and analysis in investment advisory publications, and generates more articles by academic finance researchers than any other. That question is: "Can you find an active manager who can consistently outperform an index fund?" Individually and collectively, investors have a great deal riding on how they have answered this question in organizing their own portfolios: there is far more money invested in actively managed mutual funds than in index funds. The purpose of this chapter is to examine the joint tasks of finding a superior active manager and getting money invested with her while she represents an outstanding investment opportunity—before she becomes a highlight of financial history.

Unlike the children of Lake Wobegon, not all—not even most—active managers can be above-average performers when the comparison is to an appropriately structured and well-managed index fund. In a classic article, "The Arithmetic of Active Management," William Sharpe (1991) explains why the *average* investor cannot hope to beat a comprehensive equity index. Sharpe's argument is unassailable: "If 'active' and 'passive' management styles are defined in sensible ways,[1] it *must* be the case that: (1) before costs, the return on the average actively managed dollar will equal the return on the average passively managed dollar and (2) after costs, the return on the average actively managed dollar will be less than the return on the average passively managed dollar."

The discussion of indexing in Chapter 6 suggests that a number of the assumptions in Sharpe's explanation of the compelling case for indexing do not hold as well in a world where most indexed assets are dedicated to a few popular, but inefficient, indexes—indexes that are not comprehensive and that have substantial embedded transaction costs. The transaction cost drag associated with implementation of index portfolio composition changes caused by concentrated index trading activity has penalized some popular index funds to a degree unanticipated by the indexing pioneers— and unanticipated by Sharpe in 1991. Given the level of their embedded transaction costs, Russell 2000 index funds no longer offer investors assurance of outperforming most competitive actively managed funds operating in their capitalization space. S&P 500 index funds are a little better. However, if the comparison is consistent with Sharpe's assumptions (e.g., the comprehensive index is the Dow Jones Wilshire 5000), the *average* active manager will inevitably trail the index fund.

The potential reward from a successful active manager search is obvious: superior performance. The daunting obstacles to success are just as clear: higher costs. There are opportunities to add value with active management. A determined effort to find a good active manager in some market segments is not outside the scope of what a determined investor can accomplish. Given the simple but certain mathematics of investment performance calculations, investors need to find market segments where an active manager's cost disadvantages are least oppressive and where the range of results from best to worst is wide. You will have to decide if the necessary effort is worth the commitment you will have to make. With reasonable care, you can avoid many of the mistakes the average investor makes. The fact that the manager selection process undertaken by most investors and promoted by fund rating services is doomed from the start leaves space for you to do better. Like many other aspects of life, success in active manager selection is likely to be the result of making fewer mistakes than other people make.[2] This chapter is partly about avoiding the major mistakes.

Some types of assets offer better prospects than others for active management if an investor can find the right manager. Against the background of the research that has been done in the academic community and the frustrations that investors have experienced in their search for superior managers, here are a few suggestions on how to make the difficult search for an active manager as promising as possible.

There are two issues a search for an active manager has to confront. The first issue is: Are there active managers who can add value for the investors who entrust them with their assets? The answer to this question is, rather clearly, yes. A few skeptical comments directed at some managers with excellent records aside, Peter Lynch, Warren Buffett, William Miller, and a number of other successful investors and investment managers have demonstrated performance that cannot be attributed entirely to a random process. There may be some disagreement with this statement, but I believe it reflects the consensus of both academic researchers and practitioners who have studied investment management records. Unfortunately, even accepting this conclusion, a far more difficult task remains for the investor seeking an outstanding manager: "How do I find one or more of these managers at the beginning of their careers and give them my assets to manage during the period of their outstanding performance?" That is a much harder problem to solve.

But, let's begin with Sharpe's cost challenge.

Cost Arguments Against Active Management

Anyone familiar with the literature of index funds or with any of the better books on mutual funds or indexing will be acquainted with most of the arguments against the average investor's ability to achieve superior performance with actively managed mutual funds or separate accounts. The most compelling of these arguments is that matching the market (as the market is represented by a broad market index) costs at least a small amount of money—even the lowest-cost index fund incurs some costs. These costs are exemplified by the fund's expense ratio, but other costs were discussed at length in Chapters 5 and 6.

Active investment management is a more labor-intensive process than indexing and, of course, active managers do not work pro bono. In addition to higher costs for some of the same services an index fund requires, an actively managed fund has to pay for things the index fund does not need. Even an active manager with average credentials commands a substantial salary and benefits package. A good index fund manager is well paid, but not paid as well as the typical active fund manager. Superior managers will be even more expensive as soon as their capabilities are recognized by others. Any active management process involves research and the development and implementation of an investment plan. Total costs, including an actively managed fund's expense ratio, and transaction costs (which are typically higher in an actively managed fund than in an index fund) bring the total annual costs of all but the most efficient actively managed funds above 200 basis points or 2 percent per year. Many actively managed funds with high portfolio turnover have much higher total annual costs.

The comparison of active management costs to the costs of an index fund is the basis for most of the arguments for the probability of superior long-term performance with indexing. To the extent that the index is (more or less) the market, an index fund can replicate the market at a lower cost than an active manager can operate. If the average active manager does not add material value in the form of superior investment selection, most investors would be better off investing in total market index funds than they would be entrusting their assets to the average active manager. The logic of this argument is incontrovertible, but the "Index

Fundamentalism" text box offers an amusing contrary example. This example, based on Vanguard's experience, suggests that the rules for finding a good actively managed fund are not all that different from the rules for finding a good index fund. The Vanguard example suggests that an actively managed fund that avoids most of the cost penalties that hurt the average mutual fund's performance—marketing costs, high portfolio turnover, and costly flow trading from late-arriving fund share orders—will start off much closer to matching or beating the benchmark return than the average active fund.

Index Fundamentalism

Of all the studies that have compared index fund and active management performance, perhaps the most intriguing is Reinker and Tower (2004). This paper, based on Reinker's Duke University undergraduate economics honors thesis, offers an excellent example of how to conduct such a study, and also illustrates many of the obstacles to getting meaningful results. The paper compares the performance of the index funds and the actively managed funds offered by Vanguard.

Vanguard is closely associated with indexing, and the Vanguard index funds have consistently been good relative performers. One might expect that, based on Sharpe's argument and on common sense, the Vanguard index funds would have beaten the Vanguard actively managed funds. The result is considerably more complex. The significance of the paper's conclusion that Vanguard's actively managed funds beat Vanguard's index funds is clouded slightly by some significant differences in portfolio average capitalization and styles that proved difficult to completely eliminate or offset (Kizer 2005). Not to take any credit away from them, however, the portfolio managers of the actively managed Vanguard funds did some decent stock picking, and the active funds definitely won the contest.

The actively managed funds carried higher expense ratios, but, in the Vanguard tradition, the expense ratios were still quite low by actively managed fund standards. The study confirms the importance of low expense ratios and confirms other findings that some active managers have the ability to add value through stock selection.

Although no comprehensive data were developed on relative portfolio turnover in the indexed and active Vanguard funds, a spot check of some of the actively managed fund turnover statistics suggests that Vanguard's actively managed funds are not active traders.

One of the interesting aspects of the paper was the complexity of dealing with survivorship bias within a single fund company that was cooperating fully with the project. Survivorship bias is the name researchers have given to the effect on aggregate fund performance calculations when some funds close or merge with other funds and disappear from historic databases. A significant number of funds are closed or merged out of existence each year. The departing funds often have poorer performance records than the survivors, leading fund performance studies to the conclusion that the average mutual fund or the average mutual fund investor did better than a full measure of the available choices would reveal. The classic studies of fund survival bias are Malkiel (1995) and Elton, Gruber, and Blake (1996). A more recent study, Carhart, Carpenter, Lynch, and Musto (2002) finds evidence of long-term survivorship bias distorting the fund performance record by as much as 1 percent per year over long periods. A difference of this magnitude requires careful attention to data quality.

Justifying Active Management

If you decide to depart from indexing, you should insist on being satisfied on four points:

1. That a significant fraction of active managers have the ability to add value for the investors whose assets they manage before considering the costs that the managers incur.
2. That some of these active managers can add enough value to more than cover the higher costs of engaging them.
3. That there is a way to identify such managers—before they have the entire run of superior performance that will make them legends to future generations of investors.
4. That you can get one or more of the selected managers to take some of your money to manage.

On the first point, there is substantial evidence of the ability of some active investment managers with responsibility for significant portfolio assets to deliver pretax, precost returns that are better than an index fund return. One problem, of course, is that the costs of operating a fund, the transaction costs associated with managing the portfolio, and, finally, taxes—to the extent that the portfolio enjoys a superior pretax return—all impinge on a skilled manager's ability to add value for investors relative to a low turnover index fund. This, of course, is the problem raised by the second point. Again, clearly a significant number of managers have overcome the cost drag to deliver outstanding performance after all costs. However, the costs stack the probability of success against you. The number of managers still in the running after this test is much smaller than before. Proceeding with active management makes sense only if you have an edge—an advantage—in the manager selection process. If you are not discouraged, the process of finding the superior manager (point 3) and getting her to manage some of your money (point 4) are the problems that you need to address.

Rather than review the extensive literature on active manager performance in an attempt to find a guide to the manager selection process, I want to focus on two unusual academic papers that provide some powerful insights and even some guidance for an investor in search of a superior active manager. The first of these is an award-winning paper by Berk and Green (2004),[3] which ventures to explain a number of investment management phenomena that have puzzled observers for years. Berk and Green offer a model of investor and manager behavior consistent with the observations: (1) that there are superior managers; (2) that rational investors try to find those managers and give them money; (3) that the desirable managers can deliver superior performance; (4) but only for a limited time.

One key insight of the Berk and Green analysis is that, as the superior manager becomes more and more successful and attracts more and more money, it becomes increasingly difficult to deliver superior performance. Hence, they affirm the importance of finding superior managers early in their careers. The second paper, Chevalier and Ellison (1999), attempts to find indicators of the ability of a portfolio manager before the manager's record is entirely a matter of history.

First, more about the Berk and Green manager performance model. Berk and Green cite a number of earlier studies that found evidence of performance persistence in mutual funds: Gruber (1996), Carhart (1997), Zheng (1999), and Bollen and Busse (2005). They note that other researchers have found that flows into and out of mutual funds respond to excess returns (with a lag), citing Chevalier and Ellison (1997) and Sirri and Tufano (1998). They also note that there is no solid evidence of long-term persistence of superior performance and they confirm the widely held belief that money flows into funds that have performed well recently. The oft-cited tendency of most (or all) new mutual fund money to go into funds that have Morningstar four-star and five-star ratings is simply the most widely discussed evidence that investors throw money at last year's hot managers.[4]

Berk and Green cite Bollen and Busse (2005) in connection with fund selection. The latter stated, "The existence of the mutual fund selection industry is predicated on the assumptions that some mutual fund managers possess significant ability and that this ability persists, allowing the astute investor to predict future performance based on past results." Berk and Green also cite Gruber (1996) and Sirri and Tufano (1998) on the issues of performance predictability and the forces that drive fund flows into mutual funds based on recent past performance. Taking a behaviorist's perspective, Berk and Green do not describe this investor behavior as irrational. They develop a model that assumes the behavior of all the parties involved—mutual fund managers, investors, and even providers of fund advisory services—is rational. Their model explains the strengths and weaknesses of actively managed mutual funds. It explains the presence and persistence of high fees; it explains the search for performance; and it explains why talented investment managers select an occupation in which few earn lifelong laurels but many earn a great deal of income. The Berk and Green solution is a market solution that is, perhaps ironically, consistent with *both* a generally efficient market *and* differential abilities among managers.

Let's look at the Berk and Green model in some detail.

Berk and Green posit that "Skilled investment managers exist who can generate positive risk-adjusted excess returns. Managers and investors alike know who these managers are." Yet, in a market at equilibrium, "investors who choose to invest with active managers cannot expect to achieve positive excess return on a risk-adjusted basis." Attempts by investors to invest with superior managers provide these managers with an excess supply of capital. Every investor would rationally want to abandon below-average managers or indexing and invest with the superior active manager instead. However, market equilibrium depends on the expected return to investors in all funds being equal. Otherwise, "one manager would end up managing all the available investment capital leaving the manager with no investors to trade with, which contradicts the assumption that the manager can earn excess returns."

The point of all this is that, as active managers have known since the beginning of investment history, an active manager's ability to add value in terms of excess return (a premium over the average market return) tends to decline as assets under management increase. Successful managers will charge high total fees even though their expenses (per dollar of assets managed) decline. One function of high fees is to obtain *for the manager* as much as possible of the superior return that the manager can obtain.[5] Total fees rise and assets under management at these fees rise until whatever ability the manager has is swamped by an inflow of assets and an increase in costs—largely transaction costs—that cancel out the manager's ability to provide above-average performance. The behavior of the investors is rational, the behavior of the manager is rational, and the market works—but the investor's search for a superior return has been frustrated by the manager's success.

With Berk and Green's model, chasing a superior active manager's performance can lead to poor results for investors even if they are willing and able to shift from one manager to another as growing assets overwhelm the first manager's ability to deliver a superior return. If Berk and Green's model describes reality—and I believe it comes pretty close—trying to get on a skilled manager's performance bandwagon early and being willing to switch bandwagons when the manager's assets under management exceed her competence *is the only way most investors have a shot at superior performance from an active manager in today's fund marketplace.*

If that is what the investor needs to do, how does he do it?

The paper by Chevalier and Ellison (1999) uncovered a few things that investors might look for in an active manager that indicate a chance for superior future performance early in the manager's career. To summarize very briefly, they found that managers with MBAs outperformed managers without MBAs. However, the higher returns achieved by the MBAs were attributable to the greater risk the MBAs took with portfolios. They also found that younger managers outperformed older managers, although that conclusion is clouded by the fact that a substantial amount of the higher return achieved by the younger managers is attributable to their positions with funds with lower expense ratios and to survivorship biases (possibly some poorly performing younger managers were removed from their positions and, hence, from the data set). The most statistically significant performance difference they found was that managers from undergraduate schools with higher average student SAT scores delivered higher returns.

I am hesitant to encourage a manager search based on the average SAT scores of managers and their college classmates, but I can offer some additional suggestions for an active manager search that are consistent with the findings of Chevalier and Ellison and others and consistent with earlier chapters of the book:

- Choose funds that protect shareholders from the cost of providing liquidity to fund share traders.
- Look for as low an expense ratio as seems consistent with sound management and look for an investment strategy that promises low transaction costs.
- Look at funds that specialize in market segments like small-capitalization stocks and sector selection where there is evidence of pricing inefficiency and significant differences of returns across portfolios and managers.
- Look for smaller and newer funds with young managers from established management companies. The management company's other funds should have generally good records and reputations. You want

a competent organization that can select the portfolio manager for you so you don't have to research SAT scores (for example).

- Disregard any performance record from periods when the fund was not fully open to investors.
- Avoid funds with significant 12(b)(1) marketing fees.

The combined purpose of these suggestions is to find promising managers and to put off for as long as possible the point at which new assets flowing into a successful fund will cancel out the manager's ability to add incremental return. Let's look at each of the suggestions in turn.

Shareholder Protection

Edelen (1999) found that the typical fund manager in the sample of funds he studied added value with stock selection, but the fund's ongoing shareholders lost all the benefit because the funds offered free liquidity to entering and leaving fund shareholders. As we have argued elsewhere (Chapter 5, pp. 105–111, and Gastineau (2004c)), fund policies that cut off order entry earlier than 4:00 p.m. can eliminate the costs of providing this liquidity and protect ongoing shareholders. Policy changes to protect shareholders will permit more of the superior stock selection skills of the best active managers to flow through to pre-expense performance—to the benefit of the fund's shareholders.

Low Expenses

Low expenses can help delay the inevitable dilution of a great manager's talent and they increase the chance that any superior skill will show up in performance after expenses.

Inefficiently Priced Market Segments

If we accept the premise that superior active managers exist, they may be more able to ply their trade in some market segments than in others. In fact, there is evidence to that effect. Assuming that it is possible, by emphasizing cost reduction and effective risk budgeting, to focus the active management effort on the right segment(s) of the market, Exhibit 2.3, p. 37, suggests that the greatest dispersion of returns available to the manager exists in individual stock selection or, to a modestly lesser extent, in sector selection. There is independent evidence that the least efficient equity market segment is the market in small-capitalization stocks.

The argument for active management rests fundamentally on the assumption that parts of the market are not as efficiently priced as the more adamant indexing advocates claim. A useful way to look at the active manager's task, then, is to describe it as a search for inefficiently priced securities. In small-capitalization markets, the securities are less thoroughly researched, the opportunities for substantial valuation discrepancies are greatest, and the value of the skilled portfolio manager's research effort can result in the greatest value added against less intense scrutiny of any given security. As the Kritzman and Page analysis reflected in Exhibit 2.3 shows, a roughly similar range of return possibilities is present in a sector selection strategy to add value with active management.

Large-cap stocks are thoroughly analyzed by a large number of investors, and, hence, these stocks are more efficiently valued than small-capitalization stocks. Large-cap stocks tend to track their respective sectors and the overall market more closely than small-cap stocks. The available amount of information about large-cap stocks leads to smaller price movements and, generally, to more efficient pricing—leaving less opportunity for a skilled manager to find a significant valuation anomaly that can be translated into superior performance. Assigning more of the portfolio's **risk budget** to the small-cap sector increases the probability that active management can add value.

Risk Budgeting

Risk budgeting allocates active management risk to market sectors and to portfolio managers that the asset allocator expects to have the best chance to improve the performance of the overall portfolio. In practice, risk budgeting is implemented through quantitative models using value at risk and other techniques to measure and control the risk allocation. Some inefficient market segments (e.g., small-cap stocks) usually offer the greatest opportunity to use the risk budget effectively.

Smaller Funds and Younger Managers

The small-cap and sector rotation markets also have appeal because they are frequently market segments where young, untried managers will be given an opportunity to cut their teeth managing a portfolio. An established manager will be more likely to operate in the large-cap or balanced fund sector where funds are larger, but where opportunities for materially superior performance are less obvious and, in general, less dramatic.

Disregarding Performance Records from "Private" Funds

Incubating very small funds for a few years to establish a spectacular track record with generous allocations of shares from hot initial public offerings (IPOs) and a fund company's best small stock ideas has been a common practice. Find out if a fund was really offered to the public in its early, highest-performance years. The incubation text box describes some things to watch for.

Incubation—Grabbing a Head Start in the Fund Performance Derby

Bettors on a horse race would be very disturbed to learn that the winning record reported in the racing form for a particular colt had been achieved in races where the colt had started running at the head of the home stretch at the same time the other horses were leaving the starting gate. In the mutual fund world, this kind of head start happens fairly often. Mutual fund firms will often organize new funds and run them for a period of time in an "incubator" mode. These incubated funds will not have a significant number of shareholders, and none of their shareholders need to be members of the general public. In fact, all the shares might be held by associates of the fund company for the first few years of the fund's life. During their incubation period, the new funds will get positions in small stocks that one of the firm's analysts likes, but which cannot be purchased in sufficient size to have a significant effect on the firm's larger funds. Some incubated funds have had preferential access to initial public offerings during periods when the IPO market was hot. The latter practice will be less common in the future.

Investors should be wary of any small fund with an extraordinarily favorable record on a very small asset base. This can be difficult to detect, though looking at the size of the fund in prior annual and semi-annual reports filed with the SEC may offer some strong hints. If a fund with a favorable record has not operated continuously with a reasonable level of assets during the period of its posted performance record, skepticism is appropriate.

Avoiding Marketing Fees

Even if you can use marketing fees to meet other obligations, consider that marketing fees may shorten the period you might enjoy superior performance from the fund in two ways. First, they increase the costs that come out of performance. Second, if the marketing program is successful, the manager will be swamped with assets that much sooner.

A Plan for Action

Berk and Green's model is the best explanation I have seen of a market with exploitable inefficiencies. Good managers can add value until constraints dissipate their value-added performance as the size of the portfolio grows. In short, the superior manager soon spreads her skill over too large a pool of assets and any period of superior performance ends, often before more than a small number of investors can benefit from the manager's skill.[6]

The Berk and Green model suggests a commonsense strategy for detecting and profiting from the skills of a superior active manager. The small-cap or sector selection investment styles offer the greatest opportunity for manager value added. One disadvantage of small-cap stocks is that superior managers have to spread their knowledge and research over a larger number of companies. They are able to manage a smaller dollar amount of assets than they could manage in, say, a sector rotation portfolio. The fund should be relatively new in the sense that it has not accumulated a large pool of assets relative to the skill the manager can bring to the table. Ideally, the fund should have demonstrated a good short-term performance record under the current manager with no obvious performance quirks like a period of incubation when the fund was not offered to investors.

Relative to a policy of selecting a fund based on a five-star rating from an advisory service, this process is relatively ad hoc. The opportunities for false starts and disappointments are obvious. But, while there is a degree of performance persistence in top-ranked funds, simply following past performance is not a particularly good way to achieve superior future results.

An investor planning to use these suggestions will not get a great deal of help from most fund advisory services. The investor will have little choice but to dig into fund shareholder reports and SEC filings as he attempts to select a fund with some promise of superior results based on a manager's skill. Under the Berk and Green model, by the time the portfolio manager posts the opening wedge of the performance record she might be capable of, the fund will be growing toward a size that will make further superior performance improbable.

The probability that the active manager selection process described here can survive a comparison with a well-run index fund for more than a few years is not high, but it is certainly not zero, either. Most of us will continue to buck the odds against active management with large or small parts of our assets, and there is no better way to find good active managers with today's fund structures.

The text box describes a new fund manager ranking service that might make the manager search both easier and more frustrating.

Rating Fund Managers

A new portfolio manager ranking service from a new firm, The Rankings Service (www.trsreports.com), takes advantage of increased disclosure about portfolio managers implemented in 2005. The new service appears to cover portfolio manager performance records for the most recent five years. There is information on the manager's maximum cumulative loss and maximum time to recovery from a loss within the five-year window. Information on the manager's return volatility and the index volatility of the fund's benchmark relative to the S&P 500 provides an indication of the effect risk might have had on the manager's results.

The methodology used by the service appears to be as sound as limited data availability permits. Obvious shortcomings include the immeasurable significance of the investment organization behind a top-performing manager. For overall rankings, all managers are grouped together regardless of the type of funds they manage. This means that a fixed-income manager—with the possible exception of a high-yield manager—is not going to make the top rank in most periods. The service's publication of top 10 manager ratings by asset class should make up for this. If a manager is responsible for a number of portfolios, the service calculates the performance for each portfolio and weights them equally—not the best weighting method, but the easiest. To the extent that The Rankings Service does detect and bring attention to superior managers, the time period during which superior fund managers will be available before their assets under management swamp their ability is likely to end even more quickly than in the past.

Candidly, the probability of finding and engaging the services of a superior active mutual fund manager using this process is not high enough to appeal to me. I am particularly concerned about the tax inefficiency inherent in active management and the way in which a process that moves from one active manager to another will affect the after-tax return in a taxable account. As the Dammon, Spatt, and Zhang analysis in Chapter 3 indicated, most of a typical investor's equity assets will be in taxable accounts. If a conventional actively managed fund will lag a comparable index ETF by 0.5 percent to 2.5 percent because of tax inefficiency alone, this characteristic added to the inherently higher cost of active management asks too much of an active manager in overcoming both the cost and the tax advantages of an index ETF in a taxable account.

Apart from stock positions with low costs or subject to other restrictions, most of my financial assets are in efficient index funds and a hedge fund (in a tax-deferred account). However, as a former active portfolio manager, the siren song of active management still has appeal for me. Instead of trying to find the best of the available funds and managers, I have thought about a fund structure that can provide consistently better results for a limited pool of assets for a longer period of time. If this change can be made in a way that pays skilled portfolio managers well, it may be an answer to the active portfolio management problem for some investors. The new funds will have to find ways to deal with the cost problems of mutual funds and with the incentive open-end fund managers have to accept any assets that arrive on the manager's doorstep. The funds will have to be ETFs for tax efficiency. This improved fund structure is the topic of the next chapter.

Summary

This chapter examines the case for and against active management as part of the solution to most investors' portfolio requirements. In an era when most index fund assets are benchmarked to two overused indexes—the Standard & Poor's 500 and the Russell 2000—there should be an opportunity for an investor willing to do some homework on active managers to do better than simply finding a fund using a less popular index.

Berk and Green (2004) describe what I believe to be the market mechanism that creates the greatest active management performance problem. Working with this market mechanism, there may be a way to obtain the services of a superior manager who can outperform for a longer period of time.

Supplementary Information

Few topics in finance have received as much research attention as the continuity and reproducibility of superior actively managed fund performance. A bibliography of all the significant academic literature on this topic would go on for pages, and a listing of popular press discussions would fill volumes—with new material appearing all the time. The papers cited in the text and endnotes have extensive bibliographies listing some of the better research papers on active manager performance.

Three excellent books with the phrase "random walk" somewhere in each of their titles collectively summarize the case both for and against active management on a number of levels. Malkiel (1973) is in its eighth edition (2003). Complementary perspectives are offered by Lo and MacKinlay (1999) and Singal (2004).

CHAPTER 10

Reinventing the Mutual Fund: Actively Managed Exchange-Traded Funds

If the mutual fund had not been introduced into the United States in the 1920s, financial markets would be very different today. However, if the development and growth of mutual funds had not attracted $8 *trillion* to today's so-called legacy funds, no investor, no investment manager, and *certainly* no objective regulator would suggest that the primary repository of U.S. savings and investments should have the characteristics of today's mutual funds in the twenty-first century. Starting with the premise that a few features of today's mutual funds might be taken as examples of what *not* to do and taking advantage of the technology available today, I try to sketch the outline of a new or "reinvented" fund structure.[1]

The framework for the new funds is very similar to the structure of exchange-traded funds. Certain features of the existing index ETFs have been modified or, more accurately, generalized to accommodate a wider variety of funds and to overcome some of the weaknesses apparent in the existing index ETFs.

Some of the features I propose for the new fund structure are closely linked. Other features might be implemented separately or as part of a different set of fund features. Whatever the final shape of the funds that emerge from a series of changes likely to happen over the next 10 years, the result will certainly be a more flexible investment management structure that meets the needs of a wider range of individual and institutional investors.

Investors and fund managers should look forward to change with enthusiasm. Investors will enjoy better net returns because their expenses, direct and indirect combined, will be lower. Top investment managers will work in a better environment and can earn as much or more from exercising their skills as they have earned in the past. Their investment decisions will be made and implemented in an atmosphere that preserves the confidentiality of their information, and the value of their work will be clearer than ever before. In exchange for reasonable constraints on conflicts of interest, they will be able to preserve the confidentiality of their investment process and deliver better results to investors.

The new funds will increase the transparency of sales and marketing costs—something U.S. regulators have been closing in on for years without total success. The closer the regulators come to total transparency of sales and marketing costs, the easier it will be to change the fund structure. No current participant in the creation, marketing, or operation of funds will be systematically disadvantaged by the new structure. Clearly, however, fewer people will be needed in the investment management and fund distribution process. Many industry participants will have to reinvent their own roles and justify their claims to a share in the costs paid by investors.

The history of innovation in financial markets and innovation in all parts of a growing economy is largely a history of cost reduction or delivery of a better product or process at the same cost. In this context, Exhibit 10.1 is a preliminary attempt to estimate how the new fund structure might improve the return a typical investor can expect from one of the new and improved indexed or actively managed funds. There may be some overenthusiasm behind the reduced cost estimates reflected in the table, but under any reasonable assumptions, the new structure offers a marked improvement in expected performance over the funds investors own today. Note that the cost reduction estimates in Exhibit 10.1 do not include the extremely important tax-deferral advantage that the new structure will add to actively managed ETFs. I have estimated that advantage at 0.5 percent to 2.5 percent per year for a long-term taxable account. It is not listed in Exhibit 10.1 because it is significant only for taxable accounts. In those accounts, it is a critically important feature.

The failure of the fund industry and its regulators to achieve significant reform in the wake of the mutual fund scandals of 2003—2004 suggests that necessary shareholder protection in conventional mutual funds is not possible within the current regulatory framework. Exchange-traded fund (ETF) innovation is delayed by high Securities and Exchange Commission (SEC) staff turnover and an extraordinarily full agenda for both the SEC staff and the Commissioners. The virtually immediate availability of any ETF innovation to all comers reduces the incentive for entrepreneurs to undertake the investment in regulatory applications necessary for incremental ETF improvements. My objective in this chapter is to demonstrate the compelling superiority of a radically new fund structure—superiority in investor protection and superiority in expected performance.

EXHIBIT 10.1   Total Annual Shareholder Cost Comparison for Actively Managed Funds

	Equity Mutual Fund	New Equity Fund
Expense Ratio (ex (12b)(1) or service fee)	1.0%	1.0%
Portfolio Composition Trades inside the Fund	1.5%	1.5%
Fund Share Trading Liquidity Costs	1.4%	a
Leakage of Investment Information/Index Publication[b]	0.35%	
Fund Supermarket vs. Multi–Share Class ETF	0.35%	c
Performance Penalty from Oversized Funds, Net of Higher Performance-Based Fee[d]	Up to 2.00%	
Annual Total	Up to 6.60%	2.50%
Potential Shareholder Cost Difference	Up to 4.10% per year	

[a]Costs to enter and leave the ETF share class are paid by the trading shareholder only when entering or leaving.

[b]Preliminary estimate based on an estimate of half the typical annual cost of the publication effect of S&P 500 composition changes. The value of plugging leakage of trading plans for active portfolios may be greater.

[c]Costs in affected share classes equal to minimum annual supermarket preference fee charged by major brokers. Some supermarket fees are higher. There would be no ongoing annual sales or marketing fees in the new structure without specific agreement by the investor to pay them.

[d]A rough average derived from conversations with active fund managers and trading cost analysts. The estimate allows for some of the performance penalty reduction being absorbed by a higher management fee as compensation for that performance.

Problems with Mutual Funds

While mutual funds are used by many investors—individuals, institutions, endowment funds, qualified retirement plans, and others—mutual funds and their investment process are *not* generally designed to:

- Offer investors inherent protection from most of the abuses uncovered in the recent mutual fund trading scandals.
- Minimize investor costs from fund share trading and portfolio turnover.
- Require an efficient investment management process at the management company responsible for the selection of investments for a fund.
- Provide an appropriate allocation of transaction costs between entering and leaving shareholders on the one hand and ongoing shareholders on the other hand.

- Allocate marketing and service costs appropriately among various classes of fund shareholders.
- Protect the confidentiality of an investment manager's trading plans.

New actively managed and indexed ETFs can be designed to:

- Offer investors increased protection from most of the abuses uncovered in the recent mutual fund share trading scandals.
- Reduce investor costs from fund share trading and portfolio turnover.
- Increase the efficiency of the investment management process at the management company responsible for the selection of investments for a fund.
- Provide an appropriate allocation of transaction costs between entering and leaving shareholders on the one hand and ongoing shareholders on the other hand.
- Allocate marketing and service costs appropriately among various classes of fund shareholders.
- Protect the confidentiality of an investment manager's trading plans.

The new fund structure meets these requirements in ways that should appeal to investors who are unsatisfied with existing funds. There is no regulatory time bomb embedded in these proposals. In fact, this structure is as close to self-regulating or, better, "structure regulating" as any fund I can imagine will ever be. This new fund structure will not work for all types of portfolios. Unless a large investment management firm creates a number of relatively independent satellite fund management organizations to develop families of these funds, no one entity should expect to achieve the kind of market share that the five or 10 largest mutual fund management organizations have in the United States today. Of course, there is no reason why one parent organization could not create such a decentralized structure.

Listing some of the key features of this new fund product will provide a frame of reference for comparison with existing funds:

- Any notice of intention to create or redeem a domestic equity exchange-traded share class received by the fund *after* 2:30 p.m. or an appropriate earlier time on trading days with early market closings will be implemented at net asset value (NAV) on the following day. Commitments to create or redeem ETF shares received *before* 2:30 p.m. will be priced at that day's 4:00 p.m. NAV. Appropriate early cutoff times will be imposed on creation or redemption of shares in fixed-income funds or funds holding foreign securities.
- All entry of assets to and removal of assets from a fund will be through an exchange-traded share class or an equivalent procedure that pro-

tects ongoing fund shareholders from the costs of providing liquidity to entering and leaving shareholders.

■ An intraday fund share proxy NAV based on the start-of-day fund portfolio will be distributed through electronic quotation vendors during the trading day at an interval to be determined by the fund's board of directors. That interval will be no shorter than 15 seconds, and no longer than 60 minutes.

■ Except for some large-cap funds, each actively managed equity fund will announce the maximum number of shares that it will issue. Once that total is reached, no additional shares will be issued unless shares are first redeemed. A market maker that redeems shares to reduce its inventory of shares in a fund that has reached its maximum size will have the exclusive right to re-create those shares for a period set by the fund board.

■ With the concurrence of the fund's directors, the investment manager may disclose the current fund portfolio to the public by any means the SEC approves that permits low-cost access to the information by any investor. There will be no preferential disclosure of portfolio information. The portfolio disclosure will be no less frequent than the quarterly disclosure with a 60-day lag now required of conventional mutual funds. Fund managers will be encouraged by market and marketing forces to make more frequent portfolio disclosures and to disclose other information that describes the characteristics of the portfolio in a format that will help investors and market makers value the shares appropriately and hedge their positions in the shares intelligently during intervals between required portfolio composition disclosures.

■ An investment manager could manage a series of active ETFs, but after the active ETF complex reaches a size specified by the funds' prospectuses, the investment process used by the management company would have to be used exclusively for products using a fund structure. The same directors would be directors of every fund managed using a common investment process, and the directors would be responsible for determining that the investment process had adequate capacity to serve additional funds without a detrimental effect on existing funds. To clarify the exclusivity requirement, the manager would not be permitted to handle separate accounts or institutional pooled accounts except as fund share classes converted from ETF share classes. If an investment manager has excess research or idea capacity along a particular dimension, the firm can sell that capacity to another investment manager on terms that are consistent with the interests of its own funds' investors.

■ A wide range of specialized share classes would be available for conversion from and back to the ETF share class used for shareholder entry and exit. These specialized share classes would offer a variety of management fee and marketing fee arrangements designed to accommodate different types of shareholders with investment objectives that coincide with the objective pursued by the fund.

■ An innovative incentive fee program would permit the board to increase the investment manager's advisory fee to reward superior long-term performance by superior managers without overwhelming the investment process with more assets than they can manage with superior returns.

■ The popularity of being able to buy shares in a mutual fund at the day's closing NAV has been largely ignored by ETF issuers, perhaps because ETFs were originally introduced in the United States primarily to create securities for trading throughout the day on the American Stock Exchange. A new trading mechanism can appeal to traditional mutual fund investors.

Why Do It This Way?

There are a number of new features reflected in these statements that will make these funds very different from current fund offerings. The best way to understand the reasons for the changes is to describe, step-by-step, how the new funds will work.

Early Cutoff for Fund Share Creation and Redemption

The 2:30 p.m. cutoff for creation and redemption instructions for domestic equity funds is based on the need to protect ongoing shareholders from the costs of providing liquidity to fund share traders and, in the specific case of ETFs, to facilitate portfolio changes. In contrast to conventional mutual fund practice, which favors entering and leaving shareholders, I believe every fund must decide the conflict between traders and investors in favor of the fund's long-term investors.[2]

In looking for a solution to a conventional fund performance problem highlighted by a 1999 paper by Roger Edelen, I examined the best practices followed by a number of funds prior to the 2003–2004 mutual fund scandal revelations. The in-kind creation and redemption process of benchmark index ETFs is very effective with one exception: it discourages ETF managers from implementing index or portfolio composition changes aggressively. See Gastineau (2004c). With the new active ETFs, the creation and redemption baskets will not match the fund portfolio as closely as they match benchmark index ETF portfolios. Consequently, managers need trading time between the commitment to create or redeem shares and the NAV determination to adjust the portfolio to the fund composition they want to maintain.

While the costs of modifying portfolio manager behavior to implement index composition changes more aggressively are not great, the costs to maintain the appropriate portfolio in an actively managed ETF will often be significant. The simplest solution is to require a commitment to creation or redemption by 2:30 p.m. for all domestic equity ETFs, letting the portfolio manager make changes in the portfolio before the NAV at which the creation or redemption is priced must be calculated and before any change in the creation or redemption baskets for the next day will be posted.

Prior to 2004, several conventional mutual fund firms—the one with the highest profile being Vanguard—had adopted procedures to prevent fund share traders from entering orders that would come to the fund just before the 4:00 p.m. market close. A fund's acceptance of orders until 4:00 p.m. provides free liquidity to the trader at potentially high cost to the fund's ongoing shareholders. The net effect of the changes made in the wake of the scandals has been to slightly *reduce* the level of shareholder protection from the cost of afternoon orders while offering false comfort to investors.

The greatest weaknesses in today's ETF and conventional mutual fund structures can be solved by a hard 2:30 p.m. cutoff for new orders. This structural requirement is the source of the 2:30 p.m. creation/redemption cutoff. It is a simple solution to a modest problem for index ETFs, and a huge problem for conventional mutual fund investors. It is a structural necessity for active ETFs because their creation and redemption baskets may not closely reflect the contemporary fund portfolio. SEC's weakened 4:00 p.m. "hard close" proposal does nothing to protect fund shareholders from the costs of providing liquidity to market timers or to any other fund share traders.

Intraday Valuations

The principal reason for less frequent dissemination of the ETF intraday share value proxy is that frequent dissemination will permit sophisticated analysts to "back calculate" the precise composition of the current portfolio from the periodic valuations, particularly if a portfolio has relatively few positions. To protect the value of information on the fund's recent trades, less frequent dissemination of information is called for. If a proxy value calculation is disseminated every 15 seconds, more than 1,500 intraday value calculations will be published every full trading day. The average actively managed portfolio has fewer and larger positions than broad market index ETFs, making determination of portfolio composition and of recent changes relatively easy if an analyst has enough fund value data points. I am aware of proposals to base the intraday value proxy on a portfolio that does not match the fund portfolio to frustrate back calculation of portfolio composition. Accurate valuations at less frequent intervals are more useful to market participants than approximate valuations at more frequent intervals.

If more frequent but less accurate value prices are necessary, they would serve investors better if they were based on the actual portfolio with all but the hourly value adjusted by a randomly generated increment or decrement from a known distribution. There is no need for precise 15-second value updates, and they reveal information to the fund shareholders' disadvantage. I would expect the full portfolio composition of most of these funds to be disseminated voluntarily about every two weeks with a two-week lag, but that is a decision appropriately left to each fund board. There is little incremental value in most trading or investment ideas that will survive as long as two weeks after the fund begins to trade. The only valid reason for the 60-day delay on the current quarterly disclosure of conventional fund portfolios is that managers of very large aggregate portfolios may control a substantial fraction of the shares of many of their portfolio companies. Protection of their shareholders requires giving the entire fund family time to make portfolio changes without having to operate in a fishbowl. Capping the size of some or all funds in a fund complex should minimize this problem and, more importantly, preserve a superior fund manager's ability to achieve superior long-term returns.

Capping Fund Size Will Reduce Performance Dilution

With the possible exception of funds holding just large-capitalization stocks, the investment manager would state in fund prospectuses the maximum number of ETF equivalent shares that each fund in a family will issue or use a controlled share-growth formula that will prevent growth that will swamp the manager's ability to achieve superior performance. The cap could be increased or the formula modified at a future date if the management organization was comfortable with its ability to manage a larger portfolio and if the fund board or the fund shareholders approved a change. An appropriate maximum fund size offers the prospect of superior investor performance over a longer period and, if the fund performs well, a higher fee for the manager on each dollar of assets managed.

Of course, an important argument for capping fund size in some portfolios comes from the Berk and Green (2004) paper on the difficulty of finding a superior active manager and having assets managed by that manager over a long period of time as described in Chapter 9. The capping of some of these new funds should help ensure that investors can obtain higher returns for a longer period and permit portfolio managers to post better long-term performance records. With management fee increases linked to multiyear performance, managers could earn as much money on a limited asset base as they might earn on much larger portfolios today.[3]

Retaining Tax Efficiency

After a fund reaches its cap in terms of number of ETF share equivalents to be issued, the fund might see few redemptions unless the creation/redemption rules are designed to encourage occasional redemptions. The existence of a cap without some variability in the number of shares outstanding would foreclose redemptions and lead to much greater price volatility in the secondary market trading of the capped funds' shares than is necessary or appropriate. The absence of redemption in kind would reduce the tax efficiency of the fund. To permit the fund share market price to more closely reflect changes in the fund's NAV most of the time and to avoid significant fluctuations in any premium that the market price of the shares may carry over the fund's NAV, it is appropriate that a market maker with a temporary excess inventory of shares in a particular fund should be able to redeem fund shares from time to time, bringing the size of the fund below the stated ceiling on the number of shares the fund would issue.

Subsequent to such a redemption and for a short period designated in the fund's prospectus, the redeeming authorized participant would have the exclusive right to re-create the shares it had redeemed under terms established by the fund prior to its closing to new creations. These terms would be essentially a re-creation of the shares redeemed with an in-kind deposit priced at NAV plus a normal creation fee. Re-creation will be permitted for a period of, say, 10 to 45 days from the time of the redemption. If the redeemer did not re-create within that period, the fund would have the option of either shrinking the cap on the number of shares it would issue (to shrink the fund because management had determined that the capped size was too large) or to permit any authorized participant to create shares up to the posted share ceiling under standard (NAV) terms for fund share creations.

Protection of Information

A key feature of the new fund structure will conserve the value of the investment information and ideas developed by the investment manager for the fund or for a group of complementary funds. With a unified portfolio management and trading operation offering protection from inappropriate dissemination of investment information, the value of an idea should be preserved for as long as possible—ideally until the funds managed by the organization could buy or sell as much as they wanted of a particular security.

Today, most sizable investment management organizations provide a wide variety of products to investors. These investment products are usually managed independently, in the sense that each portfolio is independent in composition relative to other portfolios. However, because funds and other products from the same adviser hold numerous securities in common and because the investment manager has a responsibility to the beneficial holders of each portfolio or separately managed product to treat them fairly, management of the products is partly integrated. What this means in practice is that when the firm embarks upon the purchase of a particular security or group of securities, the securities are often purchased for many or maybe even all of the manager's accounts or funds at about the same time. To manage conflicts of interest, investment management organizations have developed techniques to handle purchases and sales for different accounts in a sequence or rotation. The rotation is designed to ensure that a particular account comes first on the list for some investment ideas, in the middle for others, and, inevitably, at the bottom of the list for still others. The starting point for purchase of a new position or liquidation of an old position is selected at random or the starting point simply moves from the top to the bottom of the list, a step at a time, recycling back to the top until a position has been either taken or liquidated for accounts as necessary. Alternatively, a trading desk that handles trades for all of the manager's accounts may calculate an average price and give each account the same average price with all accounts participating in trades over a longer period.

The problem with these procedures is that each type of account that might hold a specific position has characteristics that cause its trading practices to reveal different amounts and kinds of information, almost at random, to other market participants while the trading moves through account categories or trades are allocated to all accounts over a period of a few weeks.[4]

Clearly, one of the weaknesses of the typical active manager's investment management process—in which different types of accounts are buying or selling the same security—is information leakage that could be largely eliminated if all of the manager's clients met in a single investment pool with delayed publication of portfolio content and changes. With a single type of product—funds—there are no conflicts associated with the order in which transactions are made, and there would be no leakage to outside organizations from trade confirmations sent to owners of separate accounts and individuals associated with institutional and pooled portfolios. Effective information management can be accomplished most efficiently and most confidentially with multiple share class funds.

Multiple Share Class Exchange-Traded Funds

The preemption of the index space in the ETF market by low-cost funds using a broad range of index compositions may make it harder for higher-cost actively managed funds to make inroads without a variety of marketing strategies more or less along the lines of the marketing processes used by conventional mutual funds. In contrast to conventional mutual funds, where index funds were introduced about 50 years after actively managed funds, it is the active ETFs that must compete with established index ETFs as well as established conventional funds. Obviously, given the low fees on index ETFs, competing on fees alone is not feasible for these new actively managed funds.

An investment management structure that concentrates the investment manager's activity in a limited number of portfolios makes it both desirable and feasible to offer special institutional share classes that might have lower expense ratios than even some traditional index ETFs. Although active management will generally require higher management fees for retail funds than the fees for index ETFs, institutional investors such as pension funds and endowments are used to paying lower fees for active management than the fees charged to individuals investing in some index ETFs. In order for the investment management organization to achieve the necessary critical mass, it may offer lower-cost share classes designed to meet the needs of institutional investors who will be attracted by the efficiency of the investment management structure, its more effective use of investment information, and the possibility of an extended period of superior performance with capped fund size. These institutional investors will still expect lower rates than those charged retail actively managed fund investors.

The non-ETF share classes offered will include at least the following: (1) front-end load share classes; (2) back-end load share classes (i.e., shares with a contingent deferred sales charge); (3) level load funds, typically with a 100-basis-point 12(b)(1) fee (or its equivalent should such fees be eliminated) for the life of the investment; and (4) one or more institutional low-management-fee share classes for investors investing minimums of, say, $1 million, $10 million, or $100 million. The ETF share class and the specialized share classes will be exchangeable for one another (perhaps for a small administrative fee), probably without tax consequences.[5] Institutional investors may be attracted by the fund's approach to the use of research, by the new investment structure, and by incentives such as ownership in the investment management company and/or the opportunity to exchange their share class for the ETF share class, which might sell at a premium after a capped fund is closed to new investors.

Supplementary Portfolio Information

The dissemination of supplementary information about the characteristics of active ETF portfolios must fall short of providing information on current trading plans to protect ongoing shareholders, but certain types of supplementary information will make market makers more comfortable, and, in spite of somewhat less frequent valuation proxy publication, should encourage fund share market makers to tighten their spreads. Supplementary disclosure of portfolio characteristics can help provide appropriate transparency of portfolio features that might affect fund share trading, and, in a very general way, transparency of portfolio composition. Transparency is a desirable thing in some respects, but beyond a certain point, portfolio and trading transparency work against the interest of the fund's ongoing shareholders who, after all, are owed primary allegiance whenever there is a question as to what is fair or appropriate.

New Intraday Trading Mechanisms for ETFs

Orders to trade stocks or ETFs are usually entered as market orders or as bids or offers at a specified limit price. Quotations posted in the marketplace, largely by market makers, are represented as bids and offers at specified prices. There are other order types, probably the most important of which is the market-on-close order whereby an order entered prior to a certain time will be guaranteed execution at the closing price in some markets.

The popularity of being able to buy shares in a mutual fund at the day's closing NAV has been largely ignored by ETF issuers and trading markets, perhaps because ETFs were originally introduced in the United States primarily to create securities for trading throughout the day on the floor of the American Stock Exchange. The ability to enter an order for execution at NAV or at a small spread to the NAV reported at a stated time will permit investors to place orders with market makers through various financial intermediaries for purchase and sale of an ETF share at a price linked to an hourly posting of the intraday proxy for NAV or at the official end-of-day NAV. In some cases, these trades might be done at a spread and in others the market maker might provide a guarantee of a fill at NAV (or the NAV proxy value) with no spread or commission—the terms depending in part on the time interval between the entry of the order by the investor and the calculation of the NAV that determines the price. The spread from the NAV or hourly proxy would generally widen as the time of price determination drew closer because the market maker would have less time to hedge or offset risk with another trade.

Using the closing NAV as the target in such a trading structure would make the pricing and trading of ETFs much like the conventional mutual fund trading process. Market makers might be willing to guarantee execution with no commission at the closing NAV on orders received before trading opened for the day. Obviously, an order for execution at, say, today's NAV with no commission will not be acceptable to a market maker after a certain cutoff time. The cutoff time for such an order could vary among funds and among market makers.

Extending a Superior Manager's Period of High Performance

The investment manager would be able to require conversion of institutional share classes to the higher fee ETF share class after the fund reaches its maximum size or after the ETF share class sells at a specified average premium over NAV for a designated time period. One purpose of this provision would be to permit a superior manager to obtain higher fees while continuing to manage a small enough pool of assets to permit the manager's skills to be reflected in superior fund share performance. A further incentive to the portfolio management team to continue to manage the fund with a cap on assets under management could be a schedule of increases in the basic money management fee for the exchange-traded share class as a result of a multiyear record of superior performance. Note that this is a very different structure with different incentives from the performance fees sometimes utilized by conventional mutual funds. The structure is designed to serve the long-term interests of fund shareholders in keeping a superior portfolio management team in place without forcing them to take in more assets than they can manage effectively.

Opportunity for Superior Performance

Exhibit 10.1 compares the costs experienced by a typical investor in an actively managed domestic equity mutual fund to the costs of a domestic equity version of the new fund. The potential cost/performance difference could exceed 4 percent per year without considering the value of greater tax efficiency. The new structure offers substantial advantages to investors, largely from eliminating unnecessary or inappropriate trading costs and performance penalties related to fund size.

Summary

It would be premature to argue that the actively managed ETFs described in this chapter will be the most significant development in the fund industry over the next few years. It is clear that the fund industry's regulatory baggage has increased as a result of the 2003–2004 mutual fund scandals. The ETF model is the best framework for eliminating many of the opportunities to abuse shareholders that have surfaced in recent years.

Supplementary Information

The best available source of information today on actively managed ETFs can be found in the comments on the SEC web site for the actively managed ETF Concept Release: www.sec.gov/rules/concept/ic-25258.htm.

The SEC's Concept Release Request for Comments illustrates the Commission's thinking at the time it was published. The comments from various individuals and organizations (largely industry participants) illustrate a wide range of views.

In the period ahead, I expect to see a number of comments on actively managed ETFs from a variety of sources, including possible issuers and the American Stock Exchange.[6] The initial products may or may not be attractive and intriguing, depending on the vision of the innovators and the regulators.

CHAPTER 11

Improving the Efficiency of Custom Investment Management: Some ETF Applications

The greater an investor's personal wealth, the more complicated his tax situation, and, in all probability, the more diverse his holdings. Of course, diversity of holdings is not the same thing as effective portfolio diversification. Great wealth is commonly associated with a large low-cost position in one or a very small number of assets that account for a disproportionate share of an individual's or a family's net worth. These individuals and families usually have extensive and expensive processes in place for portfolio, risk, and tax management.

In recent years, the investment management industry has developed increasingly automated software that permits sophisticated tax, diversification, and risk management of portfolios far below the net worth level of the superrich. Indeed, these services now reach down to the "merely affluent" investor. The claims for such software and the associated investment, tax, and risk management process are impressive, but most investors find that when they add the costs at each level of overlay and management integration, the annual cost starts near 2 percent of assets for the typical account and goes higher for smaller accounts.

This chapter is about several exchange-traded fund (ETF)-based approaches to custom investment management. Investment managers offer these services to provide effective investment management of part or all of a complex account at lower cost than traditional separate account management. The first half of the chapter describes the widespread use of exchange-traded funds by specialized managers who obtain client-appropriate exposure to various asset classes at low cost and with effective capital gains tax deferral. The second half of the chapter describes how some managers are implementing tax loss harvesting programs with sector index ETFs—again, at lower cost than similar programs using individual stocks can provide and with improved near-term and long-term diversification.

Investment Managers Using Exchange-Traded Funds: Cost Savings Mean Better Performance for Investors

Early adopters of ETFs were largely do-it-yourself investors. The continued growth in ETFs has been fueled by new services offered by specialized managers. These managers use ETF portfolios as components of comprehensive customized portfolios. They use passive vehicles—index ETFs and, sometimes, index mutual funds—and traditional active management vehicles—mutual funds and specialized separate account portfolios—in eclectic combinations. They pursue most of the goals that traditional separate account managers pursue. However, these managers enjoy some unique cost advantages, which often provide a better investment service at a lower net cost to the investor than their more traditional competitors.

The basic argument for using ETFs rather than individual stocks in customized separate account portfolios is the low expense ratios and (often) lower relative trading costs for ETFs. Exchange-traded fund components in the client's portfolio permit the manager to offer a comprehensive separate account service at a lower total cost. Of course, there are some significant differences between the services provided by managers who use ETFs extensively and traditional active managers.

The cost advantage of the new approach relies on the low expense ratios of ETFs—ranging from 9.45 basis points to 75 basis points (0.0945 percent to 0.75 percent) in the United States, with expense ratios under 30 basis points (0.30 percent) on the most popular funds in the U.S. market. Expense ratios are generally higher in Europe and Asia, partly because funds tend to be smaller outside the United States. In most cases, the combination of transaction costs inside the ETF and the cost of buying, selling, and holding ETF shares is lower than the best alternative way to take the position, whether in an entirely separate account composed of individual common stocks or in conventional mutual funds. The diverse menu of available ETFs also permits a manager to take low-cost positions in asset classes or subclasses that provide useful diversification at lower cost than would be possible in a monitored investment program without the ETFs.

Many of the pioneers in ETF-based investment management have five-year or longer records of performance. Prospective clients can compare their records with the records of other managers of complex diversified portfolios. Investors can examine these records not only by comparing performance to traditional benchmarks, but also by comparing total expenses for the ETF approach with the total expenses of other management formats.

The expense comparisons will be almost uniformly favorable to the managers who use ETFs. Correspondingly, the ultimate performance comparisons will get a boost from the savings in cost from using ETFs. To put the cost issue in perspective, some U.S.-based ETF-oriented managers provide a comprehensive service with a few attractive bells and whistles for less than 100 basis points (1 percent) in annual expenses, including the expense ratios of the funds used in the portfolio. Managers providing similar services with active management of the entire portfolio typically incur higher aggregate expenses. In addition to lower combined expense ratios associated with the ETF-based portfolios, total transaction costs are generally lower in the portfolios that use ETFs as components.

The standard index portfolio in an ETF makes trading in ETF shares more economical than a basket trade in a nonstandard portfolio or separate trades in individual component securities. The ETFs based on the most popular indexes are cheaper to trade, as ETFs, than funds based on less popular indexes, but even relatively obscure index portfolios are usually less costly to trade than separate stocks. The lower total management expenses from combining the expenses of the funds and the fee for the overall manager look even better when accompanied by lower transaction costs at the component and portfolio levels.

The fact that they can obtain positions in appropriate asset classes with standardized ETF baskets also permits specialized ETF-oriented managers to meet investors' objectives and manage risks with greater precision than most conventional managers can attain. It is easier and less costly to establish, measure, and maintain appropriate allocations and diversification with a small number of ETF positions than with a changing basket of individual stocks.

Managers can provide a wide range of value-added strategies, including tax loss harvesting to facilitate realization of gains on undiversified low-cost-basis positions that dominate many investor portfolios. Some ETF-oriented managers offer other specialties ranging from sector and style rotation to more comprehensive risk budgeting approaches similar to those used by sophisticated wealth and risk managers for much larger accounts than the ETF-oriented manager usually requires.[1] Some ETF-oriented managers offer component portfolios of individual stocks that they manage themselves or farm out to specialized submanagers. In short, using ETFs, at least for core asset allocations, can reduce costs and make appropriately customized management available to investors who are affluent, but not extremely wealthy.

It is useful to devote a paragraph or two to some of the specialized services ETF-based managers offer. These specialized services may be offered separately as well as integrated into a comprehensive ETF-based asset management package.

Tax Loss Harvesting

Tax loss harvesting is a particularly interesting application, partly because it illustrates some of the differences between conventional separate account management and the ETF approach. The second half of this chapter is devoted to tax loss harvesting with sector ETFs, but it is useful to look at the relative economics of ETFs and individual stocks for tax loss harvesting in the context of an ETF-based portfolio management offering.

Tax loss harvesting with sector ETFs can generally be achieved with management expenses (ETF sector fund expense ratio plus transaction costs plus any specialized tax manager's fee) that are about half the similar costs of a tax loss harvesting portfolio that uses individual stocks. Of course, the sector ETF returns are typically less volatile than single stock returns. Consequently, the investor and the investment manager need to discuss the relative importance of the tax loss harvesting feature. If tax loss harvesting is something that would just be nice to have, it is not likely to dominate the investment and tax objectives of the account. Unless the case for tax loss harvesting is a compelling and immediate requirement, the sector ETF tax loss harvesting approach can be more attractive. It is certainly less costly and it assures better long-term portfolio diversification. Some managers offer exactly this tax loss harvesting choice—between separate stocks and sector ETFs—to their clients.

Sector Rotation

Various techniques are used by specialty ETF managers to evaluate the relative attractiveness and likely future performance of different sectors. These managers overweight and underweight sector ETF positions relative to the aggregate index for the family of sector funds. Sector rotation is often combined with tax loss harvesting and other portfolio features. The range of principles used to select and weight sectors approximates the range of fundamental and technical approaches to individual stock selection.

Style Rotation

Style ETFs are a difficult product for individual investors to use effectively and economically. The turnover in the composition of style indexes and, consequently, the turnover within ETFs based on style indexes tends to be substantially higher than the turnover within broad market ETFs, sector ETFs, or even small-cap ETFs. Some style indexes and their associated

ETFs use index rules designed to reduce portfolio turnover, but these rules do not usually lead to as representative a style index. The reduction in turnover typically delays the portfolio changes that give separate growth and value portfolios their desired characteristics. The result is a trade-off between transaction costs and style purity.

Risk Budgeting/Core-Satellite

Professional investors and analysts recognize that asset allocation should depend primarily on the risk appetite and personal circumstances of the investor and on the timing and pattern of the investor's required cash withdrawals from the investment portfolio in future years. Asset allocation decisions are complicated by the fact that opportunities to add value beyond an unmanaged benchmark portfolio are not evenly distributed over the universe of available investments. The graph from Kritzman and Page (2003) reproduced as Exhibit 2.3 (page 37) illustrates that opportunities to add significant value with active management are largely confined to individual stock and sector selection investment processes.

Some sector and securities selection decisions provide a relatively large variation in return possibilities relative to the change in systematic portfolio risk. Consequently, any information of value can make a greater impact on portfolio return when sector and stock selections are assigned most of a portfolio's risk budget. Managers allocate the risk budget where they feel they can add value with judgments based on research information. Most commonly the risk budget is allocated to sector selection or individual stock selection in small-capitalization stocks.

An attractive feature of the ETF-oriented managed account is that the expense and transaction cost savings associated with using ETFs for basic asset allocation provides an opportunity to make intelligent use of the risk budget to take appropriate sector or separate stock exposures. The manager will try to add value where she feels that she or a selected subadviser can improve upon an indexed portfolio, while keeping the total expenses of the fund management process (and, of course, the risk) at appropriate levels.

Other Ways an Investment Manager Using ETFs Can Add Value

As earlier chapters have established, most individual investors using ETFs have limited access to good quality information that helps them:

- Distinguish among the indexes used as templates for ETFs.
- Evaluate the quality of index fund management provided by ETF issuers.

In general, the best information published on these topics is available from major investment banking firms.

Using information assembled and published by some of the leading brokerage firms with index and ETF research coverage, an ETF specialist manager can do some things that individual investors cannot do as easily for themselves. First, the manager can evaluate the indexes underlying the ETFs. Usually, the best index is a less popular index. If one of the popular indexes *must* be used, there is, for these indexes, what William Bernstein (2004) refers to as an "execution advantage" if a good index fund manager can recapture some of the embedded transaction costs associated with index changes. There are substantial differences across all types of ETFs in the quality of their index fund management and execution.

As described in Chapter 6, an astute index fund manager who transacts at a time other than the moment of the official index composition change can often add substantial value for investors.[2] Exhibit 11.1 shows the median (negative) tracking error and range of tracking errors for various categories of U.S.-based ETFs for 2002 through 2004. Tracking error data are available for the individual funds represented in Exhibit 6.2 in Chapter 6 (pp. 133–136). The median tracking errors and the ranges of the tracking errors are large. The magnitude of the median negative tracking error illustrates that most of these funds have not been managed aggressively. The dominant ETF performance determinant appears to have been fund cash balances. For more information on tracking error,

EXHIBIT 11.1   Comparison of U.S.-Based ETF Tracking Errors, 2002–2004

Fund Type	Median Tracking Error 2002	Range 2002 Best	Range 2002 Worst	Median Tracking Error 2003	Range 2003 Best	Range 2003 Worst	Median Tracking Error 2004	Range 2004 Best	Range 2004 Worst
Large-Cap Broad Market	−9	+1	−13	−30	−17	−38	−19	−5	−29
Mid-Cap Broad Market	−5	+2	−21	−33	−25	−46	−29	−19	−34
Small-Cap Broad Market	−11	−4	−24	−29	−20	−31	−20	−17	−21
Growth Style	−11	−3	−24	−31	−19	−43	−27	−18	−39
Value Style	−17	−4	−35	−37	−28	−72	−28	−21	−45
Foreign Single-Country	−33	+193	−269	−128	+573	−238	−57	−2	−384
Foreign Multi-country	−11	+136	−42	−54	−5	−358	−41	−17	−177
Sector	−26	+80	−358	−68	+552	−115	−64	−26	−175

Sources: Morgan Stanley, Barclays Global Investors, State Street Global Advisors, Thomson, Bloomberg. See Exhibit 6.2.

see the text box "Evaluating the Performance of an Investment Manager" in Chapter 6 (pp. 137–139).

Analysis of ETF performance will become a much more significant activity than these simple examples suggest. Until better information is available to all investors, fund evaluation is a place where a manager who uses ETFs can add significant value. When good ETF data and analysis are more widely available, individual investors will be better able to evaluate ETFs for themselves.

While short selling of ETF shares has been common since the launch of the S&P 500 SPDR in 1993, interest in the use of ETFs on the short side has grown substantially in portfolio applications in recent years. Individual investors are at a distinct disadvantage when it comes to selling ETF shares short because their orders are typically small and do not get the attention of the stock lending desk at their brokerage firm. An investment adviser who handles accounts for a large number of individual investors will not have this problem. An investment adviser who is a large customer of the brokerage firm and who trades in significant size will find it much easier to sell ETFs short than an individual investor who simply wants to sell 100 shares or 1,000 shares of a small or inactive ETF short.

Exchange-Traded Funds, Short Selling, and the Short Interest

The short interest in the average stock listed on the New York Stock Exchange is typically about 1 to 2 percent of the company's shares outstanding. The short interest in the average ETF typically ranges from 15 to 25 percent. One reason for the large short interest is that ETFs are exempt from the uptick rule.[3] The Securities and Exchange Commission has authorized a pilot test of a new rule to replace the uptick rule for larger-capitalization, actively traded common stocks. Under the new rule the short sale of a stock can occur only at a price above the highest posted bid. This rule has a number of nuances that are outside the scope of this book, but it may ultimately make short selling of stocks more common than it is today. Nonetheless, short selling in the average stock will probably never approach the level of short selling activity in some of the more actively traded ETFs.[4]

In general, a large short interest in an ETF means little more than that the fund's underlying index is a useful risk management tool for securities traders and portfolio managers. Short interest in an ETF will often rise when investors who are not regular users of other hedging instruments detect an opportunity to profit from a change in pricing relationships. For example, the short interest in one of the longer-term fixed-income ETFs jumped to more than 600 percent of the capitalization of the fund in early 2004 as investors sold the fund short in anticipation of an increase in interest rates and a corresponding decline in bond prices. Portfolios that can sell short but are not able to use futures contracts may find a short position in an index ETF to be the preferred vehicle for certain risk management or speculative trades. Even investors who can use futures often find that index ETFs are a lower-cost choice for a short position that might be held for longer than the life of a single futures contract. The ability to sell ETFs short in securities accounts as an alternative to futures can simplify margin and cash management issues for some investors.

The only value a large ETF short interest might have as an indicator for investors is that a very large short interest combined with a large negative tracking error may suggest that the fund's portfolio manager is doing a poor job of managing the portfolio. In the case of the two S&P 500 index ETFs, the greater size and more fully developed market in the SPDR draws more short selling to the SPDR than to the iShares fund.

Some Reported Short Interest Percentages, as of Mid-March 2005

Fund	Symbol	Short Interest as Percent of Shares Outstanding
S&P 500 SPDRs	SPY	24.6%
iShares S&P 500	IVV	3.7%
Nasdaq-100	QQQQ	34.9%
DIAMONDS	DIA	15.8%
Sector SPDRs Financial	XLF	107.8%
iShares Treasury 20+	TLT	158.6%

The large short interest in many ETFs makes any statement about growth in ETFs less useful than a similar statement about a conventional fund. When shares are sold short, the seller borrows shares from an investor who owns the shares. The borrowed shares are sold to another investor. Both the ETF share lender and the buyer of the borrowed shares have long investment positions in the same shares. The effective size of the fund from the perspective of long investors is equal to the shares issued by the fund plus the short interest. The large short interest in ETFs leads to an understatement of the investor commitment to ETFs when shares outstanding are the measure of ETF size. Statements about ETF growth rates do not include adjustments for changes in the short interest. ETF short interest data are available at www.etfconsultants.com/Short_Interest.xls.

ETFs versus Mutual Funds

Some of the managers who use ETFs in their customized portfolios for individual investor clients began by using conventional mutual funds to achieve appropriate asset class allocation and diversification before ETFs

came along. While the degree of sophistication they bring to the fund selection process is far from uniform, many of these managers show considerable understanding of the issues, which, in one instance, will make an
ETF the obvious choice versus another situation where no adequate ETF is
available and a conventional mutual fund is a better choice than a separately managed portfolio.

Tax Management and Loss Harvesting with Sector Funds

At the beginning of 2003, many observers argued that the vaunted tax efficiency of ETFs was likely to be unimportant for the foreseeable future.
Large conventional mutual funds, particularly those that had taken in significant new assets during the late 1990s, had net realized and unrealized
losses in their portfolios, reducing the probability of large capital gains distributions. To put the magnitude of taxable capital gains distributions in
perspective, the Investment Company Institute calculated in 2005 (*Mutual
Fund Fact Book*) that U.S. mutual funds distributed only $5 billion in tax-
able capital gains to households in 2002, down from a record $114 billion
in taxable capital gains distributions to households in 2000. The sharp market recovery in 2003 erased many funds' accumulated losses, making fund
tax efficiency significant again—especially for taxpayers who doubt the
longevity of the 15 percent capital gains tax rate. Taxable capital gains distribution to households rose to $22 billion in 2004.

In any sector fund tax loss harvesting program, a tax-efficient fund is
highly desirable. The reason tax efficiency is important in tax loss harvesting is that some of the fund positions in a tax-oriented investment program
will perform well and become long-term holdings. Tax-efficient funds will
shelter a shareholder's embedded capital gains indefinitely and provide
consistent diversification over the sector. This section is not just about the
tax efficiency of sector funds, but rather about all the characteristics of a
sector ETF that can allow an investor to generate tax-deferred returns more
efficiently. For example, high volatility, low expenses, and good long-term
performance are all highly desirable characteristics in a sector ETF used for
tax loss harvesting.

Tax loss harvesting relies on the principle that, while most stocks go
up and down together, individual securities and sectors have significant
movements that are independent of the direction of the overall market. An
investor who owns a diversified equity fund may have average pretax and
pre-expense performance similar to the average performance of the portfolio of sector funds in the tax loss harvesting program. However, the
holder of a single broad market fund will not have a dependable source of
tax losses. In fact, investors in broad market funds will generally find that
they have either more realizable tax losses than they need to harvest—or

no tax losses at all. If some stocks or market sectors are down when the overall market is up, the investor with diversified *separate* investments in stock or sector funds will have opportunities for tax loss harvesting.

Prior to the introduction of sector ETFs, most tax loss harvesting programs used separate portfolios of individual stocks. While these separate stock portfolios may be able to generate more tax loss opportunities than a diversified portfolio of sector funds, a separate stock portfolio will also incur somewhat higher tax management, trading, and administrative costs compared to a program using sector funds. Because they can reduce these costs and offer better long-term diversification, sector ETFs can provide an efficient alternative to individual stock tax loss strategies.

In many cases, an adviser will offer an investor the choice of a separate stock or a sector fund–based tax loss harvesting program. The overall cost of a sector fund–based tax loss harvesting portfolio will be approximately half the cost of a separate stock tax loss harvesting program. The supplementary fee for an individual stock tax loss harvesting program typically runs about 55 basis points. The sector fund expense ratios, about 26 basis points on the Sector SPDRs, are about half the 55-basis-point fee. ETF specialty managers usually do not charge extra fees to do sector fund tax loss harvesting. Also, trading costs will typically be lower for the Sector SPDRs than for individual stock positions that might be used to harvest losses.

Choosing a Sector Fund Family

All sector ETFs are not equally useful in tax loss harvesting programs. The exhibits should be of help in selecting an appropriate family of sector funds and in getting comfortable with the sector fund approach. Exhibit 11.2 lists some attributes of the three available families of sector funds that reflect upon their effectiveness for tax loss harvesting. For the most part, the funds covering the sectors are roughly interchangeable in coverage. The choice will turn largely on cost and net performance, with volatility an additional consideration that is harder to quantify.

The available ETF fund families are the Sector SPDRs managed by State Street Global Advisors, the iShares sector funds managed by Barclays Global Investors, and the Vanguard Index Participation Equity Receipts (VIPERs) sector funds managed by Vanguard. In terms of sector definitions, both the Sector SPDRs and the use the Global Industry Classification Standard (GICS) jointly developed by Standard & Poor's (which provides the indexes for the Sector SPDRs) and Morgan Stanley Capital International (MSCI). MSCI provides the indexes for the Vanguard VIPERs. The iShares sector funds use the Industry Classification Benchmark (ICB) developed jointly by Dow Jones Indexes and the FTSE Group. The principal differences between the classification systems are in the two consumer indexes.

EXHIBIT 11.2   Attributes Affecting Tax Loss Harvesting

	Sector SPDRS	iShares Sector Funds	VIPERs Sectors
Sector Definitions	GICS	ICB	GICS
Companies Covered	500	About 1,600	About 2,500
Volatility	Highest	Middle	Lowest
Expense Ratio (basis points)	26	60	25
2002 Median Tracking Error[a]	(19)	(47)	N/A
2003 Median Tracking Error[a]	(49)	(78)	N/A
2004 Median Tracking Error[a]	(28)	(66)	N/A
Fund Share Transaction Costs	Lowest	Middle	Highest
Fund Tax Efficiency	High	High	Unknown

[a]Includes net effect of expense ratio, excludes iShares Telecom Sector fund in both years.

Source: Fund and index reports; Mazzilli and Kittsley (2004) and Mazzilli, Kittsley, and Maister (2005).

In GICS, the nominal emphasis is on consumer "discretionary" spending versus "staple" spending. In the ICB system, the emphasis is on "services" versus "goods." The split in the consumer stocks will continue to be slightly different for the two classification systems.

Most financial industry research and analysis is based on the S&P 500 (GICS) sector classifications. So, if research availability is important to an investor or an adviser, the Sector SPDRs or the VIPERs (with a similar classification system) might be preferable.[5] For aggregate portfolio risk management and tax loss harvesting, the classification differences are not likely to be important.

The coverage differences among the fund families may be significant for a few investors. There are nine Sector SPDR funds compared to 10 iShares sector funds and 10 VIPERs sector funds. The difference between the Sector SPDRs and the other families occurs because the Sector SPDRs are based on the S&P 500 and there are not usually enough telecommunications stocks in the S&P 500 to populate a regulated investment company (RIC) diversification-compliant telecommunications fund. RIC diversification compliance is necessary if a U.S. fund is to distribute dividend income without taxation at the fund level.[6] Any U.S. telecommunications sector fund (as well as funds in several other sectors) cannot be both RIC compliant and capitalization or float weighted. Telecommunications and technology, which are usually highly correlated, have been combined into a single fund in the Sector SPDRs.

The number of companies included in the various sector indexes and in sector funds based on the components of the various broad market indexes varies significantly over the three sector ETF families. Because the largest companies are so dominant in all the indexes, adding additional companies does not reduce the target weighting of the largest companies in an index very much. While the iShares sector funds contain a total of about 1,600 securities from the Dow Jones indexes and the 10 VIPERs sector funds could have as many as 2,500 securities in total from the MSCI indexes, the S&P 500 stocks account for at least 80 percent of the capitalization weight of these broader sector indexes. The smaller number of companies in the Sector SPDRs makes their indexes (and funds) slightly more volatile than their more diversified competitors. As Exhibit 11.3 from a Dow Jones publication illustrates, the volatility (standard deviation) for the Sector SPDRs indexes generally has been higher than the volatility of the indexes underlying the iShares sector funds.

The principal reason for higher volatility in the Sector SPDRs indexes is the difference in aggregate diversification in coverage—500 companies versus 1,600 or 2,500. Even though the large companies are weighted heavily in all the indexes, the fact of greater diversification, even within a sector, will reduce volatility. In terms of its effect on tax loss harvesting, greater volatility in a sector fund is a desirable feature because more volatile funds will usually show more diverse relative performance. Most of the volatility differences will disappear in the aggregate multisector portfolio because some of the greater sector volatility will cancel out in any of the broad market indexes that will be roughly matched by the basket of sector funds. I would expect the volatility of the VIPERs sector funds to be very slightly less than the volatility of the iShares sector funds.[7]

Expense Ratios Much more important than the volatility differences among the indexes and the funds are their expense ratios. The expense ra-

EXHIBIT 11.3 Comparative Sector Volatility—Dow Jones Sector and Indexes versus Sector SPDR Indexes (Standard Deviation Percentage 6/24/02–12/31/04)

	Dow Jones Index	Sector SPDRs Index
Materials	22.52%	27.47%
Consumer Services/Discretionary	21.08	27.60
Consumer Goods/Staples	14.32	22.76
Energy	21.26	28.26
Financial	20.52	27.54
Healthcare	19.04	26.53
Industrial	20.28	26.31
Technology and Telecommunications	27.98	32.27
Utilities	20.49	29.14
Median	20.49%	27.54%

Source: Seneker (2005).

tios on the Sector SPDRs are typically 26 basis points and on the VIPERs are 25 basis points versus 60 basis points on the iShares sector funds. A higher expense ratio makes a fund more likely to perform poorly and give rise to a tax loss harvesting opportunity, but that is clearly not the reason to focus on the expense ratio. The reason for highlighting the expense ratio is that some of the funds in the program should perform well. Tax loss harvesting investors will eventually have substantial embedded capital gains in some of the sector funds they buy. The ongoing expenses incurred in maintaining a long-term position in a fund—once the investor's embedded capital gains make selling the fund shares less attractive— should be as low as possible. As I have stressed in a variety of contexts, a low expense ratio is a very desirable characteristic in a fund.

Trading Costs   In contrast to a broad market ETF that you might expect to buy only once and hold forever, transaction costs in buying and selling fund shares matter more if your objective is tax loss harvesting. You will be paying transaction costs to buy the funds initially, to sell funds to harvest losses, and to replace the sector exposure after the 30-day wash sale period (discussed later) has passed.

There are at least three components covered in the simplest analysis of transaction costs: commissions, the bid-asked spread, and market impact. Commissions are typically the smallest component and they are usually a flat fee per trade for individual investors at most brokerage firms. The bid-asked spread and market impact costs are larger. They reflect the liquidity of the ETF shares, and more fundamentally, the liquidity of the underlying fund portfolio. While I am unaware of any published sector fund transaction cost comparisons, the lowest ETF transaction costs are generally associated with the largest average stock capitalization and most liquid portfolio. The fact that the average stock is larger and more liquid in the Sector SPDRs means that realizing losses and reestablishing positions should be less costly with the Sector SPDRs than with the other funds. The iShares sector funds will be more costly to trade than the Sector SPDRs—with the VIPERs more costly to trade than the iShares sector funds. As Exhibit 11.4 illustrates, by far the largest and the most actively traded sector ETF shares are the Sector SPDRs, followed distantly by the iShares sector funds. The trading volume comparison is a little misleading because the average price of the iShares funds is about twice the average price of the Sector SPDRs. However, even if we convert from share volume to dollar volume, the trading volume of the average Sector SPDR is more than seven times the volume of the comparable iShares sector funds. The VIPERs have few assets and an inactive trading history. The portfolio component characteristics (larger cap equals more liquid stocks) are usually more important than total assets or ETF share trading volume in determining trading costs, but the Sector SPDRs would come out on top under all these criteria.[8]

EXHIBIT 11.4   Sector Fund Year-End Assets and Average Daily Trading Volume for 2004

Assets

Sector Fund	SPDRs Symbol	Sector SPDRs Assets 12/31/04 (Millions)	iShares Symbol	iShares Assets 12/31/04 (Millions)
Materials	XLB	$ 708	IYM	$ 420
Health Care	XLV	$1,053	IYH	$ 934
Industrial	XLI	$ 780	IYJ	$ 254
Utilities	XLU	$1,687	IDU	$ 560
Energy	XLE	$1,571	IYE	$ 498
Consumer Discretionary/Services	XLY	$ 471	IYC	$ 205
Financial	XLF	$1,140	IYF	$ 303
Consumer Staples/Services	XLP	$ 761	IYK	$ 360
Technology[a]	XLK	$1,236	IYW	$ 468
Telecommunications			IYZ	$ 362
Total Assets All Funds		$9,406		$4,364
Average Assets per Fund ($ millions)		$1,045		$ 436

Trading Volume

Sector Fund		SPDR Daily Volume 2004 (Thousands)		iShares Daily Volume 2004 (Thousands)
Materials	XLB	1,066	IYM	98
Health Care	XLV	444	IYH	109
Industrial	XLI	663	IYJ	42
Utilities	XLU	831	IDU	51
Energy	XLE	1,963	IYE	84
Consumer Discretionary/Services	XLY	343	IYC	46
Financial	XLF	3,356	IYF	25
Consumer Staples/Goods	XLP	474	IYK	67
Technology[a]	XLK	619	IYW	70
Telecommunications			IYZ	160
Share Volume 2004		9,747		753
Average Daily Volume per Fund (thousands of shares)		1,084		75

[a]Sector SPDR Technology Fund includes Telecommunications.

Source: American Stock Exchange, fund issuers.

Tax Efficiency   With respect to fund tax efficiency, the efficient Sector SP-DRs and iShares creation and redemption processes make me comfortable that neither fund is likely to distribute taxable capital gains in the foreseeable future. Although a number of the iShares funds distributed capital gains in their first year, the iShares portfolio managers seem to have learned the basics of ETF tax management and I do not anticipate a recurrence of these early capital gains distributions. The tax efficiency of the VIPERs is slightly less certain. VIPERs are an exchange-traded share class that is part of a larger fund. The size of the conventional share class for the sector VIPERs is hard to predict. Vanguard has taken a number of steps to encourage investors to use the VIPERs share class in these new sector funds rather than the conventional share class, including a requirement that an initial purchase of the conventional share class must be at least $100,000. There is also a 2 percent redemption fee on conventional sector fund shares sold within a year. I argued in Chapter 3 that the combination of conventional and ETF shares in the same fund with some shareholders able to redeem fund shares for cash is likely to be less tax-efficient than a pure ETF redemption mechanism, but there is little reason to think very many investors will find the conventional Vanguard sector fund shares attractive with this combination of large initial purchases and a yearlong redemption fee period. Vanguard's problem seems to be they have created an unnecessarily complex and confusing product to compete with an established product that is easy to understand—the Secor SPDRs. Vanguard's best strategy would be to eliminate or separate the conventional share class from the Sector VIPERs ETFs.

Tracking Error   Exhibit 11.5 shows 2002 through 2004 annual tracking errors for the Sector SPDRs and the iShares sector funds. The large absolute tracking errors for the iShares Energy Sector fund and the iShares Telecom Sector fund for both years occurred primarily because the indexes for these funds are not compliant with the diversification requirements for a regulated investment company under the U.S. Internal Revenue Code. As a consequence of this feature, these funds will only coincidentally track the index closely. The key column in Exhibit 11.5 is the "Difference" column. This tracking error difference essentially reflects the net effect for the three-year period of the higher expense ratio of the iShares sector funds. The difference in total expenses over three years is about 100 basis points or 1.0 percent. Setting aside the iShares funds that have erratic tracking errors because of noncompliant indexes, the average tracking error difference is about 100 basis points. Clearly, expenses matter. Given roughly equivalent indexes, higher expenses are a cost penalty that an investor can avoid by choosing the Sector SPDRs. For more information on tracking error, see the "Evaluating Index Mutual Funds and ETFs" section in Chapter 6 (pp. 132–139).

EXHIBIT 11.5   Sector ETF Tracking Errors 2002–2004

	Tracking Error				
Sector/Fund	2002	2003	2004	Three-Year Total	Three-Year Difference[a]
Consumer Discretionary/Services					
Consumer Discretionary Select Sector SPI	(21)	(44)	(38)	(103)	
iShares DJ US Consumer Cyclical Sector	(42)	(77)	(67)	(186)	(83)
Consumer Staples/Goods					
Consumer Staples Selector Sector SPDR	(16)	(35)	(30)	(81)	
iShares DJ US Consumer Goods Sector	(58)	(73)	(66)	(197)	(116)
Energy					
Energy Select Sector SPDR	(19)	(49)	(52)	(120)	
iShares DJ US Energy Sector	(196)	138	(72)	(130)	(10)
Financials					
Financial Select Sector SPDR	(19)	(53)	(26)	(98)	
iShares DJ US Financial Sector	(46)	(86)	(66)	(198)	(100)
Health Care					
Health Care Select Sector SPDR	(26)	(36)	(28)	(90)	
iShares DJ US Health Care Sector	(39)	(73)	(64)	(176)	(86)
Industrials					
Industrial Select Sector SPDR	(22)	(59)	(36)	(117)	
iShares DJ US Industrial Sector	(57)	(84)	(84)	(225)	(108)
Technology					
Technology Select Sector SPDR	(15)	(46)	(28)	(89)	
iShares DJ US Technology Sector	(36)	(90)	(61)	(187)	(98)
Materials					
Materials Select Sector SPDR	(18)	(71)	(40)	(129)	
iShares DJ US Basic Materials Sector	(48)	(85)	(72)	(205)	(76)
Utilities					
Utilities Select Sector SPDR Fund	(21)	(51)	(78)	(150)	
iShares DJ US Utilities Sector	(43)	(80)	(45)	(168)	(18)
Telecommunications					
iShares DJ US Telecom Sector	(358)	552	(57)	137	N/A

[a]A negative number measures how much greater the negative tracking error was for the iShares fund than for the comoparable Sector SPDR over the three-year period.

Sources: Morgan Stanley, Barclays Global Investors, State Street Global Advisors, Thomson, Bloomberg.

Small Company Effect   In 2002, smaller companies, which are more heavily represented in the iShares (and even more heavily represented in the VIPERs sector funds) than in the Sector SPDRs, *under*performed larger-capitalization stocks. In 2003, and to a lesser extent in 2004, the smaller-capitalization stocks *out*performed the large-cap stocks. Any difference in expense ratios will always favor the low-cost fund's performance in the long run, but the relative performance of these sector funds in a particular year is likely to turn on the relative performance of small-cap versus large-cap stocks.

What Sectors Are Most Volatile?

Exhibit 11.6 provides some information on volatilities and correlations of stocks based on the Global Industry Classification Standard (GICS). As the first column indicates, the average single stock standard deviation (volatility) is highest in information technology, telecommunications services, and health care. When you have a 25- or 50-stock basket based on the population of these indexes, the volatility drops materially. All of the sectors are positively correlated with the S&P 500, some more closely than others. On average, the stocks in a sector will have broad market correlations similar to their sector correlations. The high standard deviation of a 25- or 50-stock basket suggests that the information technology, telecommunications, and health care sectors are most likely

EXHIBIT 11.6   Volatilities and Correlations—Global Industry Classification Standard (GICS)/Sector Stocks in S&P 500

Sector	Average Single Stock Standard Deviation	25-Stock Basket Standard Deviation	50-Stock Basket Standard Deviation	GICS Sector Correlation with S&P 500
Information Technology	91%	51%	50%	0.89
Telecommunication Services	57%	35%	35%	0.68
Health Care	56%	32%	31%	0.57
Consumer Discretionary	46%	25%	24%	0.91
Industrials	39%	18%	17%	0.94
Energy	37%	26%	26%	0.72
Financials	36%	29%	29%	0.84
Utilities	35%	24%	23%	0.46
Consumer Staples	33%	19%	19%	0.50
Materials	27%	15%	15%	0.62
Correlations based on quarterly data for Q1 1995 to Q3 2003				

Source: Bloomberg.

to contribute volatility to a tax loss harvesting program. When correlation with the broad market is measured, health care, utilities, and consumer staples are the most likely contributors to the success of a tax loss harvesting strategy, which relies for its success on divergent performance among the sectors.

Wash Sale Rule

Tax loss harvesters should be fully aware of a provision in the tax code called the wash sale rule. A wash sale occurs when, within 30 days of the realization of a loss, an investor acquires securities "substantially identical" to the securities that were sold at a loss. In the event of a wash sale, the loss is not immediately recognized, but is added to the basis of the purchased securities and recognized when those securities are sold, presumably without being tainted with another wash sale. Wash sales *may* enter the picture for a sector fund tax loss harvester if the investor realizes a significant loss on the shares of a sector fund and decides to maintain the portfolio's exposure to that sector by buying a similar sector fund.

The question is: Does the purchase of a similar sector fund trigger a wash sale? Many observers argue that buying a fund with a different manager or based on a different index is enough to avoid the effect of the wash sale rule, but there is certainly no unanimity that buying a similar fund is risk free. The Internal Revenue Service has steadfastly declined to define "substantially identical." The reader should check with a personal tax adviser to get appropriate comfort before making a similar fund purchase within a period of 30 days before or after realizing a loss on the sale of sector fund shares. An investor who, after such a conversation with a tax adviser, concludes that there is some cause for concern might decide that the remaining sector funds in the portfolio provide enough diversification to justify doing nothing for the 30-day interval.

Conclusion—Tax Loss Harvesting

On the basis of higher sector volatilities, lower fund expenses, lower trading costs, and long-term tax efficiency, the Sector SPDRs are the obvious choice for sector fund–based risk management and tax loss harvesting. Apart from the inherent volatility and cost differences, there is relatively little to distinguish among the available sector fund families and likely entrants. There is ample room for one of these fund providers to distinguish its offerings by more aggressive fund management. Ultimately, the manager that delivers the best net investment performance should dominate the sector ETF market.

Summary

This chapter focuses largely on how a number of advisers have developed customized investment programs that utilize ETFs to deliver effective asset management at significant cost savings to the investor. Examples include risk budgeting and tax loss harvesting strategies. While statistics are hard to come by because most of the participants in this market are relatively small firms, this is one of the fastest growing segments of the investment advisory business.

Supplementary Information

While mainstream consumer finance publications have occasional material on customized management of portfolios using ETFs, most of the useful material has appeared in publications designed primarily for financial planners and brokers or advisers who help their clients find appropriate money managers.

I have not found a single source, such as a web site, that lists these specialized managers, but a Google search using "exchange-traded funds money managers" comes up with a number of listings that yield names of some of these managers. I plan to keep looking, and if I find a useful and reasonably comprehensive list, I will post its location on my web site, www.etfconsultants.com.

Sources of Additional Information on the Internet

Supplementary sources on many of the topics covered in the text are listed at the end of most chapters. This annotated list of Internet sites does not include all sites. For example, I have not tried to list all of the conventional mutual fund issuers' sites.

Listing Internet links is a much chancier proposition than compiling a conventional print bibliography. With a traditional bibliography, the author, title, and publication date will generally take you to exactly what the author who prepared the bibliography was looking at when his own work was done. The same cannot be said of Internet links. On the plus side, old information is updated. On the minus side, the control of web sites changes, and perishable information that was timely when the link was selected may not be updated as the nature of the site might lead one to expect. Equally important, a single web site may have a few gems and a lot of dross. With these reservations, I offer a variety of links that you might want to click on.

If you have found this book useful, you may want to consult my web site, www.etfconsultants.com, for additional material on funds in general, ETFs in particular, and indexes and indexing.

ETF Basics—and Beyond

American Association of Individual Investors (AAII): www.aaii.com /guides/etfs. "The Individual Investor's Guide to Exchange-Traded Funds" (membership required for access to this guide).

American Stock Exchange: www.amex.com. Click on Education.

ETF Consultants LLC: www.etfconsultants.com/An%20Introduction%20 to%20ETFs%20JPM.pdf. "Introduction to ETFs."

Farmcreek Securities: http://farmcreeksecurities.com. This brokerage firm/investment manager web site is an excellent source of solid, unbiased information on ETFs. "Farmer Ed" is a thoughtful analyst. His observations always stimulate my thinking, and you may profit from a similar effect.

IndexFunds.com's ETF basics: www.indexfunds.com/articleSelection .php?stype=All&stopic=ETFs&sauthor=All&spub_date=All&skwds= Basics.

Tech Uncovered: www.techuncovered.com/ch17.html. "The Seven Advantages of ETFs Over Index Mutual Funds."

Specific ETFs and Families

The American Stock Exchange's listing of ETFs: www.amex.com /?href=/etf/EtMain.jsp. Select product category from drop-down list.

Barclays' iShares: www.ishares.com/splash.jhtml?_requestid=155549.

ETF Connect: www.etfconnect.com.

Fidelity: http://personal.fidelity.com/global/search/resultsindex.shtml ?quser=Exchange-traded_funds.

PowerShares: www.powershares.com.

Rydex: www.rydexfunds.com/etfs/?etfsection=sites8.

Select Sector SPDRs: www.spdrindex.com.

StreetTracks: http://advisors.ssga.com/streettracks/index.jsp.

Vanguard VIPERs: http://flagship3.vanguard.com/VGApp/hnw/Funds VIPERByName.

Indexing Literature

Bogle Financial Markets Research Center: www.vanguard.com/bogle _site/bogle_home.html.

Dimensional Fund Advisors: www.dfaus.com.

Gastineau, Gary L., "The Benchmark Index ETF Performance Problem." www.etfconsultants.com/Benchmark_Index_ETF_Problem _JPM.pdf.

Gastineau, Gary L., "Equity Index Funds Have Lost Their Way." www.etfconsultants.com/Equity_Index_Funds_ JPM.pdf.

IndexFunds.com: www.indexfunds.com.

Index Universe: www.indexuniverse.com.

The *Journal of Indexes*: www.journalofindexes.com.
State Street Global Advisors: www.ssga.com.

Index Providers

Dow Jones: www.djindexes.com/jsp/industrialAverages.jsp?sideMenu=
true.html.
Morgan Stanley Capital International: www.msci.com.
Russell: www.russell.com.
Standard & Poor's: www2.standardandpoors.com/NASApp/cs/Content
Server?pagename=sp/Page/IndicesMainPg&r=1&l=EN&b=4.
Wilshire: www.wilshire.com/Indexes.

Asset Allocation Literature

Efficient Frontier: www.efficientfrontier.com.
Ibbotson Associates: www.ibbotson.com. Click on Published Research,
then Asset Allocation.
Windham Capital Management: www.wcmbllc.com/workingpapers.

Asset Allocation Questionnaires

Accutrade: www.accutrade.com/fhtml/assetallocation.fhtml.
Oppenheimer Funds Asset Allocator: www.oppenheimerfunds.com
/commonJhtml/assetAllocator.jhtml.
Deborah Owens: www.deborahowens.com/assetallocation.html.
Smart Money Asset Allocation: http://university.smartmoney.com
/Departments/TakingAction/AssetAllocation.
T.D. Waterhouse: www.tdwaterhouse.com/planning/index.html.
Vanguard: http://flagship.vanguard.com/web/planret/AdvicePTCreate
PlanStepIICompleteInvestorQuestion.html.

Retirement Planning Software

The two best and most widely used models for retirement planning I have
found are those from Financial Engines and Advisor Software. The Financial Engines model is available to customers of Vanguard and participants
in a number of 401(k) plans. The Advisor Software material is available to
customers of Fidelity, to advisers using the iShares web site and to participants in a number of 401(k) plans.

Advisor Software: www.advisorsoftware.com.

Fidelity: http://personal.fidelity.com/retirement/retcalcframe.html.

Financial Engines: www.financialengines.com.

iShares: www.ishares.com/tools/index.jhtml;jsessionid=DZQO4KAL
  HIMBOCQGMTMBBGQKAEHQGD50. Click on iShares Allocation
  Proposal Tool (APT) (registration as an financial professional is required to access this feature, so click on "About Financial Professionals' Site" to register).

Vanguard: www.vanguard.com. Log on as a Vanguard individual investor (you must be a Vanguard customer), click on the Financial
  Engines Plan link, and that will bring you to the Financial Engines
  web site.

Fund Industry Data and Ratings

Adviser Investment Management: www.adviserinvestment.com.

Appliederivatives.com: www.appliederivatives.com. Not a lot of fund
  material, but thought provoking.

Bloomberg.com: www.bloomberg.com. There is not much data available through this site, but try to get access to Bloomberg's full service. It provides the most comprehensive and most dependable
  data I have found anywhere.

ETF International Associates (ETFI): www.etfinternational.com.

Exchangetradedfunds.com: www.exchangetradedfunds.com.

Forbes.com: http://www.forbes.com.

Investment Company Institute: www.ici.org. This site is worth explor-
  ing for reliable fund industry statistics.

Investors FastTrack: www.fasttrack.net/etf.asp. FastTrack is the best
  low-cost price and limited data site for ETFs and conventional
  funds I have found.

Lipper: www.lipperweb.com. Many of this site's research studies are
  very good. Some are available only for a fee.

Lipper Leader: www.lipperleader.com. This site is moderately useful
  for screening funds by expense levels and the like, but the breakdown by ratings √ through 5 is only by fund quintile.

MarketWatch.com: www.marketwatch.com.

Morningstar.com: www.morningstar.com. Check Morningstar's data independently with another source, if possible.

The Motley Fool—Fool.com: www.fool.com. Fun, but uneven.

Personalfund.com: www.personalfund.com This web site offers an interesting paper, Sharkansky (2002), on fund expenses for free
  download and a mutual fund expense calculator. I approach the

transaction cost and tax calculations very differently, but this site is worth a visit.

The Rankings Service—TRS Repots: www.trsreports.com. Rankings of active fund managers (described in the "Rating Fund Managers" text box in Chapter 9).

SmartMoney.com: www.smartmoney.com.

Yahoo! Finance: http://finance.yahoo.com. I consider this the best of the free market sites, but check them all out and pick your own favorite.

Conventional Mutual Funds versus Exchange-Traded Funds: Making Choices

For all its virtues, the exchange-traded fund with all reasonable en-
hancements is not a candidate to replace all other types of funds. As
the liquidity in various markets improves, the scope for use of the ETF
structure will expand to market segments that are not fully suitable for
ETFs today. Other markets will be served best by new funds that may
have some features from ETFs and other features from conventional
funds. The subject of this appendix is a comparison of conventional funds
and ETFs in traditional equity market applications, the largest fund market segment in the United States and in most other countries. This comparison may have implications for other countries but some aspects of
the comparison (e.g., tax efficiency) are obviously U.S. specific. Most
readers will use this appendix as an occasional reference, not as required reading.

Comparing Fund Structures

This appendix is organized around Exhibit B.1, which shows a simple but
detailed comparison of the important features of two pairs of fund categories. The first pairing is "Current Practice"—today's *typical* equity mutual
funds with today's *typical* equity ETFs. The other pairing, "Best Practice,"
reflects what these conventional funds and ETFs, respectively, could be if
they were structured—as they eventually must be—to provide adequate

EXHIBIT B.1 A Comparison of No-Load Conventional Equity Mutual Funds and Equity Exchange-Traded Funds

	Current Practice		Best Practice	
	Conventional	ETFs	Conventional	ETFs
Entry and Exit Costs to Traders				
Direct share purchase and sale costs	Nil to small flat fee*	Similar to stock trading	Similar to stock trading	Similar to stock trading
Redemption fees for short-term trades	Yes	No*	No	No
Opportunity to market time a trade	Yes*	No	No	No
Annual Cost to Ongoing Shareholders				
Cost of share trades by other investors	From negligible to several %	Under 0.1%*	Negligible	Negligible
Cost of shareholder accounting at fund level	Yes	Usually furnished by broker at no incremental cost*	Yes	Usually furnished by broker at no incremental cost*
Index license fees	Negligible*	10–30% of expense ratio	Negligible	Negligible
Ongoing marketing or 12(b)(1) fees	0–1.0%	0–0.07%*	No	No
Non-Expense Issues				
Portfolio transparency	Quarterly disclosure, 60-days delay*	Daily	Quarterly disclosure, 60-days delay	Disclosure after portfolio change is complete
Tax efficiency (no capital gains distributions)	Rarely as good as ETFs	Excellent*	Rarely as good as ETFs	Excellent*
Inherent shareholder protection	Investor and regulatory regulatory diligence required	Good structural protection*	Investor and diligence required	Good structural protection*
Product maturity	Started 1924*	Started 1993	Amended 200?	Amended 200?

*A category winner. See the text because you may not want to own a fund that wins in this category.

protection and better economics for ongoing shareholders. The discussions of each topic will clarify the differences between current practice and best practice. Best practice will include, among other features, early order cutoff for all purchase and sale transactions for both styles of funds and it will include active management of ETFs.

Note that the table is headed "A Comparison of No-Load Conventional Equity Mutual Funds and Equity Exchange-Traded Funds." Actually, fund marketing arrangements and sales fees are so varied that I ignore marketing fee issues, except for 12(b)(1) fees, in this formal comparison.

At the risk of giving away in advance how the comparative fund evaluation is going to come out, there are stars next to a number of the entries, indicating which (if either) of the two current products or which of the two best practice products "wins" in that category. Some of the criteria for winning a star are not intuitive, so do not assume that a star on a specific point will make that fund better *for the type of investor you are.* To be sure you are making the right choice for your needs, read the text before you count the stars. Understanding what is behind the conclusion has always been a good policy when using any fund rating process that labels its results with stars.

Of course, all funds in either the conventional or ETF categories are not identical now. They will not be identical under my notion of a best practices regime. Consequently, the conclusions offered are not always simple conclusions with a favorable nod to every fund with one structure and a condemnation of every fund with the other structure. I have tried to make the evaluation process as simple as possible, but there are limits to simplification. When I take pains to qualify a conclusion in the text, please remember Albert Einstein's comment to the effect that everything should be as simple as possible—but no simpler.

I evaluate the competitive structures under three broad categories:

1. Entry and exit costs to fund share traders.
2. Annual cost to ongoing shareholders.
3. Non-expense issues.

After a few preliminary comments on each category, we will look at the specific structural issues.

Entry and Exit Costs to Traders

The first category looks at the fund share purchase and sale process from the perspective of a short-term trader—someone who will own the fund shares for only a short period of time. The reason for looking at entry and exit costs from the trader's perspective is that there is an inherent conflict between the interests of short-term traders and the interests of long-term investors. The mutual fund scandals of 2003–2004 happened because some fund companies and some fund structures took the side of the short-term traders in that conflict.

It should come as no surprise that, prior to the Securities and Exchange Commission (SEC) proposed rule that most conventional funds impose up to a 2 percent redemption fee on mutual fund shares redeemed within seven days of purchase, conventional funds were clearly more attractive than ETFs to most short-term traders. It is mildly ironic that *because* the in-kind fund share creation and redemption process of ETFs was designed to permit intraday fund share trading, ETFs do the best job of protecting ongoing fund shareholders from the cost of fund share trading. ETFs have consistently been protective of long-term shareholders since their introduction in 1993.

Annual Cost to Ongoing Shareholders

The second category reflects the perspective of the long-term shareholder. The principal objective of a long-term shareholder will be to buy a fund that operates subject to a set of rules that do not adversely affect the portfolio manager's ability to deliver favorable performance with low expenses. The fund structure should provide protection from the costs of in-and-out trading by fund share traders. The emphasis on *structural* protection is fundamental. The mutual fund abuses revealed in 2003 and 2004 were possible because there is nothing in the conventional mutual fund structure to protect a fund's ongoing shareholders from the costs of providing liquidity to short-term traders. Marketing and other decisions harmful to ongoing investors in mutual funds can still be made without blatantly breaking the rules. It is more difficult for the manager of an ETF to make a similar decision that would hurt ETF shareholders.[1]

Non-Expense Issues

This is a slightly misleading category title. Most of these issues have an effect on investor expenses either inside the fund or, as in the case of tax efficiency, on the net return the investor will earn after paying taxes on the fund's performance. My reason for calling these "non-expense issues" is that the cost is not reflected in the fund's *expense ratio*. Consequently, the expense or performance impact can be hard to measure.

Entry and Exit Costs to Traders

The perspective I take in describing the entry and exit costs to traders reflects the impact of mutual fund reforms planned through 2006. As noted, this entry and exit cost evaluation is based on the viewpoint of a short-term fund share trader. While many of the postscandal reforms were designed to prevent **late trading** and market timing in conventional funds, the aggregate effectiveness of these reforms is doubtful. Some of the reasons for doubt will be clear as we work through the specific items.

Direct Share Purchase and Sale Costs

Under current practice, the typical conventional mutual fund is purchased with an order delivered to a fund issuer by 4:00 p.m. for execution at that day's net asset value (NAV). A few funds charge a small administrative fee and some transactions through a brokerage firm carry a commission, but most transactions of any size can be accomplished at NAV if the investor deals directly with the fund or trades through a fund supermarket. In contrast, trades in ETFs work like stock trades. On ETF transactions of all sizes, the trader usually pays a commission and part or all of the spread between the bid and the offer prices quoted in the market.

I put a star in the current practice conventional fund column on direct purchase and sale costs. The SEC's requirement that all mutual fund orders be entered by 4:00 p.m. still gives a market timing advantage to the conventional fund share trader relative to the ETF trader. That advantage is also reflected in the star on the "Opportunity to market time a trade" line as described later. This continuing advantage to traders is obviously not in the best interest of ongoing shareholders.

In a best practice regime, I expect the trading processes for conventional funds and ETFs to become increasingly similar. For example, on orders entered early in the day, a dealer might offer to buy or sell ETF shares at today's NAV. The dealer could execute a fund share trade for his trading account at any time during the day or defer it to the next day—and the investor would be guaranteed an execution at the NAV computed with today's closing stock prices. The timing option that the fund share trader gives the dealer to execute the underlying trade at a time of the dealer's choosing has value and should offer the dealer enough profit potential on orders of significant size to justify the dealer's willingness to provide a guaranteed execution at NAV.

ETF execution at NAV would be comparable to the executions conventional funds will offer on orders placed early enough to permit the fund manager to trade in the fund portfolio to offset the cost of accommodating the fund share trade. Both types of funds will, thus, offer executions at the close similar to those available in the stock market to institutional investors. If the order is entered early enough, the trader can get NAV with no commissions. If the order is placed later, the fund share trader will bear the cost of liquidity to execute the trade. Without regulatory or fund management support, an ETF execution at NAV may not be readily available to small investors. An industry utility to pool small orders and make NAV execution available to all investors might be feasible.

Redemption Fees for Short-Term Trades

The only significant deterrent to conventional mutual fund market-timing traders in the reforms of 2004–2005 is the proposed redemption fee for fund share positions held less than seven days. The fact that a conventional fund share trader will be hit with up to a 2 percent redemption fee on positions held less than a week does offer a relative advantage to some ETF traders because there is no such penalty for an in-and-out ETF trade. However, a short-term mutual fund share trader should be able to neutralize the market risk exposure associated with a short-term holding in most funds with a variety of risk management tools including futures contracts and offsetting short positions in index ETF shares.[2] For large traders, the effective cost of sidestepping the redemption fee is much less than 2 percent of assets. The redemption fee will not deter a large trader with access to risk management opportunities from taking advantage of momentum reflected in market movement shortly before the market close. It will not deter would-be market timers in international funds where, in the absence of delayed pricing or effective fair value pricing, market timing opportunities are still sufficiently frequent and large enough in magnitude to overcome concern about holding positions for a week or hedging to avoid paying a 2 percent redemption fee.

Opportunity to Market Time a Trade

The star in the conventional mutual fund column reflects the fact that, from the perspective of a fund share trader, the reforms of 2004–2005 (including the redemption fee) do not seriously inhibit profitable market-timing trades. Under best practices for both conventional mutual funds and ETFs, purchases and sales with the fund on the other side of the transaction will be cut off by, say, 2:30 p.m. for pricing at today's NAV. Similar rules for cash and in-kind transactions will eliminate a modest disadvantage many ETFs face in making portfolio composition changes, partly as a result of laziness on the part of their portfolio managers. When the early order cutoff is implemented, with corresponding changes for international funds as described briefly in Chapter 5, there will be no material entry and exit cost disadvantage to ongoing shareholders in the competition between conventional funds and ETFs. This section of the playing field will be level, and ongoing shareholders of both fund types will be fully protected from the transaction costs imposed by fund share traders.

Annual Cost to Ongoing Shareholders

As I argued in Chapter 5 and more extensively in Gastineau (2004b), there are a number of embedded costs affecting the fortunes of ongoing shareholders that are built into the current structure of conventional funds and ETFs. The most important of these are the embedded costs of fund share trades by other investors in conventional mutual funds. The cost of shareholder accounting and servicing at the fund level in conventional funds, high index license fees in ETFs, and ongoing marketing or 12(b)(1) fees, especially in conventional funds, are other costs borne by ongoing shareholders.

Cost of Share Trades by Other Investors

For conventional funds, the principal argument for an earlier trading cutoff than 4:00 p.m. for fund share orders is the cost ongoing shareholders bear to provide liquidity to fund share traders. An order received by a domestic equity fund before 2:30 p.m. and processed promptly will give the portfolio manager an opportunity to get to the portfolio mix she wants by the close of trading. Pricing the fund share purchase or sale at NAV based on 4:00 p.m. prices will reflect any costs of getting the portfolio to the desired position. The portfolio manager's trades will help update stale prices that would otherwise distort the NAV calculation.

The cost to ongoing shareholders of providing liquidity to traders of conventional mutual funds is likely to be much less than 1 percent per year in a sizeable, low-turnover large-cap index fund. In contrast, it might run to 5 percent or more per year in a small, high-turnover, actively managed small-cap fund. Free liquidity for traders is a very real cost for most conventional funds and a very large cost for funds that are actively traded.

At-the-close notice of creations and redemptions can impose small costs on some ongoing ETF investors, justifying an early cutoff for in-kind creation and redemption commitments. Apart from this minor effect on ETF performance, under the current rules for purchase and sale of fund shares, built-in protection from the costs of providing liquidity to fund share traders is probably the greatest advantage (even greater than tax efficiency) that ETFs have over the typical conventional fund for long-term investors. With best practices—a 2:30 p.m. cutoff for all purchase and sale orders, whether in cash or in kind—this problem for ongoing shareholders will disappear in all domestic funds. Appropriate order cutoff rules can also solve this problem for international funds. (See "A Simple Solution" section in Chapter 5.)

Cost of Shareholder Accounting at Fund Level

One of the cost advantages of ETFs is that there is no shareholder accounting at the fund level. The amount a fund company might save by avoiding shareholder accounting at the fund level will vary, but data available on the fees Vanguard imposes on its Investor Shares, on the one hand, and its Admiral Shares ($100,000 account minimum) and VIPERs (ETFs), on the other hand, suggests that for Vanguard, at least, the cost of shareholder accounting on relatively small accounts is approximately 6 basis points (0.06 percent) per year. Smaller and less efficient fund companies or companies that provide a higher level of service than Vanguard may have appreciably higher shareholder accounting costs.

But a 6-basis-point cost estimate significantly understates the cost of having some fund shares carried in brokerage firm accounts or accounts with other financial intermediaries. Fund companies whose shares are listed in fund supermarkets as no transaction fee (NTF) funds pay the brokerage firm proprietors of these supermarkets a fee of 35 basis points (0.35 percent) per year or more as a so-called service fee. In addition to the cost of providing basic accounting services, there is clearly a significant marketing cost component in the 35-basis-point or greater compensation paid to the financial intermediary.

Most financial intermediaries do not impose a charge or line item fee on their customers for carrying an ETF position in an account. Should such fees become common, they will almost certainly be lower than 35 basis points per year for most accounts. The service fees paid to brokers are part of the total fees charged by the mutual fund adviser. These fees tend to be less obvious to the investor than fees charged directly to the brokerage account—which helps account for their popularity. A cost-conscious investor will want to look at all such fees carefully.

Index License Fees

As noted in the discussion of index license fees in Chapter 6, index license fees for conventional mutual funds have typically been negligible. Early index mutual fund license fees were usually fixed amounts regardless of fund size rather than a percentage of assets. The cost allocation effect of a flat fee declines sharply as the size of the fund grows. In contrast, ETF index license fees are typically a fixed percentage of the fund's expense ratio or a fixed number of basis points per year calculated on the total assets of the fund. ETF index license fees typically range between 10 percent and 30 percent of an index ETF's expense ratio. While these license fees are usually paid by the fund management company, their net impact is embedded in a unitary fee charged by the manager.

As suggested in Chapter 6, there is no good reason to license a benchmark index and a lot of economic reasons not to license a benchmark index as the template for a fund. When best practices are adopted and silent index funds become the industry standard, index license fees for ETFs should begin to decline.

Ongoing Marketing or 12(b)(1) Fees

While most ETFs have the authority (subject to board approval) to implement 12(b)(1) marketing fees, few ETFs have them, and the existing ETF
12(b)(1) fees are small. In contrast, conventional funds may have 12(b)(1)
fees ranging upward to 1 percent of assets per year. The SEC has not eliminated these ongoing marketing fees, but the pressure to drop them grows.
I would expect either the SEC or shareholder pressure to eliminate most
12(b)(1) fees in a best practice environment. There will continue to be
fund share classes with embedded marketing fees, whether or not they are
collected as part of the management fee.

Non-Expense Issues

As noted, these are really non-expense *ratio* issues. Most choices in fund
structure or disclosure have an economic effect on shareholder performance. In dealing with these issues, therefore, I try to put at least a rough
estimate on their cost or performance impact.

Portfolio Transparency

In 2004 the SEC began requiring quarterly portfolio disclosure for conventional mutual funds with a 60-day delay from the date of the portfolio reported to the date the report goes to the SEC. This information is available
to the public on the SEC web site.[3] The current portfolio disclosure requirement for index ETFs is essentially daily disclosure. This daily disclosure is usually provided by publishing changes in the fund's creation and
redemption baskets to reflect changes in the composition of a published
benchmark index. Daily portfolio disclosure subjects an ETF to front-
running of portfolio changes. Daily disclosure can frustrate attempts to
change the composition of the portfolio on a day other than the date on
which the index change is official under the rules of the index publisher.

Actively managed ETFs are still no more than a gleam in the eye of
many investors and fund issuers. Unless regulators can begin to understand the problems that stem from immediate disclosure of index ETF
portfolios, they will not be able to approve sound, actively managed ETFs.
Without going into possible ETF disclosure changes, we expect changes in
portfolio strategy and investment management structure to eliminate most
of the disclosure disadvantages under which many ETFs labor today.[4]

Tax Efficiency (No Cap Gains Distributions)

I described the tax efficiency advantage that ETFs typically enjoy in the
Chapter 3 (section entitled "Why ETFs Are Tax-Efficient" on pp. 42–44).

I also argued in that section that a hybrid fund that combines a conventional fund share class with an ETF share class covering a single portfolio is unlikely to be as tax-efficient, particularly in the long run, as a fund where all entry and exit is through an ETF share class. Unless the tax law is changed to protect all fund shareholders from the capital gains distributions that occur because of portfolio changes rather than because they sell their own shares in a fund, the ETF advantage seems likely to be perennial, even under a full best practices regime for conventional funds.

Inherent Shareholder Protection

The shareholder protection embedded in the structure of conventional mutual funds is significantly inferior to the investor protection embedded in ETFs. The fund scandals of 2003 and 2004 leave no doubt on this point. The fact that so many regulatory changes have been made in an attempt to correct flaws and reduce predation on conventional mutual fund shareholders highlights the weaknesses in the conventional mutual fund structure. Even with the 2004–2006 reforms, conventional mutual fund shareholders need to exercise personal vigilance to ensure that they will not be adversely affected by market timing trades. ETF investors should be equally vigilant on general principles, but it is harder for financial predators to rip them off because of the safeguards inherent in the ETF share creation/redemption process. The in-kind creation and redemption process, though not perfect from the point of view of either shareholder protection or fund performance, is dramatically superior to the best shareholder protection feasible in conventional mutual funds. I expect this structural difference to remain important even as both types of funds move to best practices in the years ahead.

Product Maturity

One of the substantial operating advantages that conventional funds enjoy over ETFs is that the Investment Company Act of 1940 was written to provide some conventional mutual fund investor protection, without destroying the industry, in the light of some earlier abuses of mutual fund investors. Specifically, mutual funds started in 1924. The 1940 Act was designed to fix problems highlighted in Congressional hearings held in the 1930s. Exchange-traded funds were started in 1993, and have operated without scandal under specific exemptions from a few provisions of the Investment Company Act of 1940.

The sponsors of existing ETFs had to persuade the SEC that the exemptions from the 1940 Act provisions they needed to operate ETFs would not, given the structure of ETFs, create shareholder protection issues. The SEC understood the unique features of ETFs, including their structural advantages in providing shareholder protection, well enough to grant the necessary exemptions. The 1940 Act, however, has a great many provisions in it, and the SEC has implemented so many rules and regulations under the 1940 Act that it is hard for the SEC to adopt enough piecemeal changes to facilitate further ETF development.

ETFs Will Be the Long-Term Winners

The SEC staff personnel who must evaluate the regulatory changes necessary to expand the scope of ETFs have been dealing with the conventional mutual fund scandals. In a highly charged environment where existing fund regulation has proven grossly inadequate, it is hard to get attention for regulatory relief to develop a better fund product, no matter how superior its structure. On the other side of the table, the incentive for entrepreneurs to push for ETF innovation is small because of the way the SEC exemptive process works. The first applicant who incurs the substantial legal bills necessary to obtain approval for a more flexible ETF format will provide a great service to all applicants who follow the same path. The followers will be able to launch similar funds at about the same time as the innovator—and they will save millions of dollars in legal fees. In spite of these obstacles, changes in best practices will occur over the next few years. Substantial additional changes need to be made in the conventional mutual fund structure in the interest of shareholder protection, just as changes to increase investment flexibility need to be made for ETFs. Conventional fund problems will continue to clarify the superior investor protection inherent in the ETF structure.

In the best practices environment, there will be essentially three substantive differences between conventional funds and ETFs. Exchange-traded funds will retain their cost advantage from not having shareholder accounting at the fund level. They will retain their superior tax efficiency, and they will retain better inherent structural protection for shareholders than conventional mutual funds can provide. In the long run, these features will be a tough combination for conventional funds to compete against. The only edge conventional funds might have in some applications is a longer period of portfolio confidentiality.

Supplementary Information

The best general mutual fund references for investors and advisers are *Mutual Funds for Dummies*, 4th Edition, by Eric Tyson (John Wiley & Sons, 2004), *The Mutual Fund Business*, and by Robert C. Pozen (MIT Press, 1998). The latter book was written when Pozen, now chairman of Putnam Investments, was vice chairman of Fidelity.

The best comprehensive book on conventional fund operations is *A Purely American Invention*, by Lee Gremillion (National Investment Company Service Association, 2001).

Gregory A. Baer and Gary Gensler's book, *The Great Mutual Fund Trap* (Broadway Books, 2002), provides a perspective more critical of funds.

For exchange-traded funds, I offer my own book, *The Exchange-Traded Funds Manual*, (John Wiley & Sons, 2002), and Jim Wiandt and Will McClatchy's *Exchange-Traded Funds* (John Wiley & Sons, 2001).

Most of the major financial publications, with special emphasis on the *Wall Street Journal* and *Barron's*, have printed a great deal about the recent scandals.

GLOSSARY

For definitions of other financial terms, see the source of this glossary, the *Dictionary of Financial Risk Management* by Gary L. Gastineau and Mark P. Kritzman (John Wiley & Sons, 1999) or online at: www.amex.com/dictionary/frinit.html.

401(k) plan   A defined contribution, income tax-deferred retirement plan under which employees of a corporation may elect to make pretax contributions to an employer-sponsored plan in lieu of receiving currently taxable income. In some plans, part or all of the employee contribution is matched by an employer contribution.

403(b) plan   A defined contribution, income tax-deferred retirement plan similar to a 401(k) plan for employees of certain not-for-profit organizations.

408(k) plan   See *simplified employee pension (SEP) plan.*

457 plan   A defined contribution, income tax-deferred retirement plan similar to a 401(k) plan for employees of state and local government and tax-exempt organizations. These plans are not subject to ERISA. The funds belong to the employer and are subject to the claims of the employer's general creditors.

A shares   When referring to a mutual fund, usually means shares of a class with a front-end load. See also *B shares, C shares, institutional shares class.*

active manager   A portfolio manager who takes an active role in any aspect of the investment process, including asset allocation, style exposures, security selection, and risk management in an attempt to improve a portfolio's risk-adjusted return.

adviser   (1) An organization employed by a mutual fund's board to give professional advice on the fund's investments and asset management practices. (2) An investment counselor who assists investors in the establishment and execution of an investment program.

advisory fee   (1) The amount a fund pays to its investment adviser for the investment management associated with overseeing a fund's portfolio. Also referred to as management fee. (2) The compensation of some investment counselors.

Alpha (1), (2)

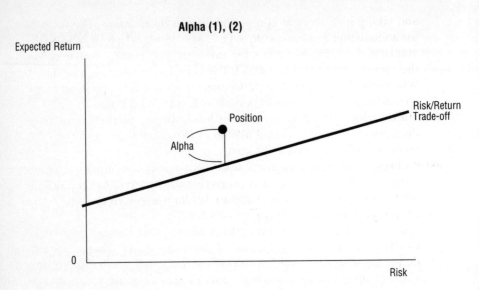

EXHIBIT G.1   Alpha

alpha (α)   (1) The net risk-adjusted premium or excess return from a position or a portfolio. Calculated by subtracting the risk-adjusted return
consistent with the position or portfolio's place on the capital asset
pricing model (CAPM) security market line from the actual return. Alpha can be negative if the return falls below the security market line.
(2) The average nonsystematic deviation from any performance
benchmark. (See Exhibit G.1.)

alternative asset   Any nontraditional investment instrument, style, or category—especially an asset class with returns that are not highly correlated with stock and bond returns. Examples can include precious
metals, real estate, and managed accounts using currency, commodity,
and long/short stock accounts, or even hedge funds using stock index
and debt futures.

Alternative Minimum Tax (AMT)   A tax calculation made as a supple-
ment to the standard income tax calculation for individuals and corporations in the United States. The AMT was designed to ensure that
wealthy individuals and successful corporations pay a minimum percentage of their income in taxes in spite of any tax shelters or tax-exempt
investments they may have. The AMT can make certain standard tax
benefits unattractive to taxpayers affected by it. As incomes rise, the
AMT has begun to affect the returns of far less affluent taxpayers that
it was designed for.

annualized return   The rate of return that would occur on average per
year given a cumulative multiyear return or a fractional year return

and taking into account compounding and discounting. The formula for annualizing a return is: $R_a = (1 + R_u)^{(1/n)} - 1$, where R_a equals the annualized return, R_u equals the unannualized return, and n equals the number of years over which the cumulative return is calculated. When reporting investment performance, it is not appropriate to annualize returns calculated over periods of less than one year.

asset allocation   Dividing investment funds among markets to achieve diversification and/or a combination of expected return and risk consistent with the investor's objectives.

asset class   A grouping of investable assets with the following characteristics: (1) nonzero exposure (positive or negative) has the potential to raise the utility of a portfolio; (2) its risk/return characteristics cannot be duplicated by some combination of other assets; (3) it is relatively homogeneous internally; and (4) it has the capacity (size) to absorb a meaningful fraction of portfolio assets. There is a tendency toward asset class pollution—a tendency to divide the universe of investments into more asset classes than are warranted or useful.

B shares   In a mutual fund, usually shares of a class that carries a back-end load.

back-end load   A mutual fund sales charge imposed when an investor sells fund shares rather than when he purchases them. The back-end load generally decreases the longer the investor holds the shares because the annual fee charged to the account covers the commission paid the salesman, usually in about five years. Also called *contingent deferred sales charge.*

backward pricing   Setting a net asset value for a mutual fund share trade using a stale price based on portfolio securities values determined before the commitment to trade was firm. This was legal until 1968 when SEC Rule 22c-1 requiring *forward pricing* became effective. Backward pricing became an issue in the *late trading* mutual fund scandals that emerged in late 2003.

basis point (bp)   One-hundredth of a percentage point, also expressed as 0.01 percent. The difference between a yield of 7.90 percent and 8 percent is 10 basis points. When applied to a price rather than a rate, the term is often expressed as annualized basis points.

benchmark index   A reference index or rate that serves as a basis for portfolio composition, performance comparison, or return calculation.

beta (β) factor   A measurement of stock price volatility relative to a broad market index. If a stock moves up and down twice as much as the market index, it has a beta of 2. If it moves one-half as much as the market, its beta is 0.5. Because beta assumes a linear relationship, it can be seriously misleading if used inappropriately. (See Exhibit G.2.)

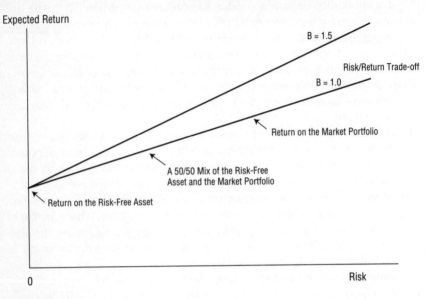

EXHIBIT G.2   Beta Factor

bid-asked spread   The difference between the bid and offer price in a market. The size of the spread is the most widely used comparative measure of market quality.

C shares   Fund shares that carry an ongoing sales or marketing fee. The ongoing fee is often a 12(b)(1) fee, named for the rule under the Investment Company Act of 1940 that authorizes these fees.

capital gains distribution   A distribution from a mutual fund or an exchange-traded fund of taxable long-term capital gains, usually from the sale of common stocks held for more than a year. Note that short-term capital gains are included with the income distributions of a regulated investment company. Capital gains distributions are taxed at long-term capital gains rates no matter how long the shareholder has owned shares in the mutual fund. Capital gains distributions are taxable in the year in which they are declared, which is not necessarily the same as the year in which they are paid.

capital gains overhang   A reference to net unrealized capital gains in the securities held by a *mutual fund* or *exchange-traded fund*. The greater the unrealized gains as a percent of fund assets, the greater the probability of a significant future *capital gains distribution*.

capital loss carryover   A capital loss not deductible to reduce taxes in the current year that may be deductible against gains realized in future years.

capitalization The market value of a company's outstanding securities, usually equity securities. Under $250 million is generally considered small-cap; $250 million to $2 billion is mid-cap; and over $2 billion is large-cap.

churn A measure of mutual fund share turnover that is captured in a combination of two ratios. Churn is measured as fund redemptions as a percentage of average net assets—with a minimum of at least 200 percent—accompanied by a ratio of redemptions to sales close to 100 percent. See also *flow*.

closed fund A mutual fund that no longer offers shares for sale to the public, often because management believes that it cannot manage additional assets effectively. In some cases, a fund will be closed to new shareholders but present shareholders may buy more shares.

closed-end mutual fund An investment company with a fixed number of shares outstanding. Shares purchased in such a fund are purchased from another shareholder rather than issued in response to demand for new shares. In contrast to shares in an open-end fund, which can usually be redeemed at net asset value, a closed-end fund's shares can trade at a material premium or discount to net asset value.

closet index fund A fund described by its adviser as an actively managed fund and that charges active management fees, but is constructed to track a benchmark index very closely.

contingent deferred sales charge (CDSC) A fee imposed when mutual fund shares are redeemed (sold back to the fund) during the first few years of ownership. The CDSC declines over time and is usually eliminated after, say, five years. Also called *back-end load*.

contingent redemption fee A redemption fee charged by a mutual fund that is contingent upon some feature of the transaction, usually imposed on a redemption that occurs shortly after the purchase of the shares being redeemed. In contrast to a *contingent deferred sales charge (CDSC)*, which goes to a salesperson, a contingent redemption fee is paid into the fund. The purpose of this type of redemption fee is usually to discourage short-term or market-timing trades in the fund shares. Also called conditional redemption fee.

core-satellite investment strategy An exchange-traded fund (ETF) asset allocation program using broad index fund (core) and separate securities or style and sector funds (satellites) in an attempt to enhance overall portfolio performance or diversification while controlling risks. See also *risk budget*.

creation unit The minimum module for issue or redemption of shares in an open-end exchange-traded fund (ETF), usually between 25,000 and 300,000 fund shares, depending on the fund's policy. Most existing ETFs issue their shares in return for portfolio deposits of securities in multiples of the creation unit basket specified by the fund's adviser.

With minor exceptions related primarily to accrued dividend payments, cash balancing amounts, and loss realizations, creations and redemptions are in kind, not in cash. ETF trading on the secondary market is in the individual fund shares issued in the creation, not in creation units.

defined benefit pension plan A retirement plan committed to paying a specified amount to a given recipient based on term of service and, perhaps, annual salary at or near retirement. The plan may be funded by employee contributions, employer contributions, or some combination. Usually the employer retains primary responsibility for the solvency and funding of the plan with a backstop from the Pension Benefit Guaranty Corporation (PBGC). Defined benefit plans have become less popular in recent years, in part because of stricter regulation and in part because of increasing longevity, which extends pension benefits over a longer time after an employee's contribution to the success of the employer's business ceases.

defined contribution pension plan A retirement plan in which the level of contributions is fixed, usually at a level determined by tax deductibility. Ordinarily, most contributions are made by employees, but these plans have become a repository for employer contributions as well with the decline in defined benefit pension plan popularity. The contributions in an employee's account and the amount the employee can earn from the investment of those contributions determine the employee's benefits after retirement.

diversification An approach to investment management analyzed and popularized by Harry Markowitz and encouraged by widespread acceptance of the usefulness of the capital asset pricing model (CAPM). With diversification, risk can be reduced relative to the average return of a portfolio by distributing assets among a variety of asset classes, such as stocks, bonds, money market instruments, and physical commodities, as well as by diversifying within these categories and across international boundaries. Diversification usually reduces portfolio risk (measured by return variability) because the returns (both positive and negative) on various asset classes are not perfectly correlated. (See Exhibit G.3.)

dividend drag Dividend drag is attributed primarily to several of the older, unit trust–based ETFs (SPDRs, MidCap SPDRs, and DIAMONDS). Because of the passively invested nature of these unit trusts and the absence of a board of directors, the SEC has required that cash dividends received by the trust not be reinvested in portfolio stocks. Dividends are accumulated in cash and paid out periodically to investors. During the accumulation period, dividend cash may be invested by the trustee. Any interest earned by the trustee (at a short-term rate) is deducted from the expenses of the trust. During

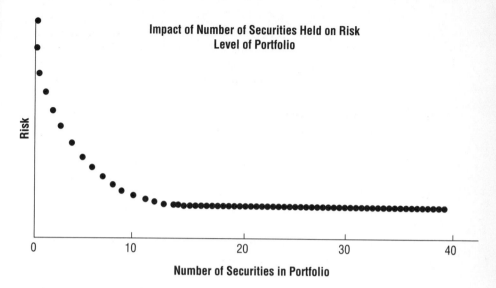

EXHIBIT G.3   Diversification—Number of Securities Held

a rising market, a dividend-paying portfolio using the unit trust structure will lag a few basis points behind a comparable fund based on a mutual fund structure that can equitize dividends (invest in stocks) until the fund is ready to pay the net dividends to shareholders. In a declining market, the fact that dividends are not equitized leads to outperformance by the unit trusts. The SEC is expected to permit the unit trust ETFs to equitize dividends in the near future. Also called cash drag.

donor advised fund   A mechanism for charitable giving that makes a full charitable deduction available at the time the investment account is funded. The donor recommends qualified charities as recipients of the assets in the account, with final approval of donations in the hands of a third-party fiduciary.

electronic data gathering, analysis, and retrieval (EDGAR)   An electronic system developed by the Securities and Exchange Commission that permits companies to file electronically all documents required for securities offerings and ongoing disclosure obligations. See also *Securities and Exchange Commission (SEC).*

Employee Retirement Income Security Act of 1974 (ERISA)   The legislation that established regulation of the administration, investment, and risk management policies of pension (defined benefit) and profit-sharing (defined contribution) employee benefit plans in the United States.

enhanced indexing   A modified indexing strategy that attempts to exceed the total return of the benchmark index, usually with quantitative tools.

equity fund   A mutual fund that invests primarily in stocks.

equity funding   A combination of a life insurance policy and a mutual fund. The insurance premium is paid by borrowing against the collateral value of the fund shares.

exchange-traded fund (ETF)   A modified unit trust or investment company characterized by a dual trading process. Fund shares are created or redeemed in large blocks through the deposit of securities to, or delivery of securities from, the fund's portfolio. Secondary trading, in lots as small as a single fund share, takes place on a stock market. The dual trading process permits (and potential arbitrage requires) the fund shares to trade close to net asset value at all times. ETFs trade at prices very close to their current underlying value throughout the trading day and are usually more tax- efficient than comparable conventional funds. *HOLDRs* and *folios*, two alternative basket or portfolio products, are sometimes compared to ETFs. In contrast to HOLDRs and folios, ETFs are subject to investment company regulation and regulated investment company tax treatment, and the product structures are quite different.

expense ratio   For a mutual fund or other investment company, a charge to fund assets for investment management, specified marketing, custody, administration, and other related costs but not for sales charges, for unusual outlays, for lawsuits, or for trading expenses like brokerage commissions and noncash market impact costs. Usually expressed in basis points or as a percentage of net assets.

fair value pricing   A price that may differ from reported prices is assigned to a portfolio component under rules set by the directors or trustees of the fund. Fair value pricing is used when accurate or up-to-date market prices are not available for some portfolio components.

fat-tailed distribution   A reference to the tendency of many financial instrument price and return distributions to have more observations in the tails and to be thinner in the midrange than a normal distribution. Assets or markets prone to price jumps tend to exhibit fat-tailed distributions. (See Exhibit G.4.)

financial planner   Trained specialist who evaluates and selects investments for individuals and firms to achieve a variety of defined short- and long-term goals with risk control and tax benefits.

fixed-income security   An investment that provides a return in the form of fixed periodic payments and/or scheduled payment of a preset principal amount at maturity.

flow   Investments moving into and out of a mutual fund as a result of investor purchases of fund shares and redemptions of fund shares

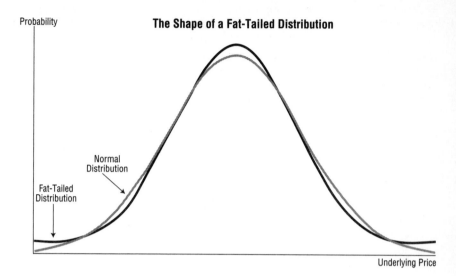

The Shape of a Fat-Tailed Distribution

Probability

Normal
Distribution

Fat-Tailed
Distribution

Underlying Price

EXHIBIT G.4   Fat-Tailed Distribution

for cash with the fund as counterparty. Flow for a share class is measured as the number of shares purchased from the fund plus the number of shares redeemed, all divided by the average shares outstanding during the period and expressed as a percent. If the period over which flow is measured is a quarter or half year, the percentage is multiplied by 4 or 2, respectively, to obtain an annual rate. See also *churn* and *turnover.*

folio   An unstructured basket of common stock that may represent a stock index, a sector or theme, or even an actively managed portfolio at inception, but which may be modified by an investor or an adviser to meet the tax and spending needs of its owner. The rationale for the folio is to take advantage of diversification and the ability to realize tax losses in a separately managed account. In most cases, an investor will have to devote a fair amount of time to the folio or engage the services of a specialized adviser to maintain appropriate diversification.

forward pricing   The valuation process for a conventional mutual fund transaction. All orders to buy or sell shares are based on the next net asset value calculation.

front-end load   A sales commission charged at the time of purchase of some mutual funds and other investment products.

fulcrum fees   Incentive fees in mutual funds that must be symmetrical. On the downside, the fund manager must refund part or all of its base management fee to match the incentive fee it can earn for superior performance relative to the fund benchmark on the upside.

fund family   A group of funds with different investment objectives offered by the same management company.

fund-friendly index   An index with one or more features designed to improve the performance of a fund based on the index relative to a fund based on a standard *benchmark index*. The fund-friendly feature may reduce portfolio turnover, attempt to avoid rebalancing at times likely to increase transaction costs disproportionately, or simply delay announcement of index changes until the fund has had an opportunity to implement the changes.

fund manager   The adviser of a conventional mutual fund, an exchange-traded fund, a pension fund, an insurance fund, or some other personal or institutional portfolio.

fund of funds   A financial intermediary organized as a corporation, business trust, or partnership that accepts equity investments and buys shares of other funds that, in turn, hold securities or commodities.

fund/SERV   A service of the National Securities Clearing Corporation (NSCC) that automates and standardizes the processing of mutual fund purchase and redemption orders, settlements, and account registrations. Fund/SERV is integrated with the continuous net settlement (CNS) system in contributing to a daily net money settlement with each firm.

HOLDRS   Shares in a grantor trust that represent an undivided interest in a specific portfolio of stocks, usually in a particular industry, sector, or group. HOLDRS (HOLding company Depositary ReceiptS) were developed by Merrill Lynch to allow an investor to own a moderately diversified group of stocks in a single investment that is transparent and liquid. HOLDRS are characterized by low ongoing expenses and by a high degree of tax flexibility that leads to tax efficiency as long as the investor does not sell highly appreciated component shares. The holder of HOLDRS can separate the portfolio into its component securities at modest cost to realize losses. The principal disadvantage of HOLDRS is that an investor may find that keeping track of the tax basis and tax consequences associated with subsequent transactions can be relatively complex.

institutional share class   A special low-fee mutual fund share designed for sale to very large investors. This share class typically has no embedded marketing charges. Sometimes called Y Shares.

intraday indicative value (IIV)   Value published for each ETF, typically every 15 seconds throughout the trading day, based on the last sale prices or current bids and offers of the securities specified for creation and redemption baskets plus any estimated cash amounts associated with the creation unit, all on a per-ETF-share basis. Also called intraday proxy value (IDPV), intraday value, indicative optimized portfolio value (IOPV), indicative per-share portfolio value (IPSPV), and underlying trading value.

Investment Company Act of 1940 (or 40 Act)   Legislation enacted in 1940 (with subsequent amendments and regulations under the legislation) that governs the operation of the fund (open-end mutual, closed-end, exchange-traded) and investment advisory industries. This act stipulates the conditions that funds and investment advisers have to meet in order to distribute their products and services to the general public.

investment objective   The goal that a mutual fund pursues on behalf of its shareholders.

Keogh plan   A qualified retirement plan that covers a self-employed person and, in some cases, a limited number of employees. May include a defined contribution or a defined benefit plan or both.

late trading   The illegal entry of mutual fund purchase or sale orders after 4:00 p.m. for execution at the net asset value calculated from 4:00 p.m. prices. In some instances, late traders have entered orders prior to 4:00 p.m. and canceled them hours after the close when the course of prices changed.

life strategy fund   One of a variety of asset allocation funds. These funds are typically structured to modify asset allocation opportunistically as relative bond and stock values change or over time as their shareholders age and prefer a less volatile (less risky) investment strategy.

Lipper Leaders ratings   A mutual fund ranking system published by the Lipper division of Reuters. Funds in a variety of categories are ranked by quintiles from √ (best) to 5 (worst) on five characteristics: total return, consistent return, preservation, tax efficiency, and expenses.

load fund   A fund that levies a sales charge when shares are bought (a front-end load) or sold (a back-end load). A level load fund charges a sales fee each year, possibly with an eventual cutoff.

long-term capital gain (LTCG)   A profit on the sale of a security or fund share that has been held for more than one year. Generally LTCGs are taxed at a preferential rate in the United States.

low-load fund   A fund that charges a sales commission of 3.5 percent or less for the purchase of its shares.

management company   The firm that organizes, manages, and administers a fund.

management investment company   A mutual fund.

market-on-close (MOC) order   A type of order that instructs the broker to execute the trade at the closing price for the day. In futures markets, a market-on-close order is executed within the closing range. Under current New York Stock Exchange and American Stock Exchange rules, an MOC order is almost assured of execution at the closing price if it is entered by a certain time. Investors using MOC orders should be aware of the probable effect a large order will have on the closing price.

market timing   (1) Entry of an order to buy or sell shares of a mutual fund close to the time securities prices are determined for calculation of the fund's net asset value. Many traders have learned that they can earn high returns when market momentum near the close is not reflected in stale prices used to price fund portfolios. While stale prices have been a greater problem in some funds holding foreign securities, market timers have also profited from trades in domestic funds. Market timing will be difficult to stop as long as funds offer free liquidity to orders that arrive just before the market close. (2) Shifting in and out of asset groups and specific instruments on the basis of expectations that some are undervalued or overvalued relative to others, and that these discrepancies will soon be corrected.

mean   The arithmetic average of a population or a sample of observations.

median   The middle observation in an ordered distribution. After the mean, the most common measure of central tendency. It is often used instead of the mean because it is less sensitive to extreme values.

microcap stock   Stock issued by companies with very small or micro capitalizations, usually less than $100 million in equity value.

money market fund   A fund designed to provide safety of principal and current income by investing in securities that mature in one year or less, such as bank certificates of deposit, commercial paper, and U.S. Treasury bills. The price per share is usually fixed at $1.00.

Morningstar ratings   For every mutual fund with at least a three-year history, Morningstar calculates a rating based on a Morningstar risk-adjusted return measure that accounts for variation in a fund's monthly performance (including the effects of sales charges, loads, and redemption fees), placing more emphasis on downward variations and rewarding consistent performance. The top 10 percent of funds in each category receive five stars, the next 22.5 percent receive four stars, the next 35 percent receive three stars, the next 22.5 percent receive two stars, and the bottom 10 percent receive one star. Highly rated funds are defined as those that have a four- or five-star Morningstar rating. High ratings attract investor assets, but are not reliable indicators of future investment results.

mutual fund   A diversified, managed portfolio of securities that pools the assets of individuals and organizations to invest toward a common objective such as tracking an index, current income, or long-term growth.

net asset value (NAV)   The market value of a fund's total assets, minus liabilities, divided by the number of shares outstanding. The official NAV is usually expressed as a value per share and it is calculated officially once a day by most U.S. funds at 4:00 p.m. Eastern time. Partly in response to the growth of open-end exchange-traded funds, some conventional funds have begun calculating an NAV several times a day or, in a few cases, hourly. The more frequent values calculated for exchange-traded funds are not official NAVs.

no-load fund A mutual fund whose shares are sold without a sales commission and without a 12(b)(1) fee of more than 0.25 percent per year.

open-end investment company Mutual fund. Most open-end companies constantly offer new shares for sale and undertake to redeem outstanding shares on any business day at their NAV. Participants can buy and sell shares on any business day, and the size of the fund is usually not limited. Most exchange-traded funds are a variant of the traditional open-end company even though their shares are not individually redeemable.

passive managers Asset managers who invest assets in index portfolios or unmanaged baskets of securities and other instruments without attempting to select individual securities. Some passive managers who made little or no effort to outperform an index in the past now try to improve upon index returns with derivatives and return-enhancement strategies, blurring the line between passive and active managers.

portfolio composition file (PCF) An electronic listing of the securities in an exchange-traded fund creation or redemption unit. ETF market participants use the PCF basket as a proxy for the fund portfolio in intraday pricing calculations and as a list of the securities they need to deposit to create more shares of the ETF or will receive if they redeem ETF shares.

qualified retirement plan A retirement plan established by employers for their employees meeting the requirements of Internal Revenue Code Section 401(a) or 403(a). Plan assets and earnings are not taxed until they are paid out as benefits.

redemption In exchange-traded funds (ETFs) the cancellation of fund shares deposited by an authorized participant in exchange for a basket of the fund's portfolio securities and a balancing cash payment. Mutual fund shares are redeemed at net asset value, usually for cash, when a shareholder's holdings are liquidated.

redemption charge (1) *Back-end load.* Also called *contingent deferred sales charge (CDSC).* (2) A charge imposed on a mutual fund investor for sale of fund shares within a predetermined time period after they were purchased. Also called redemption fee or *contingent redemption fee.*

registration statement Document filed with the SEC to register securities for a public offering.

representative sample Sample in which the relative sizes of subpopulation samples are selected in a manner designed to ensure that the weight of representatives of the subpopulations will be appropriate in the total sample taken. Also called stratified random sampling.

risk budget   Output from one of a number of quantitative models used by asset or liability managers. The models are designed to control the aggregate risk of the asset or liability portfolio and to allocate acceptance of risk in a way that will optimize risk acceptance to give the portfolio the maximum return possible on the risks accepted.

securities and exchange commission (SEC)   The regulatory agency charged with regulation of securities and securities markets in the United States.

Sharpe ratio   A risk-adjusted measure of return that divides a portfolio's return in excess of the riskless return by the portfolio's standard deviation. Because it adjusts return for total portfolio risk, an implicit assumption of the Sharpe ratio is that the portfolio will not be combined with other risky portfolios. It is relevant for performance evaluation when comparing mutually exclusive portfolios. A more recent construct, the M^2 measure, is based on the same principle and gives identical portfolio rankings.

silent index   An index used as a fund template with index changes announced only after the fund has had an opportunity to implement the changes.

simplified employee pension (SEP) plan   A retirement program that offers individual retirement accounts (IRAs) to all eligible employees. The employer and each employee can contribute under rules that are often simpler than the rules of larger qualified plans. Also called *408(k) plan*.

tax-aware portfolio management   A commitment by a portfolio's adviser to exercise a reasonable effort to achieve fund tax efficiency, but less commitment than an investor would expect in a tax-managed fund.

tax loss harvesting   Selling loss positions from a portfolio to eliminate taxable gains. In a separate account or multiple fund portfolio, the investor's total gain and loss position will be considered in deciding what losses to harvest.

tax-managed fund   An open-end mutual fund managed with the objective of minimizing taxes even at the expense of benchmark tracking, diversification, or pretax return.

tracking error   A measure of the difference between the performance of a fund and the performance of its benchmark index. See text box, pp. 137–139.

turnover   (1) As defined by the Securities and Exchange Commission for mutual fund reports, the lesser of securities purchases or sales during the reporting period divided by the average assets of the fund at each month end from the latest month before the period began to the last month end in the period. Securities and other financial instruments with a remaining life of less than one year at the time of acquisition are excluded. This measure substantially understates portfolio activity in many funds. See also *flow*. (2) Traditionally calculated as (Purchases + Sales)/(Beginning Portfolio Value + Ending Portfolio Value). If a portfolio has an average turnover of 50 percent by this measure, approximately half the securities (in a portfolio with modest contributions and withdrawals) are replaced with new positions each year.

unit investment trust (UIT)   An investment company that is organized under a trust indenture or similar instrument, does not have a board of directors, and issues only redeemable securities, each of which represents an undivided interest in a unit of specified securities.

wash sale rule   Under U.S. tax law, wash sales occur when substantially identical stock or other securities are bought within 30 days before or after a sale. Losses realized on wash sales are added to the basis of the reacquired securities, and are not immediately deductible for tax purposes.

NOTES

Introduction

1. This example is suggested by an example in Bogle (1999, 113). John Bogle uses arguments for fund cost cutting similar to some of the arguments in this book. In addition to Bogle, Jane Bryant Quinn (2005) and many others have stressed the importance of reducing fund costs to improve investment results. See, for example, Gluck (2005).
2. There are some simplifying assumptions behind these calculations. For example, I have not assumed any fluctuations in annual returns, and I have ignored any effect of taxes. Joe's investment process is extremely simple. It consists solely of selecting the best available funds—mutual funds or exchange-traded funds—for his tax-deferred retirement accounts and his taxable personal portfolio. Implicitly, any sensible steps Joe takes to maintain a consistent asset allocation may make his rate of return *less* volatile than Pete's. Retirement planning software with a Monte Carlo risk simulation (discussed in Chapter 2) can add the realism of return uncertainty to calculations of this nature.
3. Financial instruments that provided diversification and pooled the investments of numerous small investors were introduced in Amsterdam shortly before the American Revolution, a century and a half before their introduction in the United States. See Rouwenhorst (2004).
4. Palmer (2004) reports that the directors of one small fund have approved an increase in the fund's expense ratio of 6 basis points (0.06 percent) per year to pay for this required compliance function. This compliance requirement will increase the obstacles to entry by new fund managers, reducing competition.
5. Investment Company Institute's *Mutual Fund Fact Book 2004* and web site (www.ici.org). As impressive as it is, this comparison actually understates investor commitment to ETFs by about 20 percent. There is relatively little short selling of mutual funds, but the short interest in ETFs averages about 20 percent of a fund's capitalization. Shares are borrowed from some ETF investors so the short seller can sell them to another investor. This means that ETF positions reflected in investor accounts are about 20 percent greater than the number of shares the

fund has issued. For more information about short selling in ETFs, see the "Exchange-Traded Funds, Short Selling, and the Short Interest" subsection in Chapter 11, p. 209.

Chapter 1   A Framework for Saving and Investment

1. Readers interested in more information on this risk/compound return link should see Gastineau (1988, 310–312), Kritzman (2000, 65–75), and Michaud (1981) for progressively more technical discussions. Other useful volatility discussions are in Wilcox (2001) and Campbell et al. (2001).
2. See, for example, Palmeri (2005), which describes California governor Arnold Schwarzenegger's plan to end guaranteed annual pensions for state and local government employees hired after June 2007.
3. Other notable software offerings are available from Fidelity Investments and the Society of Actuaries. The latter's Retirement Probability Analyzer software at www.soa.org focuses on applications for life annuities.

Chapter 2   Assets, Liabilities, and Financial Planning

1. STRIPS is an acronym for Separately Traded Registered Interest and Principal Securities. Zero-coupon notes and bonds are created by trading note and bond coupon and principal payments stripped from Treasury securities.
2. The effect of the asset/liability mismatch on the valuation of securities illustrated by the Ryan ALM, Inc. asset/liability return data in Exhibit 2.1 can have a substantial effect on economic and investment cycles. The magnitude of this effect has not been studied as thoroughly as it should be.
3. See also Staub (2004) and Kritzman and Page (2004) for further discussions of the relative value of spending time on asset allocation.
4. The appropriateness of adopting a more conservative portfolio at retirement is considered in more detail in the "Changing Asset Allocation at Retirement" subsection in Chapter 3.
5. See Fuerbringer (2004) for evidence of the growing performance correlations among international equity markets.

Chapter 3   Tax-Efficient Financial Planning and Investing

1. A fund that experiences net redemptions can be forced to make large capital gains distributions. Along this line, Dickson and Shoven (1993) show that a fund's after-tax performance ranking can change dramatically from its pretax ranking.

2. Subchapter M, Section 852(b)(6) of the Internal Revenue Code (1986).
3. Conventional funds have another tool, called equalization, which offers some protection from capital gains distributions caused by the sale of appreciated securities to meet redemptions. Equalization is generally less effective than in-kind redemption.
4. Dickson, Shoven, and Sialm (2000) describe some of the more sophisticated tax-deferral techniques used by the more tax-aware conventional funds. It is worth noting that these funds seek only to maximize deferral, not to avoid all capital gains distributions. Avoiding all capital gains distributions is a reasonable objective for an ETF manager.
5. The adjustment does not incorporate new money invested in the SPDR in the last quarter of 2004 or the effect of redemptions during that quarter.
6. Morningstar reports a figure that it calls "potential capital gains exposure" as a secondary measure of tax exposure under the Tax Analysis tab of its basic fund reports (accessible by entering the fund's ticker symbol and clicking on Quotes/Reports). This figure is defined as "the percentage of a fund's total assets that would be subject to taxation if the fund were to liquidate today." This is identical to the definition of capital gains overhang. In the third quarter of 2004, Morningstar reported this as "0" as of the 12/31/03 statement for the Vanguard 500 Investor Shares and Admiral Shares—in contrast to the correct figure of 17.76 percent. E-mail messages pointing out this error did not persuade Morningstar to make an appropriate correction. In February 2005, before the data were updated for the 12/31/04 Vanguard annual report, Morningstar showed the Vanguard 500's potential capital gains exposure as 3 percent. In March, after updating for Vanguard's 12/31/04 annual report, Morningstar reported potential capital gains exposure as 4 percent for the Vanguard 500. Errors in Morningstar data are not uncommon, as its recent contretemps with the Securities and Exchange Commission (SEC) (Urbanowicz 2004) indicates. See also Stein (2005).
7. See Gastineau (2002b) and Chapter 6, pp. 122–129, "Recognition of Index Fund Transaction Costs."
8. Cross-border mergers, which seem more likely in the future than in the past, could also increase S&P 500 index turnover.
9. Barclay, Pearson, and Weisbach (1998) offer evidence that fund managers intentionally realize and distribute some capital gains to avoid a capital gains overhang that will exceed 30 to 40 percent and discourage new investment by taxable investors. The Vanguard 500 could support a higher capital gains overhang than 30 to 40 percent, at least temporarily. In contrast to the estimates by Barclay, Pearson, and Weisbach, Vanguard will probably attempt to defer capital gains distributions as long as possible.

10. See note 6 infra with respect to Morningstar's tax evaluation. Lipper's tax efficiency ratings are also based on the SEC after-tax return calculation; see Lipper (2002). Another aspect of tax efficiency in Vanguard index funds concerns Vanguard's VIPERs ETF share classes. This is as much an index fund fee issue as a tax issue, so it is covered in Chapter 6, pp. 142–145.

11. The step-up of basis at death is currently scheduled to expire in 2010 and to be reinstated in 2011.

12. I ignore the complications introduced by the estate's option to base estate taxation on values from a later date.

13. Most investors (as a percentage of the population) hold most of the liquid financial asset positions they plan to use to meet long-term investment goals in tax-deferred retirement and educational savings accounts. However, most long-term financial *assets* are held by a smaller number of investors who have accumulated substantially more wealth than contribution limits permit them to accumulate in tax-deferred accounts. To state this another way, wealthy investors usually have a larger fraction of their wealth in taxable accounts.

14. I discuss the highly attractive but typically small Roth IRA accounts later in this chapter. I exclude variable annuities (VAs) which have been declining in popularity from the discussion because ETFs are more useful and attractive than variable annuities for nearly all investors who have used VAs in the past.

15. The paper won the 2004 TIAA-CREF Paul A. Samuelson Award for Outstanding Scholarly Writing on Lifelong Financial Security.

16. I follow the common practice, also followed by DSZ (2004), of distinguishing only between fixed-income holdings and equity holdings in evaluating what goes where. This choice reflects the major tax distinctions.

17. Before age 59½.

18. Porter and Garland (2005) is a comprehensive review of these funds.

19. Watson Wyatt (2004). The return calculations in this study are only approximate because of data limitations, but there is no reason to believe the results are materially distorted.

20. See, for example, Brown and Oster (2004) and Oster and Damato (2004).

21. Updegrave (2004, pp. 78–79) illustrates the range of costs and features in 401(k) plans.

22. Every investor should thoroughly understand the magic of compound interest in building assets. The Joe and Pete example I have used only scratches the surface. Excellent discussions of compound returns are available, in increasing order of complexity in Wagner and Winnikoff (2001); Bogle (1999, 2001a, 2001b); and Kritzman (2000).

23. Naming a charity as the secondary beneficiary (after your spouse) of a 401(k) or non-Roth IRA is an increasingly popular way to make a relatively tax-efficient charitable bequest.
24. The on-and-off character of the scheduled estate tax changes has led most estate planners to assume that the changes will expire after 2011 and that estate planning will still be necessary along pre-2003 lines.
25. Welch (2001), Gordon (2001), and Stein et al. (2000) do an excellent job of summarizing the options open to an investor whose portfolio is dominated by a large position that carries a tax penalty or other impediment to diversification. Some of these options were foreclosed by tax reform legislation in 2003, but there are usually new ones available after each tax law change.

Chapter 4 Controlling Investment Costs

1. Commissions are, theoretically at least, negotiable—though I am not aware of any retail investor who has actually negotiated commission rates recently. Unless you are a day trader, commission differences among firms will rarely determine your choice of a broker. Brokerage firms advertise free trades and low trading commissions, but when you analyze how your brokerage firm gets paid, you will realize that shopping for lower commissions among discount brokers rarely makes economic sense unless you are doing hundreds of trades per year.
2. Lucchetti (2005) describes a warning the New York Stock Exchange has issued to its members that better disclosure of interest rates on cash balances in brokerage accounts is necessary.
3. This rebate will be taxable income to the investor unless it is rebated to a tax-deferred account. A better strategy for E*Trade or one of its competitors might be to offer financial planning or other services to supermarket accounts rather than a cash rebate. See: https://us.etrade.com/e/t/invest/mfstatic?gxml=mfrefunder_jump3.html&rightrail=disable.
4. Statman (2004) describes the cost and value of adding diversification with a low-cost fund, and Chapter 6 discusses index fund selection.
5. This kind of optimization usually bears only a superficial resemblance to other types of portfolio optimization.

Chapter 5 How to Cut Your Fund Costs

1. The fund adviser may also pay some marketing expenses out of its management fee.

2. Vanguard offers expense ratios as low as 7 basis points (0.07 percent) on its VIPERs ETF share classes, but these are not full substitutes for pure ETFs in taxable accounts. See "Fidelity, Vanguard, and the Great Index Fund Price War" in Chapter 6.

3. The largest variable cost element for most ETFs is the index licensing fee. For most ETFs, this will be close to the minimum shareholder accounting costs for a conventional mutual fund.

4. An interesting exception is the Sector SPDR Trust, which has experienced a small but steady decline in its fund's expense ratios as assets have grown.

5. A footnote from a Fidelity ad that appeared in the *Wall Street Journal*, October 26, 2004, page A5, reads, "The Industry Average Expense Ratio, calculated by Fidelity, represents the median total expense ratio of no-load or front-end load index funds that are in the same Morningstar fund categories as each of the Fidelity Spartan Index Funds listed. We excluded certain funds from this calculation if they had a back-end sales load, expenses exceeding 1.50 percent, and/or initial minimum investments of $250,000 or more. Although Fidelity has reviewed this data for accuracy, it does not guarantee that the information is accurate or complete or that Fidelity retail index funds will continue to have the lowest expense ratios among a comparison universe. Morningstar Data is as of 9/30/04." This methodology led to industry average expense ratios of 36 to 66 basis points for four fund categories.

6. Most fund management companies are parts of asset management divisions of diversified financial companies or else they are privately held. In either case, meaningful cost and profit information is hard to find.

7. See Whitehouse (2004) and Standard & Poor's (2004) for more information.

8. Schwartz and Francioni (2004). Other estimates—Karceski, Livingston, and O'Neal (2004); Bessembinder (2003); Domowitz, Glen, and Madhavan (2001); Keim (2003); Keim and Madhavan (1997 and 1998) (a survey article); and Peterson and Sirri (2003)—often show lower trading costs. The data used in these other studies comes from the period before price quotes were in pennies and do not adequately reflect the increased cost of institutional trading in more recent years.

9. See Form N-SAR, U.S. Securities and Exchange Commission, at www.sec.gov/about/forms/formn-sar.pdf. The definition of turnover in the document is:

   The rate of portfolio turnover shall be calculated by dividing (a) the lesser of purchases or sales of portfolio securities for the reporting period by (b) the monthly average of the value of the portfolio securities owned by the registrant during the reporting period. This monthly average shall be calculated by totaling the market values of the portfolio securities as of the beginning and end of the first month of the reporting period plus 1. A money market fund should enter a portfolio turnover rate of "0" even if it owns securities that have maturities in excess of one year.

Sub-items 71A and B should be rounded to zero, if appropriate; however, unless A or B is a true zero, rather than a rounded zero, sub-item 71D should have an answer greater than zero.

For purposes of this item, there shall be excluded from both the numerator and denominator all securities, including options, whose maturity or expiration date at the time of acquisitions were one year or less. All long-term U.S. Government securities should be included. Purchases shall include any cash paid upon the conversion of one portfolio security into another. Purchases shall also include the cost of rights or warrants purchased.

Sales shall include any cash proceeds from the sale of rights or warrants, or other dispositions such as tender offers. Sales shall also include the proceeds of portfolio securities which have been called, or for which payment has been made through redemption or maturity.

If, during the reporting period, the registrant acquired the assets of another investment company or of a personal holding company in exchange for its own shares, it shall exclude from purchases the value of securities so acquired and from sales, all sales of such securities made following a purchase-of-assets transaction to realign the registrant's portfolio. In such event, the registrant shall also make appropriate adjustment in the denominator of the portfolio turnover computation.

Short sales which the registrant intends to maintain for more than one year and put and call options where the expiration date is more than one year from the date of acquisition should be included in purchases and sales for purposes of this item. The proceeds from a short sale should be included in the value of the portfolio securities which the registrant sold during the reporting period and the cost of covering a short sale should be included in the value of the portfolio securities which the registrant purchased during the period. The premiums paid to purchase options should be included in the value of the portfolio securities which the registrant purchased during the reporting period and the premiums received from the sale of options should be included in the value of the portfolio securities which the registrant sold during the period.

10. One would think that futures contracts, which are widely used to adjust fund investment exposures, should be considered in calculating portfolio turnover.

11. The definition of turnover was obviously designed to show a portfolio manager's or index publisher's impact on portfolio changes after somewhat canceling out the effects of net fund share sales or purchases and net portfolio appreciation or depreciation.

12. Chalmers, Edelen, and Kadlec (2001a) found turnover to be a poor indicator of both fund transaction costs and fund returns. Exhibit 5.4 indicates that turnover provided no clue to the rate of flow (fund share) trading in some of the funds used by market timers. See also text pp. 101–110.

13. The extensive literature on the cost to ongoing shareholders of providing free liquidity to ongoing shareholders includes Chalmers, Edelen, and Kadlec (2001a and b); Edelen (1999); Gastineau (2004c); Goetzmann, Ivkovic, and Rouwenhorst (2001); Greene and Hodges (2002); and Zitzewitz (2003).

14. Hulbert (2003) and Keim (2003) discuss the challenge of earning a profit as a momentum trader. Under most circumstances, momentum traders must buy into a rising market and sell into a declining market, accepting the prices they find. If the momentum occurs near a market close, as it often does, mutual funds offer free liquidity to traders at the expense of their ongoing shareholders and the momentum trader gets the benefit of stale prices.

15. The Securities and Exchange Commission implemented requirements for quarterly portfolio reporting in 2004.

16. See Cassidy (2005). This paper illustrates the kind of analysis that is possible with a comprehensive and accurate database.

17. Edelen (1999) found, as we might expect, that cash *inflows* were the most costly fund share transactions because it is usually easiest for a timer to buy fund shares to capture positive market momentum.

18. If a fund service calculated flow, it would probably use the average of the fund's monthly shares outstanding, but the difference is likely to be small.

19. Chalmers, Edelen, and Kadlec (2001a) discussed some of the differences in trading costs by fund type. My estimates in this paragraph are not necessarily consistent with theirs, which do not fully reflect market impact effects. These estimates are not greatly different from the Plexus Group transaction cost estimates cited earlier, considering that the fund's trade is involuntary.

20. Johnson suggests that because different types of shareholders impose statistically different costs on a fund, they might be charged different fees when they enter and/or leave a fund (Hoffman 2004). The problem with this characterization, which some fund companies use to screen for market timers, is that the discrimination is imperfect and even long-term holders can impose inappropriate costs on their fellow shareholders when they enter or leave a fund.

21. For additional discussion of this solution, see Gastineau (2004d).
22. A fund accepting new investments.
23. Different times would be used on days with early market closings.
24. There are a few funds that are designed for use by traders that may not need a redemption fee. If you are a long-term investor you will not be looking at these funds anyway.
25. If you doubt the SEC web site can be this daunting, see Baldwin (2004) and Tyson (2004, 342). Tyson (2004) suggests www.freeedgar .com as a more user-friendly source than the SEC. Unfortunately, FreeEDGAR has been replaced with EDGAR Online Pro, which costs $1,200 per year after a one-week free trial.

Chapter 6   Reducing Costs with Index Funds

1. For example, Peter Bernstein (1956 and 1992); Bogle (1999 and 2001a); Ellis (1975, 1995, and 2002); Malkiel (1973 and later editions); Sharpe (1991); and Wagner and Winnikoff (2001).
2. References to some of the less attractive features of indexing and index funds include Peter Bernstein (2003); William Bernstein (2004); Blake (2002); Blume and Edelen (2002, 2003, and 2004); Chen, Noronha, and Singal (2004); Elton, Gruber, and Busse (2004); Garnick, Davi, Kim, and Lotufo (2001); Gastineau (2002a, b, c, and d); Lazzara (2002); Madhavan (2002); Plexus Group (2001); and Quinn and Wang (2003).
3. Cost reduction has been an important force behind many financial market innovations. Derivatives, for example, have grown primarily because they often reduce trading or carrying costs or taxes.
4. See Jacques (1988) and hundreds of articles and brokerage firm reports published since.
5. This estimate apparently originated with Charles Ellis's firm, Greenwich Associates.
6. See, for example, Chapter 6 of Gastineau (2002c), including the endnotes; Blake (2002); and Madhavan (2002).
7. See, for example, Bogle (1999, 134) and Blume and Edelen (2003 and 2004).
8. Chen, Noronha, and Singal (2004) conservatively estimate the annual cost of these index changes at $3.75 billion to $6.0 billion for S&P 500 and Russell 2000 investors. They found it difficult to isolate the effect of some index changes and, consequently, do not include the effect of all index changes in their summary calculation of the embedded transaction costs.
9. See Sinquefield (1991) for an excellent discussion of the advantages of patient trading.
10. See, for example, Garnick et al. (2001).

11. The index membership effect attributes a rise or fall in a stock's price around the time it is added to or removed from an index to various changes in demand and research coverage associated with index membership.
12. See also the discussion of probable future tax inefficiency in the Vanguard 500 Index Fund on pp. 44–48.
13. See, for example, Plexus Group (2001), which measures average price changes relative to preannouncement prices or effective membership prices.
14. Chen, Noronha, and Singal (2004) use a different methodology and reach a lower estimate, particularly for the S&P 500, but they still conclude that index composition changes are costly to investors in S&P 500 and Russell 2000 portfolios.
15. A capitalization-weighted index assigns each stock a percentage share in the portfolio equal to the value of the company's common stock divided by the total value of all the stocks in the index.
16. A float-weighted index is like a capitalization-weighted index except all the capitalizations are reduced by excluding shares that are not free to trade.
17. If the index is based on published rules, anyone with the rules and appropriate data can determine changes as soon as anyone else. If the index is managed by a committee, knowledgeable outsiders should be as able to anticipate changes as readily as the fund manager. Fund shareholders are appropriately protected only if the fund manager can trade before an index change is public knowledge.
18. There are numerous examples of such funds among the iShares MSCI country funds and iShares Dow Jones and Vanguard VIPERs sector funds.
19. Proposed changes might relax some of the diversification restrictions on UCITS index funds.
20. The current 10 basis point fee in the international fund will be in effect indefinitely.
21. Few 401(k) accounts can use ETFs shares today, but that is changing and will continue to change gradually over time. IRA accounts can use ETFs.
22. This conversion can go only one way. You cannot convert back to conventional shares. The prospectus indicates that the conversion is not taxable except for any sale of fractional shares that cannot be converted to VIPERs.
23. The only VIPERs that might be candidates for a fee increase are the funds with higher fees for Admiral Shares. Vanguard's intentions on Admiral Shares fees should be clear by the end of 2005.
24. I would expect the Fidelity index funds to be managed about as well as Vanguard's.

25. As a very broad generalization, the MSCI indexes will tend to have better relative returns when large-cap stocks do well and worse relative returns when small-cap stocks do well.
26. Source: Vanguard fund reports and the American Stock Exchange.
27. The fund redeemed out $144 million in net capital gains in 2004, but some of these came from redemptions of other share classes. See the discussion of in-kind redemption by the Vanguard 500 fund in Chapter 3, p. 46.
28. Relative to the size of their stock universe.
29. The extra costs include various custody and tax charges in both conventional and ETF shares.
30. Some of the additional cross-border ETF costs will be reflected in the bid-asked spread on the shares, rather than in the expense ratio.
31. The fact that ETFs trade throughout the trading day does not have an adverse effect on ongoing ETF investors. The advantage of early cutoff for notification of ETF creation and redemption is a negligible issue for index ETFs. It will be a bigger issue for actively managed ETFs.

Chapter 7 Fund Advisory Services—or Do-It-Yourself?

1. Investors FastTrack (www.fasttrack.net) offers accurate but limited data at low cost.
2. See also an interview with Sharpe in Picerno (2004).
3. Some other systems (e.g., Ibbotson) apparently do this as well. I have not undertaken an exhaustive search.
4. Morningstar Associates (2004, 3) indicates that Advice Online breaks fund composition down on the basis of how portfolio positions fall into the Morningstar style boxes, not on the full range of individual stock characteristics.
5. Roseen (2004) mentions a closely related concept, tax overhang, that includes undistributed investment income, but Lipper evaluates a fund's tax efficiency on the basis of the SEC calculations.
6. For example, Mazzilli, Kittsley, and Maister (2005).
7. For example, reports from Dennis Emanuel, Frank Sileo, Joy Chiu, and Julie Denisenko of Citigroup–Smith Barney. Many other firms also publish excellent closed-end fund reports.
8. See Lipper (2002) for Lipper's methodology.
9. Buying a fund with a star manager may be comforting, but a record compiled running a small fund is hard to maintain with a fund 10 or 20 times as large. This topic will come up again in Chapters 9 and 10.
10. Many fund companies will cap a high-performance fund or close it to new investors and immediately open a cloned fund using the same

investment process and some or all of the same staff to take in new money. The rationality of this cloning process escapes me because it circumvents the value of capping the original fund.
11. All currently offered ETFs are index funds.

Chapter 8   Some Winning Funds—and Why They Win

1. The list does not include style (growth and value) funds, single country funds, high-dividend equity funds, and other specialty funds. Some of these omitted funds may be useful to specific investors but the funds now available in these categories are not essential or even useful building blocks for *most* portfolios.
2. See the discussion of Fidelity's fee cuts in "Fidelity, Vanguard, and the Great Index Fund Price War" in Chapter 6 (pp. 142–145).
3. Redemption fees are not the best way to protect conventional fund investors from market timers, but they are essential if better solutions like an early order cutoff are politically impractical.

Chapter 9   Active Investment Management

1. See text box "Evaluating the Performance of an Investment Manager" in Chapter 6 (pp. 137–139) for a sensible definition.
2. The best explanation of this path to success is Charles Ellis's "The Loser's Game," (1975 and 1995) or Ellis (2002), Chapters 1 and 2.
3. FAME Research Prize 2003, International Center for Financial Asset Management and Engineering, Geneva, Switzerland. The Berk and Green quotations in subsequent paragraphs are from an earlier version of this paper dated December 9, 2002. The earlier version, which was distributed as a National Bureau of Economic Research working paper, is more reader-friendly than the final version, but there are no substantive differences.
4. Not all of the citations attribute this cash flow to the star ratings. Many see the stars as no more than a label that relieves some investors from the need to inquire deeply into recent relative performance.
5. Thus, the Berk and Green model provides an explanation of the observed stability of fees per dollar managed as a fund's assets under management increase.
6. Affirming the Berk and Green model, Stein (2004) attributes the popularity of the open-end mutual fund structure among investment managers to the fact that assets can pour in rapidly when the fund performs well—increasing income for the managers. Other papers with findings that support the Berk and Green thesis include Chen, Hong, Huang, and Kubik (2004) and Clark (2004a).

ffffgg faffafsfafdf

Chapter 10 Reinventing the Mutual Fund

1. Several of the proposals in the chapter were first suggested in Gastineau and Lazzara (2004).
2. I discussed the issue of early cutoff times for fund share trading extensively in Gastineau (2004c).
3. Bernstein (2004) and Stein (2004) address the interaction of fund structure with fund size, growth, open-endedness and performance from different perspectives. Both stress the often dysfunctional effect of the totally open-end fund structure on performance. Chen, Hong, Huang, and Kubik (2004) find significantly better performance in small funds that hold small cap stocks. The Berk and Green model is not the only evidence that keeping the fund small can lead to better performance. Of course, a fund which is capped may be small for different reasons than the funds studied by Chen et al. Hechinger (2005) describes plans by several very large fund managers to create separate investment units to broaden and segment the coverage of their research and portfolio management.
4. Examples of this information leakage include trades done for institutional accounts where trustees, consultants, and others learn of trades almost immediately and separately managed accounts (SMAs) for individual investors where advance notice of trades is widely dispersed before execution.
5. Tax consequences will rarely matter because most such exchanges will occur in connection with the purchase or sale of the fund shares.
6. See, for example, Porter (2004a and b).

Chapter 11 Improving the Efficiency of Custom Investment Management

1. What most investment managers call risk budgeting is often called core-satellite management, particularly in ETF implementations. See the "Risk Budgeting" text box in Chapter 9.
2. See Gastineau (2002b). Other observations along this line include Blume and Edelen (2002 and 2003) and Quinn and Wang (2003).
3. Under the uptick rule, securities listed on a U.S. national securities exchange cannot be sold short unless the last trade at a different price prior to the short sale was at a price lower than the price at which the short sale is executed.
4. For more information on short selling, see Fabozzi (2004).
5. The data in Exhibit 11.6 is based on the S&P 500 and the GICS sectors because that is what most analysts use. Mazzilli, Kittsley, and Maister (2004a), for example, make their ETF sector recommendations based on GICS sector compositions.

6. For a more detailed description of regulated investment company diversification requirements, see Gastineau (2002c, 138–144).
7. Because several of the Dow Jones sector indexes are not constructed to be RIC diversification compliant, the *index* data in Exhibit 11.3 *overstate* the likely volatility of the iShares sector *funds*, some of which will have smaller positions in some of their larger-capitalization stocks and, hence, more diversification and lower volatility than their indexes. The Sector SPDR indexes already reflect the smaller positions in some large-capitalization stocks necessary to achieve RIC diversification compliance in the funds. The Sector SPDRs are the only sector family with all RIC-compliant indexes and, hence, the only family where tracking error should always be a clear indication of manager performance.
8. For an explanation of the factors affecting ETF trading and trading costs, see Gastineau (2002c, 219–259).

Appendix B Conventional Mutual Funds versus Exchange-Traded Funds

1. It is *not* impossible for an ETF manager to abuse shareholders. Reasonable vigilance by shareholders and regulators will always be necessary.
2. Selling ETF shares short is not an appropriate trade for a small investor because borrowing a small number of shares of any security to sell short is often impractical.
3. Reports sent to shareholders do not have to provide as much detail on holdings as the SEC filings.
4. Desirable changes in investment management structure for actively managed ETFs are discussed at length in Chapter 10.

REFERENCES

Armstrong, David. 2004. "A New Way to Rate Mutual Funds." *Wall Street Journal* (December 23): D1.

Arnott, Robert D., Jason Hsu, and Philip Moore. 2005. "Fundamental Indexation." *Financial Analysts Journal* (March/April): 83–99.

Baer, Gregory A., and Gary Gensler. 2002. *The Great Mutual Fund Trap.* New York: Broadway Books.

Baldwin, William. 2004. "Peekaboo." *Forbes* (September 20): 26.

Barclay, Michael J., Neil D. Pearson, and Michael S. Weisbach. 1998. "Open-End Mutual Funds and Capital-Gains Taxes." *Journal of Financial Economics* 49: 3–43.

Berk, Jonathan B., and Richard C. Green. 2004. "Mutual Fund Flows and Performance in Rational Markets." *Journal of Political Economy* 112, no. 6 (December): 1269–1295; www.journals.uchicago.edu/JPE/journal /contents/v112n6.html. An earlier version (December 2002) was published as an NBER working paper, http://papers.ssrn.com/sol3/papers .cfm?abstract_id=338881.

Bernstein, Peter L. 1956. "Growth Companies vs. Growth Stocks." *Harvard Business Review* (September–October). Reprinted in *Classics: An Investor's Anthology*, ed. Charles D. Ellis and James R. Vertin, Homewood, IL: Business One Review Association for Investment Management and Research, 1989, 192–214.

Bernstein, Peter L. 1992. *Capital Ideas.* New York: Free Press.

Bernstein, Peter L. 2003. "Points of Inflection: Investment Management Tomorrow." *Financial Analysts Journal* (July/August): 18–23.

Bernstein, Peter L. 2004. "What's It All About, Alpha?" *Institutional Investor* (May): 48–52.

Bernstein, William J. 2004. "It's the Execution, Stupid." *Efficient Frontier* (Winter); www.efficientfrontier.com/ef/104/stupid.htm.

Bessembinder, Hendrik. 2003. "Issues in Assessing Trade Execution Costs." *Journal of Financial Markets* 6: 233–257.

Blake, Rich. 2002. "Is Time Running Out for the S&P 500?" *Institutional Investor* (May): 52–64.

Blume, Marshall E. 1998. "An Anatomy of Morningstar Ratings." *Financial Analysts Journal* (March/April): 19–27.

Blume, Marshall E., and Roger M. Edelen. 2002. "On Replicating the S&P 500 Index." Working Paper, The Wharton School, University of Pennsylvania, http://finance.wharton.upenn.edu/~edelen/PDFs/BE_050902.pdf.

Blume, Marshall E., and Roger M. Edelen. 2003. "S&P 500 Indexers, Delegation Costs and Liquidity Mechanisms." Working Paper, The Wharton School, University of Pennsylvania, http://finance.wharton.upenn.edu/~rlwctr/papers/0304.pdf.

Blume, Marshall E., and Roger M. Edelen. 2004. "S&P 500 Indexers, Tracking Error, and Liquidity." *Journal of Portfolio Management* (Spring): 37–46.

Bogle, John C. 1999. *Common Sense on Mutual Funds*. New York: John Wiley & Sons.

Bogle, John C. 2001a. *John Bogle on Investing—The First 50 Years*. New York: McGraw-Hill.

Bogle, John C. 2001b. "The Twelve Pillars of Wisdom." Speech given to the Arizona Republic Investment Strategies Forum, Phoenix, Arizona, April 27; www.vanguard.com/bogle_site/april272001.html.

Bollen, N. P. B., and J. A. Busse. 2005. "Short-Term Persistence in Mutual Fund Performance." *Review of Financial Studies*. Forthcoming.

Brenner, Lynn. 1997. *Smart Questions to Ask Your Financial Advisers*. Princeton, NJ: Bloomberg.

Brenner, Lynn. 2001. "The Right Advice." *Bloomberg Personal Finance* (September): 64–71.

Brinson, Gary P., L. Randolph Hood, and Gilbert L. Beebower. 1986. "Determinants of Portfolio Performance." *Financial Analysts Journal* (July/August): 39–48.

Brinson, Gary P., Brian D. Singer, and Gilbert L. Beebower. 1991. "Determinants of Portfolio Performance II: An Update." *Financial Analysts Journal* (May/June): 40–48.

Brown, Ken, and Christopher Oster. 2004. "As Returns Sag, Employers Turn Up Heat on 401(k) Fees." *Wall Street Journal* (September 14): A1, A12.

Brown, Stephen J., William N. Goetzmann, and Stephen A. Ross. 1995. "Survival." *Journal of Finance* 50, no. 3: 853–873.

Campbell, John Y., Martin Lettau, Burton G. Malkiel and Yexiao Xu. 2001. "Have Individual Stocks Become More Volatile? An Empirical Exploration of Idiosyncratic Risk." The *Journal of Finance* (February): 1–43.

Carhart, Mark M. 1997. "On Persistence in Mutual Fund Performance," *Journal of Finance* (March): 57–82.

Carhart, M., J. N. Carpenter, A. W. Lynch, and D. K. Musto. 2002. "Mutual Fund Survivorship." *Review of Financial Studies* 15: 1439–1463.

Cassidy, Donald. 2005. "Observations on Frequent Trading at Mutual Funds." *Lipper Fund Industry Insight Report* (January 3); www.research.lipper.wallst.com/fundIndustryOverview.asp.

Chalmers, John M. R., Roger M. Edelen, and Gregory B. Kadlec. 2001a. "Fund Returns and Trading Expenses: Evidence on the Value of Active Fund Management." Working Paper (October 15).

Chalmers, John M. R., Roger M. Edelen, and Gregory B. Kadlec. 2001b. "On the Perils of Financial Intermediaries Setting Security Prices: The Mutual Fund Wild Card Option." *Journal of Finance* 56, no. 6 (December): 2209–2236.

Chen, Honghui, Gregory Noronha, and Vijay Singal. 2004. "Pre-announced Index Changes and Losses to Investors in S&P 500 and Russell 2000 Index Funds." Unpublished Working Paper (May).

Chen, Joseph, Harrison Hong, Ming Huang, and Jeffrey Kubik. 2004. "Does Fund Size Erode Performance? Liquidity, Organizational Diseconomies and Active Money Management." Working Paper (May) (forthcoming in the *American Economic Review*); www-rcf.usc.edu/~josephsc/files /fundsize.pdf.

Chevalier, Judith, and Glenn Ellison. 1997. "Risk Taking by Mutual Funds as a Response to Incentives." *Journal of Political Economy* (December).

Chevalier, Judith, and Glenn Ellison. 1999. "Are Some Mutual Fund Managers Better Than Others?" *Journal of Finance* (June): 875–899.

Clark, Andrew. 2004a. "For Benchmark-Beating Funds, Does Fund Size Affect Performance?" Lipper Research Study (January 5); www.research .lipper.wallst.com/researchStudiesOverview.asp.

Clark, Andrew. 2004b. "How Well Do Expenses and Net Returns Predict Future Performance?" Lipper Research Study (May 3); www.research .lipper.wallst.com/researchStudiesOverview.asp.

Clowes, Mike. 2004. "The Long Road to Extinction." *Pensions & Investments* (August 9): 10.

Dale, Arden. 2005. "For Morningstar, the Light Is Harsh," *Wall Street Journal* (January 5): C-13.

Damato, Karen. 2004. "All I Want for Christmas: A Change in Taxes." *Wall Street Journal* (December 17): C1, C13.

Dammon, Robert M., Chester S. Spatt, and Harold H. Zhang. 2004. "Optimal Asset Location and Allocation with Taxable and Tax-Deferred Investing." *Journal of Finance* (June): 999–1037.

Dickson, Joel M., and John B. Shoven. 1993. "Ranking Mutual Funds on an After-Tax Basis." Center for Economic Policy Research, Publication No. 344, Stanford University.

Dickson, Joel M., John B. Shoven, and Clemens Sialm. 2000. "Tax Externalities of Equity Mutual Funds." *National Tax Journal* 53, no. 3, pt. 2 (September).

Domowitz, Ian, Jack Glen, and Ananth Madhavan. 2001. "Global Equity Trading Costs." ITG White Paper (May 8); www.itginc.com/research /whitepapers/domowitz/globaleqcost.pdf.

Edelen, Roger M. 1999. "Investor Flows and the Assessed Performance of Open-End Mutual Funds." *Journal of Financial Economics* 53: 439–466.

Ellis, Charles D. 1975. "The Loser's Game." *Financial Analysts Journal* (July/August): 19–26. Reprinted in *Financial Analysts Journal* (January/February 1995): 95–100. Also reprinted in *Classics: An Investor's Anthology*, ed. Charles D. Ellis and James R. Vertin, Association for Investment Management and Research, Homewood, IL: Business One Irwin, 1989, 524–535.

Ellis, Charles D. 2002. *Winning the Loser's Game*. New York: McGraw-Hill.

Elton, Edwin J., Martin J. Gruber, and Christopher R. Blake. 1996. "Survivorship Bias and Mutual Fund Performance." *Review of Financial Studies* 9, no. 4 (Winter): 1097–1120.

Elton, Edwin J., Martin J. Gruber, and Jeffrey A. Busse. 2004. "Are Investors Rational? Choices among Index Funds." *Journal of Finance* (February): 261–288.

Elton, Edwin J., Martin J. Gruber, Sanjiv Das, and Matthew Hlavka. 1993. "Efficiency with Costly Information: A Reinterpretation of Evidence from Managed Portfolios." *Review of Financial Studies* (January): 1–22.

E*Trade Financial. 2004. Get the Facts, 12b-1 Fees, Getting Started/Research/Mutual Funds/ETFs/Automatic Investing; https://us.etrade.com/e/t/invest/mfstatic?gxml=mfrefunder_jump3.html&rightrail=disable.

Fabozzi, Frank J. 2004. *Short Selling; Strategies, Risks and Rewards*, Hoboken, NJ: John Wiley & Sons.

Fidelity Investments. n.d. "Planning for Retirement Income." http://personal.fidelity.com/retirement/index.html?refhp=pr.

Fuerbringer, Jonathan. 2004. "Investors Look Abroad, but Not for the Usual Reason." *New York Times* (December 12): sec. 3, 8.

Gabriel, Fred. 2004. "Is Fidelity's Plan to Cut Index Fees a Bid to Steal Investors from Vanguard?" *Investment News* (September 6): 2, 28.

Garnick, Diane M., John Davi, Steve Kim, and Silvio Lotufo. 2001. "Index Dynamics: S&P Turnover Accelerated in Y2K." Merrill Lynch (January 11).

Gastineau, Gary L. 1988. *The Options Manual*. New York: McGraw-Hill.

Gastineau, Gary L. 2002a. "Comments on SEC Concept Release: Actively Managed Exchange-Traded Funds." S7 20-01 (January 14); www.sec.gov/rules/concept/s72001/gastineau1.htm.

Gastineau, Gary L. 2002b. "Equity Index Funds Have Lost Their Way." *Journal of Portfolio Management* (Winter): 55–64.

Gastineau, Gary L. 2002c. *The Exchange-Traded Funds Manual*. John Wiley & Sons.

Gastineau, Gary L. 2002d. "Silence Is Golden." *Journal of Indexes* (Second Quarter): 8–13.

Gastineau, Gary L. 2004a. "The Benchmark Index ETF Performance Problem: A Simple Solution." *Journal of Portfolio Management* (Winter): 96–103. Also reprinted in "An Investor's Guide to ETFs and Tradable Index Products," *Institutional Investor* (Fall 2004): 62–70; www.etfconsultants.com/Benchmark_Index_ETF_Problem_ JPM.pdf.

Gastineau, Gary L. 2004b. "An Exchange-Traded Fund or a Conventional Fund—You Can't Really Have It Both Ways." *Journal of Indexes* (First Quarter): 32–34. Also appears online at www.etfconsultants.com /ETF_or_Conventional_Fund_ JOI.pdf.

Gastineau, Gary L. 2004c. "Protecting Fund Shareholders from Costly Share Trading." *Financial Analysts Journal* (May/June): 22–32; www.etf consultants.com/Protecting%20Fund%20Shareholders%20FAJ.pdf.

Gastineau, Gary L., and Mark P. Kritzman. 1999. *Dictionary of Financial Risk Management.* John Wiley & Sons. Also accessible online at www.amex.com/dictionary/frinit.html.

Gastineau, Gary L., and Craig J. Lazzara. 2004. "Reinventing the Investment Fund." In *The Investment Think Tank: Theory, Strategy, and Practice for Advisers,* ed. Harold Evensky and Deena Katz, Princeton, NJ: Bloomberg Press, 153–178. Also appeared in *Bloomberg Wealth Manager* under the title of "Extreme Makeover" (November 2004): 57–68.

Gluck, Andrew. 2005. "Why Investing Costs Matter." *Investment Advisor* (March): 37–40.

Goetzmann, William N., Zoran Ivkovic, and K. Geert Rouwenhorst. 2001. "Day Trading International Mutual Funds: Evidence and Policy Solutions." *Journal of Financial and Quantitative Analysis* 36, no. 3 (September): 287–309.

Gollier, Christian. 2001. *The Economics of Risk and Time.* Cambridge, MA: MIT Press.

Gollier, Christian, and R. J. Zeckhauser. 1998. "Horizon Length and Portfolio Risk." Working Paper, University of Toulouse.

Gordon, Robert N. 2001. "Hedging Low-Cost-Basis Stock." *AIMR Conference Proceedings* 4: 36–41, 42–44.

Greene, Jason T., and Charles W. Hodges. 2002. "The Dilution Impact of Daily Fund Flows on Open-End Mutual Funds." *Journal of Financial Economics* 65, no. 1 (July): 131–158.

Gremillion, Lee. 2001. *A Purely American Invention.* National Investment Company Service Association.

Grossman, Sanford. 1976. "On the Efficiency of Competitive Stock Markets Where Trades Have Diverse Information." *Journal of Finance* 31: 573–585.

Grossman, Sanford, and Joseph Stiglitz. 1980. "On the Impossibility of Informationally Efficient Markets." *American Economic Review* 70: 393–408.

Gruber, Martin J. 1996. "Another Puzzle: The Growth in Actively Managed Mutual Funds." *Journal of Finance* 51: 783–810.

Gulko, Les. 2002. "Decoupling." *Journal of Portfolio Management* (Spring): 59–66. Also available online at: www.gloriamundi.org/picsresources /lg.pdf.

Harper, Richard B. 2003. "Asset Allocation, Decoupling, and the Opportunity Cost of Cash." *Journal of Portfolio Management* (Summer): 25–35.

Hechinger, John. 2005. "Fidelity to Woo Institutional Clients." *Wall Street Journal* (March 17): C15.

Hellerstein, Judge Alvin K. 2001. "Memorandum and Order of Judgment." In *The McGraw-Hill Companies vs. Vanguard Index Trust, et al.*, 00 Civ. 4247 (AKH), United States District Court, Southern District of New York, April 25.

Hoffman, David. 2004. "A Quick Fix for Funds? Industry Is Skeptical." *Investment News* (October 18): 2, 53.

Hulbert, Mark. 2003. "The Big Mo in Stocks Hits a Wall of Trading Costs." *New York Times*, Strategies Column—Business Section (August 17).

Ibbotson, Roger G., and Paul D. Kaplan. 2000. "Does Asset Allocation Policy Explain 40, 90, or 100 Percent of Performance?" *Financial Analysts Journal* (January/February): 26–33; www.ibbotson.com/download /research/Does_Asset_Allocation_Explain_Performance.pdf.

Investment Company Institute. 2004. *Mutual Fund Fact Book 2004*; www.ici.org/stats/mf/2004_factbook.pdf.

Investment Company Institute. 2005. *Mutual Fund Fact Book 2005*.

Jacques, William E. 1988. "The S&P Membership Anomaly, or Would You Join This Club?" *Financial Analysts Journal* (November/December): 73–75.

Jaffe, Charles A. 1998. *The Right Way to Hire Financial Help*. Cambridge, MA: MIT Press.

Jahnke, William W. 2004. "Death to the Policy Portfolio." In *The Investment Think Tank: Theory, Strategy, and Practice for Advisers*, ed. Harold Evensky and Deena Katz, Princeton, NJ: Bloomberg Press, 17–37.

Johnson, Woodrow T. 2004. "Predictable Investment Horizons and Wealth Transfers among Mutual Fund Shareholders." *Journal of Finance* (October): 1979–2012.

Karceski, Jason, Miles Livingston, and Edward S. O'Neal. 2004. "Portfolio Transactions Costs at U.S. Equity Mutual Funds." Zero Alpha Group; www.zeroalphagroup.com/headlines/Execution_Costs%20Paper_Nov _15_2004.pdf.

Keim, Donald B. 2003. "The Cost of Trend Chasing and the Illusion of Momentum Profits." Working Paper, The Wharton School, University of Pennsylvania (July 29).

Keim, Donald B., and Ananth Madhavan. 1997. "Transaction Costs and Investment Style: An Interexchange Analysis of Institutional Equity Trades." *Journal of Financial Economics* 46: 265–292.

Keim, Donald B., and Ananth Madhavan. 1998. "The Cost of Institutional Equity Trades." *Financial Analysts Journal* 54 (July/August): 50–69.

Kizer, Jared. 2005. "Index Fundamentalism Revisited." *Journal of Portfolio Management* (Winter). Forthcoming.

Kotlikoff, Laurence J., and Scott Burns. 2004. *The Coming Generational Storm: What You Need to Know about America's Economic Future.* Cambridge, MA: MIT Press.

Kritzman, Mark P. 2000. *Puzzles of Finance.* John Wiley & Sons.

Kritzman, Mark P., and Sebastien Page. 2002. "Asset Allocation vs. Security Selection: Evidence from Global Markets." *Journal of Asset Management* (December): 202–212.

Kritzman, Mark P., and Sebastien Page. 2003. "The Hierarchy of Investment Choice: A Normative Interpretation." *Journal of Portfolio Management* (Summer): 11–23. Also published as a working paper at www.wcmbllc.com/workingpapers/pdfs/Hierarchy%20Invest%20Choice%205-03.pdf.

Kritzman, Mark P., and Sebastien Page. 2004. "Response to 'The Hierarchy of Investment Choice: Comment.' " *Journal of Portfolio Management* (Fall): 121–123.

Lazzara, Craig. 2002. "Index Construction Issues for Exchange-Traded Funds." Available at www.etfconsultants.com/Indexconstructionissues.pdf.

Lipper. 2002. "The Lipper Leader System."

Lo, Andrew, and Craig MacKinlay. 1999. *A Non-Random Walk Down Wall Street.* Princeton, NJ: Princeton University Press.

Longo, Tracey. 2001. "How to Pick a Planner." *Mutual Funds* (October): 44–47.

Lucchetti, Aaron. 2001. "For Some Mutual-Fund Investors, Losses Are Getting Rubbed In by Penalty Fees." *Wall Street Journal* (August 3): C1.

Lucchetti, Aaron. 2005. "Investors Get Shortchanged on Interest." *Wall Street Journal* (February 17): D1, D4.

Lucchetti, Aaron, and Tom Lauricella. 2001. "Vanguard and S&P Seem Such a Nice Pair; Why the Nasty Spat?" *Wall Street Journal* (August 23): A-1, A-18.

Madhavan, Ananth. 2002. "Index Reconstitution and Equity Returns." ITG Inc. (April 24); www.itginc.com/research/whitepapers/madhavan/RussellStudy.pdf.

Malkiel, Burton. 1973; 8th ed. 2003. *A Random Walk Down Wall Street.* New York: W. W. Norton.

Malkiel, Burton. 1995. "Returns from Investing in Equity Mutual Funds 1971 to 1991." *Journal of Finance* (June): 549–572.

Mansueto, Joe. 2005. "Letters to *Fortune*: Morningstar Responds." *Fortune* (February 21): 18.

Mazzilli, Paul J., and Dodd F. Kittsley. 2003. "Low Historical Tracking Error for Most ETFs." Morgan Stanley Equity Research Report (February 27).

Mazzilli, Paul J., and Dodd F. Kittsley. 2004. "Most ETFs Have Exhibited Low Tracking Error." Morgan Stanley Equity Research Report (January 22).

Mazzilli, Paul J., Dodd F. Kittsley, and Dominic Maister. 2004a. "ETF Sector Allocation Model: Changes in Recommended Weightings." Morgan Stanley Equity Research Report (November 2).

Mazzilli, Paul J., Dodd F. Kittsley, and Dominic Maister. 2004b. "ETF Sector Asset Allocation: Changes in Recommended Weightings." Morgan Stanley Equity Research Report (December 9).

Mazzilli, Paul J., Dodd F. Kittsley, and Dominic Maister. 2005. "Most ETFs Exhibited Low Tracking Error in 2004." Morgan Stanley Equity Research Report (January 28).

Merton, Robert C. 1969. "Lifetime Portfolio Selection under Uncertainty: The Continuous-Time Case." *Review of Economics and Statistics* 51: 247–57.

Michaud, Richard O. 1981. "Risk Policy and Long-Term Investment." *Journal of Financial and Quantitative Analysis* (June): 147–167.

Morey, Matthew R. 2002. "Mutual Fund Age and Morningstar Ratings." *Financial Analyssts Journal* (March/April): 56–63.

Morey, Matthew R. 2005. "The Kiss of Death: A 5-Star Morningstar Mutual Fund Rating?" *Journal of Investment Management* 3, no. 2 (Second Quarter).

Morgenson, Gretchen. 1997. "What the Sales Brochure Didn't Tell You." *Forbes* (April 7): 90–96.

Morningstar Associates. 2004. "Our Methodology: How the Morningstar Online Service Works." Pages 1–5.

Oeppen, Jim, and James W. Vaupel. 2002. "Broken Limits to Life Expectancy." *Science Magazine* 296, issue 5570 (May 10): 1029–1031.

Oster, Christopher, and Karen Damato. 2004. "Big Fees Hit Small Plans." *Wall Street Journal* (October 21): D1.

Palmer, Kimberly. 2004. "New Mutual-Fund Cops Will Come at a Cost." *Wall Street Journal* (August 20): C1, C13.

Palmeri, Christopher. 2005. "The Terminator of Public Pensions?" *BusinessWeek* (January 31): 82.

Peterson, Mark A., and Erik Sirri. 2003. "Evaluation of the Biases in Execution Cost Estimation Using Trade and Quote Data." *Journal of Financial Markets* (May): 259–280.

Peterson, Peter G. 2004. *Running on Empty: How the Democratic and Republican Parties Are Bankrupting Our Future and What Americans Can Do about It.* New York: Farrar, Straus & Giroux.

Picerno, James. 2004. "Fundamentals: Bill Sharpe Talks about Asset Allocation, Pricing Theory, and Hedge Funds." *Bloomberg Wealth Manager*
(November): 105–108.

Plan Sponsor. 2004. "2004 DC Survey Eye on the Prize: No Signs of Panic"
(November 2004): 40–85.

Plan Sponsor. 2005. "How Much Does Your DC Plan Cost?" (January
2005): 12.

Plexus Group. 2001. "Is Eliminating Tracking Error Hazardous to Your
Client's Wealth?" Commentary 64 (January); www.plexusgroup.com/fs
_research.html.

Porter, Michael. 2004a. "Actively Managed Exchange-Traded Funds Can Be
the Greatest Thing Since Money Market Funds." Lipper Fund Industry
Insight Reports (November 23); www.research.lipper.wallst.com
/fundIndustryOverview.asp, ($15 payment required to view article).

Porter, Michael. 2004b. "The Future Is Now: The AMEX's Solution to the
Active ETF Riddle." Lipper Fund Industry Insight Reports (December
6); www.research.lipper.wallst.com/fundIndustryOverview.asp ($15
payment required to view article).

Porter, Michael, and Lucas Garland. 2005. "Life Cycle Funds Fit for Life."
Lipper Fund Industry Insight Reports (March 14); www.research
.lipper.wallst.com/fundIndustryOverview.asp ($15 payment required
to view article).

Poterba, James M., John B. Shoven, and Clemens Sialm 2000. "Asset Location for Retirement Savers." In *Private Pensions and Public Policies*,
Washington, DC: Brookings Institution Press, 2004. An earlier version
was presented at the Conference on Public Policies and Private Pensions, Sponsored by the Brookings Institution, Stanford Institute for
Economic Policy Research, and TIAA-CREF Institute, Washington, DC,
September 21–22, 2000; www.brook.edu/es/events/pension/10pot
_shov_sialm.pdf.

Pozen, Robert C. 1998. *The Mutual Fund Business*. Cambridge, MA: MIT
Press.

Quinn, Jane Bryant. 2005. "A Gold Mine in Low Fund Fees." *Newsweek*
(January 31): 35.

Quinn, Jim, and Frank Wang. 2003. "How Is Your Reconstitution? Has Rebalancing Become a Drag?" *Journal of Indexes* (Fourth Quarter):
34–38.

Reinker, Kenneth S., and Edward Tower. 2004. "Index Fundamentalism Revisited." *Journal of Portfolio Management* (Summer): 37–50.

Roseen, Tom. 2004. "Taxes in the Mutual Fund Industry—2004." Lipper
Research Study (April 15); www.research.lipper.wallst.com/research
StudiesOverview.asp.

Rouwenhorst, K. Geert. 2004. "The Origins of Mutual Funds." Yale ICF
Working Paper No. 04-48 (December 12).

Ryan Asset Liability Management. n.d. *Asset/Liability Scoreboard*; www
   .ryanalm.com/Research.asp.

Safian, Ken, Daniel P. Dillon, and Lorraine T. Corbett. 2005. "A Deteriora-
   tion in the Valuation of Capital Goods Stocks and an Important Coming Transition in Sector Profits." *Safian Investment Research Report* 17,
   no. 1 (March 17): 1–8.

Samuelson, Paul A. 1969. "Lifetime Portfolio Selection by Dynamic Sto-
   chastic Programming." *Review of Economics and Statistics* 51: 239–246.

Samuelson, Paul A. 1974. "A Challenge to Judgment." *Journal of Portfolio
   Management* 1 (Fall): 17–19.

Schoenfeld, Steven A. 2004. *Active Index Investing, Maximizing Portfolio
   Performance and Minimizing Risk Through Global Index Strategies.*
   Hoboken, NJ: John Wiley & Sons.

Schwartz, Robert, and Reto Francioni. 2004. *Equity Markets in Action: The
   Fundamentals of Liquidity, Market Structure and Trading.* Hoboken,
   NJ: John Wiley & Sons.

Securities and Exchange Commission. n.d. *Concept Release: Actively Managed Exchange-Traded Funds.* 17 CFR Part 270, Release No. IC-25258;
   File No. S7-20-01; www.sec.gov/rules/concept/ic-25258.htm.

Securities and Exchange Commission. n.d. Form N-SAR, Semi-Annual Report for Registered Investment Companies, Item 71, p. 66; www.sec
   .gov/about/forms/formn-sar.pdf.

Seneker, Harry. 2005. "Comparing Apples: Sector Indexes Are Not All
   the Same," *Dow Jones Indexes/Barclays Global Investors* Research
   Report (February). Replaces an earlier paper with the same issued in
   2003.

Sharkansky, Stefan. 2002. "Mutual Fund Costs: Risk without Reward." *Person-
   alFund.com* (July); www.personalfund.com/RiskWithoutReward.pdf.

Sharpe, William F. 1991. "The Arithmetic of Active Management." *Financial Analysts Journal* (January/February): 7–9.

Sharpe, William F. 1997. "Morningstar's Performance Measures." Working
   Paper, www.stanford.edu/~wfsharpe/art/stars/stars0.htm.

Sharpe, William F. 1998. "Morningstar's Risk-Adjusted Ratings." *Financial
   Analysts Journal* (July/August): 21–33. Also available online: www
   .aimrpubs.org/faj/issues/v54n4/pdf/f0540021a.pdf.

Shoven, John B., and Clemens Sialm. 1998. "Long Run Asset Allocation for
   Retirement Savings." *Journal of Private Portfolio Management* (Summer): 13–26.

Silverman, Rachel Emma. 2004. "New IRA Protects Against Lawsuits, Bank-
   ruptcy." *Wall Street Journal* (October 13): D2.

Singal, Vijay. 2004. *Beyond the Random Walk.* New York: Oxford University Press.

Sinquefield, Rex. 1991. "Are Small-Stock Returns Achievable?" *Financial
   Analysts Journal* (January/February): 45–50.

Sirri, E. R., and P. Tufano. 1998. "Costly Search and Mutual Fund Flows." *Journal of Finance* 53: 1589–1622.

Slott, Ed. 2003. *The Retirement Savings Time Bomb . . . and How to Defuse It.* New York: Penguin Books.

Slott, Ed. 2005. *Parlay Your IRA into a Family Fortune.* New York: Viking Penguin.

Society of Actuaries. n.d. "Retirement Probability Analyzer Software." www.soa.org/ccm/content/areas-of-practice/special-interest -sections/pension/retirement-probability-analyzer-software/.

Standard & Poor's. 2004. "S&P Research on Fees Show Cheaper Funds Continuing to Outperform Their More Expense Peers." *PR Newswire.com* (June 29); www.prnewswire.com/news/index_mail.shtml?ACCT=105 &STORY=/www/story/06-29-2004/0002202199.

Statman, Meir. 2004. "The Diversification Puzzle." *Financial Analysts Journal* (July/August): 44–53.

Staub, Renato. 2004. "The Hierarchy of Investment Choice: Comment." *Journal of Portfolio Management* (Fall): 118–120.

Stein, David M., Andrew F. Siegel, Premkumar Narasimhan, and Charles E. Appeadu. 2000. "Diversification in the Presence of Taxes." *Journal of Portfolio Management* 27, no. 1 (Fall).

Stein, Jeremy C. 2004. "Why Are Most Funds Open-End? Competition and the Limits of Arbitrage." Working Paper, Harvard University (January); http://post.economics.harvard.edu/faculty/stein/papers/OpenEnd Jan04revision.pdf.

Stein, Nicholas. 2005. "Investing: Morningstar's Bright Future Turns Cloudy." *Fortune* (January 10): 94–95.

Stires, David. 2003. "Don't Get Burned by Churn." *Fortune* (November 24). Available online at www.fortune.com/fortune/subs/article /0,15114,549543,00.html.

Trone, Donald B., William R., Allbright, and Philip R. Taylor. 1996. *The Management of Investment Decisions.* New York: McGraw-Hill.

Tyson, Eric. 2004. *Mutual Funds for Dummies.* 4th ed., Hoboken, NJ: John Wiley & Sons.

Updegrave, Walter. 2004. *We're Not in Kansas Anymore.* New York: Crown Business.

Urbanowicz, Nicole. 2004. "Morningstar Announces SEC Investigation." *Dow Jones Newswires* (September 24).

Wagner, Wayne, and Al Winnikoff. 2001. *Millionaire.* Renaissance Books.

Watson Wyatt. 2004. "Defined Benefit vs. 401(k): The Returns for 2000–2002." *Insider* (October). Available online at www.watson wyatt.com/us/pubs/insider/showarticle.asp?ArticleID=13811& Component=The+Insider.

Welch, Scott D. 2001. "Diversifying Concentrated Holdings." *AIMR Conference Proceedings* 4: 30–35, 42–44.

Whitehouse, Kaja. 2004. "Low-Fee Stock Funds Hold an Edge." Fund Track, *Wall Street Journal* (July 6).

Wiandt, Jim. 2004. "News—S&P 500 Exceeds $1 Trillion in Indexed Assets." *Journal of Indexes* (June/July): 46.

Wiandt, Jim, and Will McClatchy. 2001. *Exchange-Traded Funds*. John Wiley & Sons.

Wiener, Daniel P., and James H. Lowell. 2004. "Fidelity Slashes Index Fund Fees." Adviser Fund Update, *Adviser Investment Management* (September 9); www.adviserinvestment.com/pdfs/updates/0909.pdf.

Wilcox, Jarrod W. 2001. "Risks and Benchmarks." *Journal of Index Issues* (Third Quarter): 54–62.

Zheng, L. 1999. "Is Money Smart? A Study of Mutual Fund Investors' Fund Selection Ability." *Journal of Finance* 54: 901–933.

Zitzewitz, Eric. 2003. "Who Cares about Shareholders? Arbitrage-Proofing Mutual Funds." *Journal of Law, Economics, & Organization* 19 (October): 245–280.

INDEX

Liquidity shock, 50
Load funds, 98, 251
Long-term capital gain (LTCG), 47,
    49–50, 61, 73, 251
Long-term investors, 41, 125,
    231–232, 235
Longevity, 20–22, 53
Low-load fund, 251
Low-management-fee share classes,
    199
Lynch, Peter, 174

Make-or-buy decisions, 13, 29–30
Malkiel, Burton, 118–119
Management company, 251
Management quality, 95, 162, 201,
    207–208
Manager evaluation, 117
Mandatory withdrawal, 49, 60
Market capitalization, 121, 124
Market capitalization index funds,
    167–168
Marketing expenses, 87, 92
Marketing fees:
    avoidance strategies, 183–184
    types of, 181, 237
Market makers, 200–201
Market-on-close (MOC) order, 122,
    200, 251
Market risk, 17
Market segments, pricing strategy,
    181–182
Market stress, 35–36
Market timing, 75, 105, 234,
    252
Market trends, 149
Maturity, 30, 238–239
Mean, 21, 252
Median, 21, 132, 252
Microcap stock, 252
Mid-cap funds, 167–168
Miller, William, 174
Momentum, 101–102
Money management fee, 201

Money market mutual funds,
    generally:
    characteristics of, 67–69
    defined, 1, 252
    service fees, 71–72
Morgan Stanley Capital
    International (MSCI), 120,
    212
    Europe, Australasia, Far East
        (EAFE) index, 32
    U.S. Investable Market 2500,
        141–142
Morningstar:
    database, as information
        resource, 153, 155–158
    fund category, 156
    ratings, 156, 252
Multi-asset class funds, 132
Multiple share class exchange-
    traded funds (ETFs), 199
Municipal bond funds, 52, 82
Municipal securities, 40
Mutual fund(s):
    after-tax returns, 55
    conventional, 6, 39–40, 55, 90,
        160, 195, 200–201, 229–238
    defined, 252
    exchange-traded funds (ETFs)
        compared with, 210–211
    problems with, 191–195
    reinventing, 189
    scandals, 87, 101, 160, 232
    "zero cost," 6

Nasdaq-100 index, 15
NAV proxy value, 200
Net assets, 46
Net asset value (NAV), 6, 53,
    101–102, 107, 160–161,
    192–194, 197, 200–201,
    233–234, 252–253
Net worth, 149
No-load fund, 74, 253
Normal distribution, 23–24

ABOUT THE AUTHOR

G ary Gastineau is a Senior Portfolio Manager in the Dickerson Division of H. G. Wellington & Co., Inc., and Managing Director of ETF Consultants LLC, a firm that provides specialized exchange-traded fund consulting services to ETF issuers, exchanges and other markets, market makers, research organizations, and investors. He is also a director of Skyhawk Management LLC, an investment management firm that uses ETFs in its investment strategies.

Gastineau is a recognized expert on funds. Prior to joining ETF Advisors, LP, an ETF management firm, as Managing Director in May 2002, he was Managing Director for ETF Product Development at Nuveen Investments. Preceding his tenure at Nuveen, he directed product development at the American Stock Exchange for approximately five years. As Senior Vice President in New Product Development, Gastineau was instrumental in the introduction of many of the popular ETF products, which have grown rapidly since their first appearance in 1993. Previously, he held senior positions in research, product development, and portfolio management at major investment banking firms.

His earlier fund book, *The Exchange-Traded Funds Manual*, was published in February 2002 by John Wiley & Sons. Gary is also the author of *The Options Manual* (Third Edition, McGraw-Hill, 1988), and co-author of the *Dictionary of Financial Risk Management* (Fabozzi, 1999) and *Equity Flex Options* (Fabozzi, 1999), as well as numerous journal articles. He received the Bernstein Fabozzi/Jacobs Levy Award for an Outstanding Article for "Equity Index Funds Have Lost Their Way," which appeared in the Winter 2002 issue of the *Journal of Portfolio Management*.

Gary serves on the editorial boards of the *Journal of Portfolio Management*, the *Journal of Derivatives*, and the *Journal of Indexes*, and is a member of a number of advisory boards including the Research Review Board for the Research Foundation of CFA Institute. He is an honors graduate of both Harvard College and Harvard Business School.